Learning Smarter

The New Science of Teaching

Learning Smarter

The New Science of Teaching

Eric Jensen with Michael Dabney

Learning Smarter

©2000 Eric Jensen

Layout and Design: Tracy Linares
Managing Editor: Karen Markowitz
Assistant Editor: Gail Olsen

Printed in the United States of America
Published by The Brain Store, Inc.
San Diego, CA, USA

ISBN #1-890460-09-5

For additional copies or bulk discounts contact:

The Brain Store, Inc.
4202 Sorrento Valley Blvd., #B
San Diego, CA 92121
Phone (858) 546-7555 • Fax (858) 546-7560
www.thebrainstore.com

Table of Contents

Preface

Learning Smarter represents new territory. It is a unique compilation of research findings that collectively inform the teaching practice we have come to know as "brain compatible." The articles, most of them published online by The Brain Store over the past year, summarize recent discoveries about the brain and learning while translating them into practical solutions for educators.

With the advent of neuroimaging devices in the 1970s (such as PET scans), we began a new journey—one that took scientists for the first time into the inner sanctum of the human brain *during* the process of learning. Based on these studies, we can now quantitatively identify sound teaching practices supported by empirical evidence. The benefit of this new technology for those of us charged with the weighty responsibility of educating others is profound. Finally, some of what we have known intuitively all along can now be substantiated. Some teaching methods definitely *discourage* quality learning, just as some clearly *encourage* it. At this juncture, it is the encouraging, "brain-compatible" methods that *Learning Smarter* is all about!

The book is organized around learning themes that most of us confront every day. Whether we're classroom teachers, staff developers, school administrators, managers, corporate trainers, or coaches, such critical issues as improving attention span and memory, engaging learners, providing feedback, enhancing achievement, coping with behavioral problems, and enriching the learning environment are essential to our collective success. Not only do we present the fully cited research here, each article delivers related strategies for immediate application in the classroom or training environment, as well.

Due to the dynamic nature of the research (it's happening even now as we read) and its multidisciplinary character (biology alone doesn't provide all the answers), brain-compatible teaching and learning ought to be viewed as an evolving approach rather than a static formula or recipe. Certainly it is not a panacea for all of our academic ills. However, it does reflect a dose of good common sense backed by solid research.

If we agree that our schools are about learning, than shouldn't we be learning everything we can about *what* makes our brain thrive? School failures are not about bad schools, bad kids, or bad teachers; they're rather about the violation of the brain's basic operating principles. Most of us are already working as hard as we can on behalf of our learners. At this stage of the game, it's no longer about working *harder*; it's about working *smarter*. This book promises to help you make a powerful difference by working *with*, rather than *against* the brain. The primary purpose of this resource is to enhance your success. Here's to the power of knowledge...Seek it and thrive!

Give me a spark
of Nature's fire,
That's the learning
I desire.

—Robert Burns
1759-1796

Chapter 1
Enhancing Cognition

hat happens inside the brain during learning? What magic occurs in the mind as we acquire, store, and subsequently retrieve information—the process we call learning? What mix of ingredients—neurological, physical, environmental, and emotional—contribute to the cognition formula? Why do these factors play such a pivotal role? And finally, how much can we, as educators, influence them? The articles in this chapter address these central questions.

Scientists know that learning occurs on many different levels. It may be a simple reflex response (hand on a hot stove) or a more complex procedure (deciding how to remodel your house). Learning may be explicit, such as when we learn facts, numbers, faces, and names in a history lesson. However, much of it is implicit or unconscious, a process that occurs through generalizations, locations, gut feelings, experiences, reflection, and role modeling. These actions taken together represent the act of cognition—knowing and perceiving.

Most neuroscientists agree that *all* learning occurs on the level of neuron-to-neuron. Although individual neurons are not very smart, when connected to one another critical networks occur that transform information into meaningful units of learning. The newest studies suggest humans have about 40-50 billion neurons. Each of these cells has the potential of making contact with another 5,000 to 50,000 neighboring neurons. The result is a multitude of complex networks that very effectively store and activate our learning. The success of this process, however, is dependent upon many factors, including stress, diet, health, emotion, trial and error, timing, repetition, prior knowledge, meaningfulness, and motivation. The good news is that sound educational practices that respect how the brain naturally learns best strongly influence these mediating factors.

Cognition and the Power to Choose

Does learner choice play a role in cognition and motivation? As researchers learn more about how the brain goes about making decisions, the answer seems to be yes. Studies by Platt and Glimcher (1999) found that when humans and monkeys are allowed to choose freely between two alternative responses, their choices are directly related to the amount of gain they can expect from each response. This finding reflects a direct relationship with learner motivation and self-determination. The researchers also determined that during decision-making, the parietal cortex—a region of the cerebrum that is responsible for reception of sensory information (especially transforming visual signals into eye-movement commands), in addition to reading, writing and calculation—was primarily activated.

The Brain and Cognition

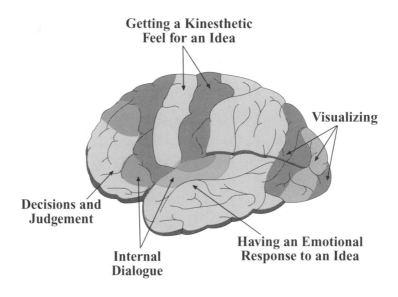

When given the freedom of choice and adequate information, the brain's prefrontal cortex (decision-making, planning, critical thinking) and amygdala (fear response) have been found to respond positively (Bechara, et al. 1999). This effect is likely triggered by the increased production of serotonin, dopamine, and noradrenaline, which enhance well-being and motivation. So, it turns out that choice may, indeed, "feed the brain."

Janelle (1997) reported that when given the opportunity to control feedback in their learning environment, high-school athletes required relatively less feedback to acquire skills, and they retained those skills at a level equal to or surpassing those who were given more feedback but received it passively. Kinzie and colleagues (1992) noted similar results among students in a computer-assisted learning environment.

Action Steps

* It is best to provide choices when learners have sufficient knowledge of the subject matter to choose wisely.
* Narrow the choices for learners. For example, allow students to choose from a pre-selected and appropriate list of books for reading assignments, or ask them which of the two testing modes (i.e., essay or multiple choice) they prefer.
* Solicit the ideas and opinions of your learning audience when planning learning tasks, especially when various options and approaches will work just as well.
* When appropriate, utilize learner discussion groups, cooperative teams, and suggestion boxes.

Sources:
Bechara, Antoine; Hanna Damasio; Antonio Damasio; Gregory Lee. 1999. Different contributions of the human amygdala and ventromedial prefrontal cortex to decision-making. *Journal of Neuroscience*. 19(13): 5473-81.
Janelle, C.M. 1997. Maximizing performance feedback effectiveness through videotape replay and self-controlled learning environment. *Research Quarterly for Exercise and Sport*. 68(4): 269-79.
Kinzie, Mable; H. Sullivan; Richard Berdel. 1992. Motivational and achievement effects of learner control over content review within CAI. *Journal of Educational Computing Research*. 8(1): 101-14.
Platt, Michael and Paul Glimcher. 1999. Neural correlates of decision variables in parietal cortex. *Nature*. July; 400(6741): 233-8.

Students Laugh Their Way to Better Learning

A well-timed joke or other appropriate display of humor not only makes us laugh and feel good, it can also promote better attention and recall while creating a conducive atmosphere for learning, claims new research (Shammin & Stuss 1999). Humor has also been shown to enhance students' abstract and creative thinking abilities while easing feelings of anxiety (Belanger, et al. 1998). In short, a good laugh can pave the road for meaningful learning.

What occurs in the brain as we react to humor? The cognitive process involves the activation and stimulation of the frontal lobes, one of the four main areas of the cerebrum (or upper brain area) concerned with intellectual functioning, including thought, language processes, behavior, and memory. A good joke also activates the frontal lobes, as well as the amygdala—the brain's center for emotional memories (Fry 1994; Johnson 1990).

More precisely, Shammin and Stuss found that reacting to verbal and visual humor requires several key abilities: language cognition, abstract reasoning, visual search, assessment of detail, and ability to keep in mind the story so that the punch line can be connected with the stem or core of the joke. In addition, scientists know that a belly laugh, like a good body massage, "wakes up" the brain and the rest of the nervous system by increasing the flow of "feel good" endorphins and cerebrospinal fluid to critical muscle areas, such as the abdominal, neck, and shoulder muscles. This is known to produce relaxation, which thereby enhances cognition.

In a study of 21 patients (aged 18-70 years) with focal damage in various parts of the brain, Shammin and Stuss reported that the right frontal lobe (the brain area responsible for such cognitive functions as creativity, discernment, recall of contextual patterns, and spatial meaning) most disrupted the ability to appreciate humor. Patients with damage to this area reacted less with laughter and smiles than a control group, and had less working memory of both verbal jokes and non-verbal (cartoon) humor, indicating an inability to focus attention on details and to comprehend the abstract meanings and mental shifting required.

In a study of 65 male and 65 female undergraduates, Johnson (1990) reported that those with higher spatial problem-solving abilities processed and comprehended humor more quickly than those with less spatial, or right frontal lobe, prowess. In the study, men were found to solve mental rotation problems faster than females, and they rated jokes as funnier. A study conducted by Belanger and colleagues (1998) suggests that listening to jokes prior to undergoing mental rotation tests can actually speed up problem-solving among men; whereas, solution times among women remained relatively unaffected.

Humor's ability to enhance recall in the classroom is well-documented. Class material relayed in the form of a simple joke was remembered better during immediate and delayed recall situations than material communicated in text sentences, research claims (Derks, et al. 1998). Similar results were reported by Lott (1994) and Deneire (1995).

In addition, according to a 1999 study by Wanzer and Frymier involving 300 university students, teachers who use humor in class are seen by their students as more "human," approachable, motivating, and productive than instructors who do not use humor.

But studies also indicate that tendentious (or biased) humor can produce undesired results. Gorham and Christophel (1990) demonstrated that teachers who used demeaning or tendentious humor were looked upon negatively by students. Research also indicates that humor often fails to enhance specific recall in non-classroom situations, such as consumer recall of commercial advertising content; although, it can positively influence overall consumer impression of the product (Fisher 1997; Michaels 1998).

A belly laugh, like a good body massage, "wakes up" the brain and the rest of the nervous system by increasing the flow of "feel good" endorphins and cerebrospinal fluid to critical muscle areas.

Action Steps

* Avoid potentially disparaging or demeaning jokes.
* Ensure that jokes and humor content are related to the learning tasks and goals of the group.
* Use humor as an "ice breaker" at the beginning of a learning session to relieve tension and to set a friendly tone.
* Don't overuse humor. Humor works best when it is appropriate and well-timed.
* If you aren't comfortable or especially adept at joke-telling or humor, don't try it. Instead, find an appropriate joke and read it to the class, or make use of an audio or visual rendering by a professional comedian or cartoonist to make your point.

Sources:

Belanger, Heather; Lee Kirkpatrick; Peter Derks. 1998. The effects of humor on verbal and imaginal problem solving. *International Journal of Humor Research*. 11(1): 21-31.

Deneire, Marc. 1995. Humor and foreign language teaching. *International Journal of Humor Research*. 8(3): 285-98.

Derks, Peter; John Gardner; R. Agarwal. 1998. Recall of innocent and tendentious humorous material. *International Journal of Humor Research*. 11(1): 5-19.

Fisher, Martin. 1997. The effect of humor on learning in a planetarium. *Science & Education*. Nov; 81(6): 703-13.

Fry, William. 1994. The biology of humor. *International Journal of Humor*. 7(2): 111-26.

Gorham, Joan and D. Christophel. 1990. The relationship of teacher's use of humor in the classroom to immediacy and student learning. *Communication Education*. Jan; 39(1): 46-62.

Johnson, Michael. 1990. A study of humor and the right hemisphere. *Perceptual & Motor Skills*. Jun; 70(3, Pt. 1): 995-1002.

Lott, Hazel. 1994. An experiment in the initial effects of humor on immediate and delayed recall. *Journal of Experimental Psychology: Learning, Memory & Cognition*. Jul; 20(4): 953-67.

Michaels, Steven. 1998. *Cognitive and Affective Responses to Humorous Advertisements*. Dissertation Abstracts International: Section B: the Sciences & Engineering. May; 58(11-B): 6282.

Shammin, P.; D.T. Stuss. 1999. Humour appreciation: A role of the right frontal lobe. *Brain*. Apr; 123(4): 657-66.

Wanzer, Melissa Bekelja and Ann Bainbridge Frymier. 1999. The relationship between student perceptions of instructor humor and student's reports of learning. *Communication Education*. Jan; 48(1): 48-62.

Downtime Adds Mental Muscle to Learning

Thomas Edison was known for taking brief naps during the day, and so is Bill Gates. Some sleep experts encourage daily naps for greater efficiency. But what are the biological implications of giving the brain and body frequent breaks on the job or in school? And what evidence supports the practice of what's been dubbed "power napping"?

Studies suggest that the brain's neural connections are strengthened and solidified when competing neural stimuli ceases for several minutes subsequent to concentrated study (Frank & Greenberg 1994; Hobson 1994; Karni, et al. 1994; Lasley 1997). Downtime during the day or night, it turns out, allows the brain to recycle a protein switch called CREB (cAMP response element-binding protein), which is known to be crucial to long-term memory formation. Known to bind with serotonin, a neurotransmitter that regulates such functions as relaxation and sleep, CREB appears to aid the recall of declarative memories concerning facts, ideas, and images. Frank and Greenberg report that beyond facilitating long-term memory in REM (rapid eye movement) sleep, CREB also plays a major role in consolidating long-term learning during non-sleep mental reflection periods.

Frydenberg and Lewis (1999) suggest that constructive reflection is important in that it allows the brain's frontal lobe region a chance to filter information and draw associations with prior learning, while aiding memory, planning, and decision-making. Other studies also substantiate the value of frequent rest and reflection intervals in reducing fatigue and aiding cognition and performance (Henning, et al. 1997; Koulack 1997; Shafir & Eagle 1995; Rossi & Nimmons 1991).

Among 19 computer operators, Henning and colleagues found that productivity and comfort relating to the eyes, legs, and feet improved significantly after taking one 3-minute break combined with stretching exercises every hour. Koulack found in a study of 40 subjects that those who learned in the afternoon and then slept prior to testing later in the day performed better on recognition tasks compared to subjects who learned in the morning and did *not* nap prior to testing later the same day. And, Shafir and Eagle found in a study of 88 fifth- and sixth-graders that students who spent periods in self-reflection after learning were not only better learners and problem solvers, but developed better corrective strategies than subjects who did not reflect. Primary school children, who, because of immature stages of brain development, are not able to focus their attention for extended periods of time especially benefit from frequent breaks (Pellegrini & Bjorklund 1997).

The Brain and Downtime

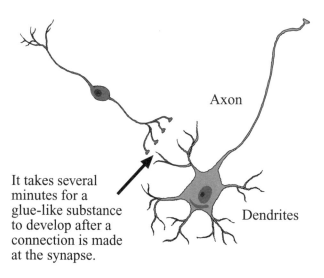

It takes several minutes for a glue-like substance to develop after a connection is made at the synapse.

Axon

Dendrites

Although the recommended frequency and duration of breaks depends on the nature of the work and on the individual, in general we need a 5- to 15-minute break every 1 to 2 hours of concentrated work (Okogbaa & Shell 1986). Webb (1982) reports that the ideal time for napping may be between noon and 3 p.m.—at the height of the circadian rhythm, and the ideal length seems to be about 30 minutes, although positive results have also been reported with 15- to 20-minute naps. The worst time to nap is at the bottom of the circadian rhythm, between 3 p.m. and 6 p.m., adds Webb.

These results add credence to the notion that both sleep and circadian rhythm (our internal clock that regulates sleep-wake cycles, hunger, and other metabolic functions) play an important role in the memory process.

Action Steps

* Establish a mutually agreeable policy with learners or employees for taking breaks. As a general guideline, if increased errors or fatigue begins to occur, take a break.

* If possible provide a brain break between problem-definition and idea-generation activities.

* The ideal break should involve some degree of exercise, such as walking, stretching, bending, or deep breathing to stimulate the body out of drowsiness or under-arousal.

* The urge to nap occurs in relation to a natural rhythm, and denying it may negatively impact cognition, productivity, and general well-being. If possible, take a 10- to 15-minute "power nap" during a lunch break to get recharged, and especially before testing and after new learning.

* Allow for sufficient quiet time during the day for yourself and your learners. Good downtime activities, beyond pure rest and reflection, include movement, stretching, meditation, walking, and deep breathing.

* Encourage workers or learners to reflect on their successes and weaknesses after learning evaluations or tests, asking them, for example, what achievements they are most proud of and what they might do differently in the future.

* Allow students to share their jokes, but screen them first.

Sources:

Frank, D.A. and M.E. Greenberg. 1994. CREB: A mediator of long-term memory from mollusks to mammals. *Cell.* 79: 5-8.

Frydenberg, Erica and Ramon Lewis. 1999. Things don't get better just because you're getting older: A case for facilitating reflection. *British Journal of Education Psychology.* Mar; 69(1): 81-94.

Henning, R.; P. Jacques; G. Kissel; A. Sullivan. 1997. Frequent short rest breaks from computer work: Effects on productivity and well-being at two field sites. *Ergonomics.* Jan; 40(1): 78-91.

Hobson, J.A. 1994. *Chemistry of Conscious States.* Boston, MA: Little Brown and Co.

Karni, A.; D. Tanne; B.S. Rubenstein. 1994. Dependence on REM sleep of overnight improvement of a perceptual skill. *Science.* 265: 679-82.

Koulack, D. 1997. Recognition memory, circadian rhythms, and sleep. *Perceptual Motor Skills.* Aug; 85(1): 99-104.

Lasley, E. 1997. How the Brain Learns and Remembers. *Brain Work.* 7(1): 9.

Okogbaa, O.G and R.L. Shell. 1986. The measurement of knowledge worker fatigue. *IEEE Transactions.* Dec; 18(4): 335-42.

Pellegrini, Anthony and D.F. Bjorklund. 1997. The role of recess in children's cognitive performance. *Educational Psychologist*. Winter; 32(1): 35-40.

Rossi, E.L. and D. Nimmons. 1991. *The 20-Minute Break: Using the New Science of Ultradian Rhythms*. Los Angeles, CA: Tarcher.

Scroth, M., et al. 1993. Role of delayed feedback on subsequent pattern recognition transfer tasks. *Contemporary Educational Psychology*. Jan; 18(1): 15-22.

Shafir, Uri and Morris Eagle. 1995. Response to failure, strategic flexibility, and learning. *International Journal of Behavioral Development*. Dec; 18(4): 677-700.

Webb, W.B. 1982. *Biological Rhythms, Sleep and Performance*. Chichester, England: Wiley.

Formatting Helps the Brain Process Written Material

Have you ever perused a seemingly interesting book, magazine, or report but had trouble sifting through the information? The problem may lie with the typography of the text and/or the page layout and design—key elements, it turns out, in how the eye and brain process written information for memory and comprehension (Metz 1999; Yager, et al. 1998).

Researchers know that when we view something our occipital lobe (the brain area responsible for visual perception) joins forces with the brain's other somatosensory areas and the frontal lobe (which controls mental focus, attention, and decision-making) to make sense of what we are seeing. During this viewing process, the perceived sights, sounds, shapes, and colors are collectively processed by the brain in an attempt to gain a sense of unity, or wholeness, from what is seen, according to Campbell (1995).

When various elements, such as unconventional or incongruous text shapes, colors, or page design techniques, interfere with the brain's effort to perceive unity, the viewer or reader can experience confusion, poor comprehension, and even mental stress, Campbell suggests.

Research indicates there are certain layout and design techniques that enhance readability. For example, Yager (1998) and others have noted that the type of fonts used in text is important. Research suggests that fonts with serifs (referring to the short lines stemming at an angle from the upper and lower ends of the stroke of a letter) increase reading speed rates when compared to sans serif fonts (without serifs). It is speculated that the stems of serif letters, when viewed as a whole in the text, promote a better sense of text unity and flow, thereby enhancing readability.

In addition, the appropriate and ample use of white space between text and graphics is equally essential, Metz and Campbell agree. A degree of white space gives the eye much needed spatial relief, which aids in comprehension.

In addition, Wallace and colleagues (1998) noted that the use of color in close proximity to words, and in groupings of shapes and forms, enhances memory of text. This is especially true of blue (which has been found to produce a calming effect conducive to deep thinking and concentration) and red (useful for creative thinking and short-term high energy).

Action Steps

* Look for materials that are not only highly informational, but also visually appealing in typography and graphic design.
* Research shows that materials which make use of serif fonts, ample white space between text, and color graphics result in increased comprehension and recall.
* Encourage your learners and colleagues to use these helpful techniques when creating computer-generated learning materials and reports.

Sources:
Campbell, Kim. 1995. Coherence, continuity, and cohesion: The theoretical foundations for document design. Hillsdale, NJ: Lawrence Erlbaum Associates, Inc.
Metz, Marilyn. 1999. *Typography preferences of consumers over 50*. Dissertation Abstracts International: Section B: the Sciences & Engineering. 59(8-B); Feb; 4502.
Wallace, David; S.W. West; A. Ware. 1998. The effect of knowledge maps that incorporate gestalt principles on learning. *Journal of Experimental Education*. Fall; 67(1): 5-16.
Yager, Dean; Kathy Aquilante; Robert Plass. 1998. High and low luminance letters, acuity reserve, and font effects on reading speed. *Vision Research*. Sept; 38(17): 2527-31.

Time of Day Impacts Comprehension

Research suggests that most schools "serve morning people best," even though most students, especially adolescents, are sharpest in mid-afternoon (Callan 1998). Callan is among a growing number of researchers who are posing the question, "Should school systems synchronize their clocks?" The answer to this question may depend on several factors, including the individual student's time of peak efficiency and comprehension. Callan and others maintain that learning would be greatly enhanced if each school district provided scheduling options—ultimately, by incorporating three parallel systems that allow students to choose a morning, afternoon, or

evening schedule. With such options, learners would be better equipped to maximize valuable learning time.

At the heart of this debate over school starting times is the important role that sleep and the body's circadian rhythm plays in memory formation and learning. In essence, some researchers suggest, early school starting times may interfere with these important memory-forming processes, which can affect reading comprehension and other cognitive tasks.

Stickgold and colleagues (2000) and Dotto (1996) report on the importance of the rapid eye movement (REM) state in sleep. REM sleep is crucial to enhancing the brain's processing of long-term memory and intense emotions. Dotto suggests that during REM sleep, the brain rehearses the prior day's learning. This "instant replay" consolidates and enhances memory. Waking up too early, however, affects REM sleep, says Stickgold, and 80 percent of REM occurs in the last few hours of sleep.

Dotto also found that the onset of hormonal changes during puberty causes a teen's biological sleep clock to generate a natural bedtime closer to midnight and a waking time closer to 8 a.m. Callan (1998) reported that most teens are unable to fall asleep at an early hour, and that 20 percent of high school students fall asleep in class. The time of peak efficiency and comprehension for *most students* is mid-morning and mid-afternoon.

Recent studies support previous findings that more meaningful learning often occurs in mid-morning and mid-afternoon:

∗ Barron and colleagues (1994) found in a study of 128 under-achieving first through fourth grade reading students that overall mean reading scores for children receiving instruction in the afternoon increased substantially compared to those who underwent instruction in the early morning.

∗ Epstein and colleagues (1998) reported in a study of more than 800 fifth graders that those students who started school at 7:10 a.m. complained more about sleepiness and concentration problems than children who began school at 8 a.m.

∗ Deficits in night sleep in kindergarten students can be compensated for by a longer afternoon nap in class the following day, research by Rodriguez and Montagner (1994) suggests.

∗ Kubow and colleagues (1999) found that among more than 7,160 students in seventeen school districts in the state, later starting times (moved from 7:15 to 8:40 a.m.) appeared to result in better achievement, less sleepiness, and fewer reports of depression, especially among high-school students.

∗ When learning sessions are matched with students' time-of-day preferences, reading and other cognitive performances improve (Ammons 1995; Natale & Lorenzetti 1997).

*The onset of hormonal changes during puberty
causes a teen's biological sleep clock to generate
a natural bedtime closer to midnight and
a waking time closer to 8 a.m.*

Action Steps

* Review past research that suggests that peak time for comprehension for most students is mid-morning and mid-afternoon.
* Allow for sufficient "downtime" or quiet time during the day for your learners and yourself. Besides rest and reflection, include movement, stretching, meditation, and deep breathing.
* Rotate various subjects, modalities, and materials. Student attention cycles normally dip and peak 45 minutes apart. In addition, suggest to students to get a good night's sleep during the school week to aid comprehension.
* Your school district may wish to consider the brain-friendly starting times adopted by the Edina School District in Minneapolis, MN. The district starts middle- and high-school classes later than usual in hopes that improved sleep patterns may result in better academic performance.

Sources:

Ammons, T.L. 1995. The effects of time of day on student attention and achievement. *Personality & Individual Differences*. Dec; 21(6): 480-510.

Barron, B.; M. Henderson; R. Spurgeon. 1994. Effects of time of day instruction on reading achievement of below-grade readers. *Reading Improvement*. Spring; 31(1): 56-60.

Callan, Roger. 1998. Giving students the (right) time of day. *Educational Leadership*. Dec-Jan; 55(4): 84-7.

Dotto, L. 1996. Sleep stages, memory, and learning. *Canadian Medical Association Journal*. Apr 15; 154(8): 1193-96.

Epstein, R.; N. Chillag; P. Lavie. 1998. Starting times of school: Effects on daytime functioning of fifth-grade children in Israel. *Sleep*. May; 21(3): 250-6.

Kubow, P.; K. Wahlstrom; A. Benis. 1999. Starting time and school life: Reflection from educators and students. *Phi Delta Kappan*. 80(6): 366-71.

Natale, Vincenzo and R. Lorenzetti. 1997. Influences of morningness-eveningness and time of day on narrative comprehension. *Personality & Individual Differences*. Oct; 23(4): 685-90.

Rodriguez, Danilo and H. Montagner. 1994. Children's biological and psychological rhythms at school and their importance for the school schedule. *Inancia y Aprendizaje*. 67-68: 221-44.

Stickgold, R.; Dana Whidbee; Beth Schirmer; Vipul Patel; J.A. Hobson. (2000). Visual discrimination task improvement: A multi-step process occurring during sleep. *Journal of Cognitive Neuroscience*. (12) 246-54.

Why We Tend to Learn Best in Groups

Research has found that supportive, safe learning environments (including those involving peer collaboration) engage the emotions in a positive way and stimulate attention, meaning, and memory in the brain. Researchers believe this enhanced learning results from both psychological and physiological components found in safe environments. Most of us experience security in numbers since the chance of being singled out is reduced. With others around us to provide a sense of social safety, the brain's fear response is less likely to be triggered.

Doughterty (1997) maintains that this freedom from fear is key to improved learning in groups. The physiological response to fear is an activated amygdala—the region of the brain that triggers the release of chemicals such as vasopressin and adrenaline. The release of these chemicals signals threat or danger, which immediately puts the body on alert. This situation can quickly shut down the brain's receptiveness to learning.

In Dougherty's study of cooperative learning among undergraduate organic chemistry students for two semesters at the University of Florida, he found that not only did learning flourish in group study situations, fewer students dropped out or had to repeat the course. In addition, spoken, written, aural, and visual information acquired in the lecture hall are reinforced in group study discussion, thereby aiding in successful retention and recall during exams. Other researchers concur that whatever the learning topic or task, small-group discussion reinforces classroom learning, aids recall, and gives students collaborative opportunities to solve problems and explore topics more thoroughly (Alexopoulou & Driver 1996; Allen & Reed 1997).

DeGrave and colleagues (1996) also noted in their study of third- and fourth-year medical students that those participating at least twice a week in small-group discussion displayed superior cognitive and metacognitive skills during problem analysis compared to non-participating students. And Karolides (1997) found in a study of elementary school classrooms that small-group discussion in literature-based reading classes promoted student interest in reading, encouraged student discussion about literature, and stimulated sophisticated literary interpretations.

Lloyd and colleagues (1996) of the University of Virginia also found results that support the benefit of group learning. In a series of two experiments comparing students' performance on Spanish vocabulary quizzes, Lloyd found that group study produced superior test scores over individual study/reward contingencies.

Action Steps

* Develop more opportunities for peer collaboration.
* Use teams during important study sessions or problem-solving tasks and provide a realistic time frame in which to realize results.
* Hold brainstorming sessions with a rotating facilitator.
* After meaningful classroom learning, break students into groups of four to further analyze and discuss the material. Encourage them to come up with their own views on the topic and/or problem at hand. Then reconvene the class for a discussion of the results.
* Provide positive reinforcement for strong analysis outcomes, problem solving, and inclusive discussion techniques.

Sources:

Allen, Shelley and Peg Reed. 1997. Talking about literature "in-depth": Teacher supported group discussions in a fifth-grade classroom. In: *Reader Response in Elementary Classrooms: Quest and Discovery*. Karolides, Nicholas (Ed). Mahwah, NJ: Lawrence Erlbaum Associates, Inc.

Alexopoulou, Evinella and Rosalind Driver. 1996. Small-group discussion in physics: Peer interaction modes in pairs and fours. *Journal of Research in Science Teaching*. 33(10): 1099-1114.

DeGrave, W.S.; H.P. Boshuizen; H.G. Schmidt. 1996. Problem-based learning: Cognitive and metacognitive processes during problem analysis. *Instructional Science*. 24(5): 321-41.

Dougherty, Ralph. 1997. Grade/study-performance contracts, enhanced communication, cooperative learning, and student performance in undergraduate organic chemistry. *Journal of Chemical Education*. June: 74(6): 722-6.

Karolides, Nicholas (Ed). 1997. *Reader Response in Elementary Classrooms: Quest and Discovery*. Mahwah, NJ: Lawrence Erlbaum Associates, Inc.

Lloyd, J.W.; Matthew Eberhardt; P. Drake, Jr. 1996. Group versus individual reinforcement contingencies within the context of group study conditions. *Journal of Applied Behavior Analysis*. Summer: 29(2): 189-200.

Enhancing Student Success Against the Odds

Why do some economically disadvantaged students perform well academically despite obstacles while others flounder? According to a recent study by Reis and Diaz (1999), the success of economically disadvantaged students may be related more to enrichment in the educational setting than to parental support at home.

Reis and Diaz found that, despite a lack of parental involvement in the academic pursuits of 9 ethnically diverse high-school females, the students continued to perform well on achievement tests and in other academic endeavors. The students attributed their success to interaction with other high-achieving students, teachers, and mentors—all which helped deepen a strong belief in self, the study reports.

Research conducted by Campbell and Ramey (1995) and others have demonstrated the brain's capability and willingness to respond positively to enriched learning environments at an early age. Scientists know that synaptic structures in human brains actually grow in such environments, and this growth continues throughout one's lifetime (including into old age) with continued enrichment.

In a long-term study of 111 children from low-income families, Campbell and Ramey concluded that the earlier such children are exposed to special childhood and academic development intervention, the better the long-term results. The study determined that, even in households where parental support was less than ideal, children who received Head Start mentoring and social worker intervention—continuously from infancy through 8 years of age—scored significantly higher on reading and math tests by age 15 than the control groups. The control groups received the intervention at later age intervals or did not receive any intervention at all. In addition, children exposed to intervention early in life repeated fewer grades and required fewer episodes of special education.

In 1997, Sharon and Craig Ramey reported that universities can also do much to enhance student performance in underprivileged schools—namely, by establishing university-community partnerships in which outreach efforts are emphasized and university resources are shared. Such cooperative environments help schools establish increased academic motivation and expectations among students.

Action Steps

* Take inventory of your learning environment and ensure that it's truly "safe" and non-threatening.
* Ask these questions: Does your classroom go beyond the traditional lecture approach to learning? Do you provide stimulating reading material that reflects your students' diverse backgrounds? Is there an active mentor program at your school that students can access? Do you convey an attitude of high, but reachable expectations?
* If you don't already have one, explore the possibility of establishing a viable university-community partnership in your area.
* Don't underestimate how peer feedback and interaction can impact academic success. Peer feedback is often more influential than teacher feedback in obtaining lasting performance results.

Sources:

Campbell, Frances and Craig Ramey. 1995. Cognitive and school outcomes for high-risk African-American students at middle adolescence: Positive effects of early intervention. *American Educational Research Journal*. Winter; 32(4): 743-72.

Ramey, Sharon Landesman and Craig Ramey. 1997. The role of universities in child development. In: *Children and Youth: Interdisciplinary Perspectives*. Herbert J. Walberg; Olga Reyes, et al. (Eds). Thousand Oaks, CA; Sage Publications, Inc.

Reis, Sally M. and Eva Diaz. 1999. Economically disadvantaged urban female students who achieve in schools. *Urban Review*. Mar; 31(1): 31-54.

The Power of Peer Tutoring

Having students help each other with class work and test preparation can serve an important cognitive function and may boost academic performance, suggests researchers Mathes and colleagues (1999) and others. In fact, peer-assisted learning in some cases has more influence on student learning than teacher instruction (Ginsburg-Block & Fantuzzo 1997) and can be used with learners of all levels, including students with disabilities, gifted students, and second-language learners (Topping & Ehly 1998).

Scientists have long been aware of the effect that peer interaction has on cognition. The fear response in the brain's amygdala region is less likely to be triggered when others provide social safety, security, common identity, and meaning. Fear is known to cause the release of critical brain chemicals such as vasopressin and adrenaline, which in abnormal amounts can impede learning.

Malone and McLaughlin (1997) found in a study of 40 middle-school students that weekly quizzes in vocabulary were significantly higher after reciprocal peer tutoring was implemented. Immediate recall and long-term memory were especially enhanced. Ginsburg-Block (1997) and her research team noted similar results in math test scores in academically at-risk students from an urban elementary school. And Mathes and colleagues (1999) demonstrated that reciprocal peer learning strategies, beginning as early as the first grade, help prevent later reading failure.

Action Steps

* Institute early and regular use of reciprocal peer tutoring. Group students with a variety of classmates who exhibit varying degrees of learning skill.
* For students with learning or reading problems, use reciprocal peer tutoring in close connection with structured teacher instruction.
* Encourage the use of peer-assisted learning, especially during classroom work and test preparation.

Sources:

Ginsburg-Block, Marika and John Fantuzzo. 1997. Reciprocal peer tutoring: An analysis of teacher and student interactions as a function of training and experience. *School Psychology Quarterly*. Summer; 12(2): 134-49.

Malone, Retta and T. McLaughlin. 1997. The effects of reciprocal peer tutoring with a group contingency on quiz performance in vocabulary with 7th and 8th grade students. *Behavioral Interventions*. Jan; 12(1): 27-40.

Mathes, Patricia; Marcia Grek; J. Howard; A. Babyak; S. Allen. 1999. Peer-assisted learning strategies for first-grade readers: A tool for preventing early reading failure. *Learning Disabilities Research & Practice*. Winter; 14(1): 50-60.

Topping, Keith and Stewart Ehly. 1998. *Peer-Assisted Learning*. Mahwah, NJ: Lawrence Erlbaum Associates, Inc.

Unstructured Study Groups Can Impede Cognition

Student study groups used for review and rehearsal of new learning have been shown to positively impact knowledge transfer, but such groups work best when they are structured and their goals and expectations are properly defined, research indicates (Gillies & Ashman 1998; Maheady 1998). Well-structured study groups are particularly important at the elementary, middle-school, and high-school levels, suggest the researchers.

In a study of 396 elementary-school children, Gillies and Ashman investigated the behaviors and interaction of children as they worked together in structured and unstructured groups for three school terms during social studies activities. Results suggest that students in structured groups with regular teacher input are consistently more cooperative in assisting other children in their group than those in unstructured settings with minimal teacher input. Middle-elementary grade students in structured groups also exhibited substantially higher reading and learning outcome scores compared to peers in unstructured groups.

In an examination of peer-assisted learning and study groups at the elementary and high-school levels, Maheady found that such groups as a whole are cognitively beneficial, but that many lack sufficient direction, especially from teachers or an appointed study group leader.

Scientists know that children's immature brains need structure to develop *optimal* cognitive skills, especially frontal-lobe skills such as planning, social conduct, and decision-making. While study groups elicit important learning in "safe" peer settings—enhancing students' sense of responsibility, well-being, and motivation—structured direction from the teacher or group leader is often essential to assure that the goals and expectations of the students are met.

Action Steps

* Encourage the use of study groups, but for optimal results help students define goals, expectations, and responsibilities for the group.
* Make sure every study group has a responsible group leader.
* Follow up on the progress of study groups and assist students when necessary to improve study group interaction.

Sources:

Gillies, Robyn and Adrian Ashman. 1998. Behavior and interactions of children in cooperative groups in lower and middle elementary grades. *Journal of Educational Psychology*. 90(4): 746-57.

Maheady, Larry. 1998. The advantages and disadvantages of peer-assisted learning strategies. In: *Peer-Assisted Learning*. Topping, Keith and Stewart Ehly (Eds). Mahwah, NJ: Lawrence Erlbaum Associates, Inc.

How Habits Are Formed in Learning

For better or worse, we are all creatures of habit. Habits are but thoughts and actions, which, through frequent repetition, have become more or less automatic. Just as in the acts of walking or using a fork, we do not pay attention to the individual steps involved. Rather, these learned actions are so ingrained and natural to us, we perform them without thinking. But what neurological mechanisms are at work in the brain as habits are formed? And what cognitive areas are involved in the process?

Scientists are just beginning to piece together the answers to these questions. What is known is that the driving force behind the formation of a habit (both good and bad) is meaningful and specific reinforcement. We exercise because it makes us look and feel better; we eat or drink too much because it seems "to pick us up" when we're stressed out and depressed; we throw temper tantrums because they help us get our way. This goal-directed behavior fuels habit formation, and with repetition, makes an impression on the brain that is often difficult to erase (Aarts & Dijksterhuis 2000).

This cognitive process is even more important when we realize that every time we think a thought or perform an act, a slight change takes place in the delicate nerve cells in some part of the brain, including the frontal and mid-brain areas (Jog, et al. 1999). Every action among these cells leaves an indelible mark or crease. Just as it is easy for paper to bend where it has been creased before, it is likewise easy for impressions to be embedded in the brain where similar action has taken place before.

Jog and colleagues shed further light on how the brain reacts when it acquires a habit. Using rats that were taught to run a maze, the researchers

found that, as the rats learned, a change occurred in the firing pattern of certain neurons in the brain, leading to speculation that there may be a network of neuron activity linked to exercising a habit, particularly in the brain's sensorimotor region known as the striatum.

The Jog study asks, "Do we use a piece of brain to learn a habit and then another part of the brain to exercise that habit?" The researchers suggest that there may be a whole network involved, and different parts of the network may be more active after the habit is learned. Ultimately, what is learned about how the brain acquires habits may help in the formulation of drugs or other therapies to treat degenerative neurological disorders and addictions that affect behavior such as Parkinson's disease and substance abuse.

The importance of meaningful and specific reinforcement in habit formation was further borne out in a 1997 study by the National Assessment of Education Progress (NAEP). The research, conducted by Vanneman (1997) found that students who were most successful in forming good study habits looked upon homework and class work as highly relevant and specific to their academic achievement and career goals. Scientists know this degree of reinforcement stimulates long-term memory and learning. We know that habits are hard to make and even harder to break, but consider the following suggestions when working with learners to counteract their bad ones:

Action Steps

* Help the learner discover why he or she performs the bad habit in the first place (i.e., habitual tardiness, lying, or turning in ill-prepared assignments). If the learner has multiple bad habits, tackle the most crucial or easily changed one first.

* Provide learners with incentives or advantages for breaking the bad habit (increased productivity, better conduct rating, and more respect from peers).

* After obtaining initial input from the learner, help him/her establish a realistic step-by-step action plan to eliminate the bad behavior. Provide appropriate follow-up, encouragement, and feedback as the plan progresses, and if appropriate, enlist the help of a peer or another person respected by the learner.

* In most cases, view the breaking of a habit as a long-term goal. The learner has probably been practicing the habit for some time, which means it's deeply ingrained. Encourage the learner to be patient with him/herself. Be patient with yourself, as well, and learn to appreciate the "little victories."

Sources:
Aarts, Henk and A. Dijksterhuis. 2000. Habits as knowledge structures: Automatically in goal-directed behavior. *Journal of Personality & Social Psychology*. Jan; 78(1): 53-63.
Jog, M.S.; Y. Kubota; C.I. Connolly; V. Hillegaart; A.M. Graybiel. 1999. Building neural representations of habits. *Science*. Nov 26; 286(5445): 1745-9.
Vanneman, Alan. 1997. Good Study Habits and Academic Performance: Findings from the NAEP History and Geography Assessments. *NAEP Publications*. Aug 2(4).

Mentoring and Tutoring Benefit At-Risk Students

Although research is sparse, evidence does suggest that students, especially educationally disadvantaged ones, can benefit significantly from interaction with positive role models through mentoring programs. However, academic gains are even more apparent when such students are exposed simultaneously to both tutoring and mentoring assistance, according to research conducted by Muscott and O'Brien (1999) and Kuehr (1997). Tutoring-mentoring interaction can often mean better test performance, improved self-esteem, and enhanced positive attitude for at-risk and learning-disabled students, the researchers found.

Previous studies by Ginsburg-Block and Fantuzzo (1997) indicate that the brain responds positively to cognitive reinforcement such as tutoring and mentoring, especially if it is relevant and specific to the needs and expectations of the learner and is followed up with constructive feedback. This is known to lessen the brain's fear response (in the amygdala) to new and difficult learning, and to increase a sense of safety, security, and meaning. These components stimulate long-term memory and learning.

Reglin (1998) found that combined mentoring and tutoring not only helped improve academic performance among 35 at-risk high-school students, it also dramatically reduced dropout rates. And in a study of at-risk elementary students who were mentored and tutored by soldiers and civilian employees at an Army base, Kuehr demonstrated that such interaction had a positive effect on students' self-defeating behavior. Muscott and O'Brien found in study of 10 learning-disabled students that mentoring enhanced social and coping skills significantly, and that the most effective mentors were those who were flexible and responsive to the needs of their students.

Action Steps

* Positive results are compounded when students are exposed to both mentoring and tutoring interaction. This is especially true for educationally at-risk students.
* Inquire about established employer or university partnerships in your area that might support a mentoring/tutoring program.
* Look for mentors and tutors who can deal effectively with the educational needs of your students and who can enhance students' goals and aspirations.

Sources:

Ginsburg-Block, Marika and J. Fantuzzo. 1997. Reciprocal peer tutoring: An analysis of teacher and student interaction as a function of training and experience. *School Psychology Quarterly*. Summer; 12(2): 134-49.

Kuehr, Wanda. 1997. *Processes and Outcomes of Mentoring Relationships in Selected At-Risk Elementary Students*. Our Lady of the Lake University, USA, UMI Order Number: AAM972483. Dissertation Abstracts International: Section B: Sciences & Engineering. Sept; 58(3-B): 1595.

Muscott, Howard and Sara Talis O'Brien. 1999. Teaching character education to students with behavioral and learning disabilities through mentoring relationships. *Education and Treatment of Children*. Aug; 22(3): 373-93.

Reglin, Gary. 1998. *Mentoring Students as Risk: An Underutilized Alternative Education Strategy*. Springfield, IL: Charles C. Thomas Publisher.

Chapter 2
Environments for Learning Smarter

veryone knows that environments influence learning. In fact, recent research has focused as much on the impact of classroom environments as on the underlying neural mechanisms of learning. In studies of rats raised in enriched environments, the subjects grew more brain cells and subsequently improved performance in problem-solving tasks. Environments do matter.

Some of the environmental elements scientists are examining include class size, furniture design, temperature, humidity, color, sound, movement, plants, air quality, aroma, and lighting. The most effective teachers are aware of the cognitive effects of these variables. For example, we know that the human brain is extremely temperature sensitive—a factor that significantly impacts cognition. In U.S. Defense Department studies, Taylor and Orlansky (1993) reported that heat stress dramatically lowered scores in both intellectual and physical tasks.

Lighting—a factor that influences all classrooms—also impacts learning. Students in brightly-lit classrooms perform better in school compared to students in dimly-lit classrooms (London 1988). This study, conducted in three states, suggests that bright classrooms—ones with massive windows and lots of natural light—provide an environment that spurs higher test scores in math (20%) and reading (26%). Ordinary fluorescent lighting has been shown to raise cortisol levels, a change likely to suppress the immune system. Although we aren't generally consciously aware of it, fluorescent lights have a flickering quality and barely audible hum, which negatively impact the central nervous system of some students.

On the positive side, certain aromas (for example lavender and lemon) can increase student attention and memory. And particular colors (for example light grays and yellows) can positively impact behavior and learning. We don't know specifically how such environmental factors physiologically alter the brain; however, with the advent of neuro-imaging devices, we are now able to view the brain in motion. Speculation centers on our stress, hormonal, and attentional systems as potential factors influenced by environment. The bottom line is that environment plays an important role in learning, and we can positively impact it. This chapter presents a variety of studies that substantiate this critical principle and the brain-compatible practices that support it.

Temperature and Learning

Did you know that the cooler your brain is, the more relaxed and receptive you are, and the warmer your brain, the more aroused you become? Researchers report that higher temperatures impact neurotransmitters levels—especially norepinephrine and serotonin, two chemicals associated with moods ranging from depression to relaxation (Donovan, et al. 1999; Howard 1994; Izard, et al. 1984). Excess levels of neurotransmitters can lead to inappropriate behavior—a persistent obstacle to learning. This basic insight sheds light on the important role temperature plays in the learning environment, and how it can affect our behavior, thoughts, and emotions.

What is the optimal temperature range for learning? Although research on this question appears limited, it is known that a moderate temperature range is more conducive to brain alertness than a room that is too hot or too cold. Harner (1974) reports that an ambient temperature of 68 to 74 degrees Fahrenheit is ideal for most learning situations, particularly those involving reading and mathematics, in which optimal focus and concentration is required. If a room's temperature cannot be perfect, however, it is better to err on the side of cool.

In animal studies, higher temperatures are known to make guppies and other fish more aggressive in feeding and predator-related behavior (Weetman, et al. 1998). And cold exposure was found to delay growth and maturation in rat pups (Gerrish, et al. 1998).

On the other end of the spectrum, however, Burke and Stewart (1980) found that with the right protective clothing, students can be exposed to temperatures as low as 50 degrees for up to 40 minutes without it adversely affecting work quality.

Other findings in studies involving humans include the following:

* Hot, humid weather was linked to increased episodes of panic attacks in an empirical study involving 154 patients at the Montefiore Medical Center in New York (Asnis 1999).
* A significant increase in body temperature in children with attention-deficit hyperactivity disorder can lead to increased aggressiveness, especially when the serotonin-enhancing drug d,l-fenfluramine (FEN) is administered (Donovan, et al. 1999).
* Acute, limited exposure to cold stimulates the immune system, which is further enhanced by prior heat treatment and physical exercise, reports Brenner and colleagues (1999).
* An empirical study suggested a link between high incidences of suicide and severe depression among the elderly during the summer months of June and July (Salib 1997).

Interestingly, the body's sensitivity to temperature fluctuates with age. Stevens and Choo (1998) examined temperature-detection thresholds to warming and cooling in 13 regions of the body, in sixty 18- to 88-year-old adults. The researchers concluded that thermal sensitivity declines with age. The greatest changes take place in the extremities, especially the feet, while central regions, such as the chest, give up their sensitivity more slowly. He also found three characteristics that remained constant regardless of age: (1) Temperature sensitivity varies approximately 100-fold over the body surface; (2) All body regions are more sensitive to cold than to warmth; and (3) The better a region is at detecting cold, the better it is at detecting warmth.

*If a room's temperature can't be perfect,
it's better to err on the side of cool.*

Action Steps

* In environments that require alertness, such as classrooms, offices, or meeting rooms, keep temperatures in the upper range of the comfort zone (Howard 1994). A room that is too cool can shut down cortical functions of the brain.

* In areas where you want individuals to be relaxed (waiting rooms, cafeterias, break rooms), keep temperatures in the lower range of the comfort zone.

* When planning and conducting sessions with the elderly, be aware of their heightened sensitivity to cool temperatures. And in sessions involving individuals with such conditions as panic disorder or ADHD, be mindful of how extremely warm temperatures can increase their anxiety or aggressiveness.

* When you are in need of refreshment, try breathing through your nose. This technique has been found to cool the brain and to promote relaxation.

Sources:

Asnis, J. 1999. Environmental factors in panic disorder. *Journal of Clinical Psychiatry*. Apr; 60(4): 264.

Brenner, I.K.; J.W. Castellani; C. Gabaree; A.J. Young; J. Zamecnik; R.J. Shephard; P.N. Shek. 1999. Immune changes in humans during cold exposure: Effects of prior heating and exercise. *Journal of Applied Physiology*. Aug; 87(2): 699-710.

Burke, Stanley and Bob R. Stewart. 1980. The effects of temperature and protective clothing upon task completion time, work quality, and student attitude toward learning. *Journal of the American Assn. of Teacher Educators in Agriculture*. Nov; 21(13): 5-13.

Donovan, A.M; J.M. Halperin; J.H. Newcorn; V. Sharma. 1999. Thermal response to serotonergic challenge and aggression in attention deficit hyperactivity disorder (in process). *Journal of Child Adolescent Psychopharmacology*. 9(2): 85-91.

Gerrish, Carolyn, et al. 1998. Acute, early thermal experiences alters weaning onset in rats. *Physiology & Behavior*. June; 64(4): 463-74.

Harner, David P. 1974. Effects of thermal environment on learning. *CEFP Journal*. Mar.-Apr; 12(2): 4-6.

Howard, Pierce, J. 2000. *The Owner's Manual for the Brain: Everyday Applications from Mind-Brain Research*. Austin, TX: Bard Press.

Izard, C.E.; J Kagan; R.B. Zajonc (Eds). 1984. *Emotions, Cognition, and Behavior*. Cambridge, England: Cambridge University Press.

London, Wayne. 1988. Brain/Mind Bulletin Collections. *New Sense Bulletin*. (Los Angeles, CA) Vol. 13, April; 7c.

Salib, Emad. 1997. Elderly suicide and weather conditions: Is there a link? *International Journal of Geriatric Psychiatry*. Sept. 12(9): 937-41.

Stevens, Joseph C. and Kenneth K. Choo. 1998. Temperature sensitivity of the body surface over the life span. *Somatosensory & Motor Research*. 15(1): 13-28.

Taylor, H.L. and J. Orlansky. 1993. The effects of wearing protective chemical warfare combat clothing on human performance. *Aviation Space and Environmental Medicine*. 64.2, A1-41.

Weetman, David; David Atkinson; James C. Chubb. 1998. Effects of temperature on anti-predator behavior in the guppy. *Animal Behaviour*. May; 55(5): 1361-72.

Odor: The Power of Common Scents

Recent research suggests that natural, everyday odors are learned and recognized by our brain with astonishing specificity, and that these odors affect cognition, mood, sleep patterns, and productivity (Pauli, et al. 1999; Laurent 1997; Kallan 1991). For example, certain smells—like fresh-baked cookies, a particular perfume, or a musty schoolbook—can almost immediately trigger memories and emotions from our past. Unpleasant odors, however, are more apt to disrupt the cognitive process and trigger our startle reflexes (Erlichman, et al. 1995).

Like the rest of our senses, smell is a key component in learning and can, in some instances, improve cognition. But our ability to *detect* odor is especially important since it represents one of the most direct pathways to the brain (Dhong, et al. 1999). For example, Pauli and colleagues (1999) reported that undergraduate psychology students experienced significant cognitive enhancement in word association and word naming tests after being exposed to background odors of vanilla. Similar results were noted by Schnaubelt (1999) in learning environments using scents of lavender. And in a 40-minute test of vigilance (similar to that needed for air traffic controllers and long-distance drivers), production workers receiving

30-second bursts of peppermint or muguet (lily of the valley) every 5 minutes showed a 15 to 20 percent improvement in performance (Dember and Parasuraman 1993).

Our sense of smell functions basically like this: Odor molecules dissolve in the mucus lining of the nose. Smell receptors there are stimulated and trigger nerve impulses that, unlike our other senses, bypass the sensory relay center of the brain called the thalamus. Our sense of smell is linked *directly* to the frontal-lobe area, which controls problem solving, will power, and planning, and to the limbic system in the mid-brain, where memory and emotion are processed and housed (van Toller 1988).

Action Steps

* Experiment with scents such as vanilla and peppermint, using them as background aromas in your classroom to enhance well-being and attention. Keep track of your results for future consideration.
* Since unpleasant odors are known to inhibit learning, be sensitive to others' complaints about bothersome smells. Also, be aware that some people may be allergic to specific odors, such as perfume or cigarette smoke.
* Consider supplying tea bags with scents such as peppermint, lemon, jasmine, chamomile, and spiced apple in break/lunch areas or as a beverage alternative to soft drinks and coffee.
* Consider using naturally fragrant wood furniture (i.e., cedar) or home-style fragrances such as potpourri in school office waiting rooms, and other areas where you would like to put people at ease.

Sources:

Dember, W. and R. Parasuraman. 1993. Remarks before the American Association for the Advancement of Science. In: Pierce J. Howard, Ph.D., *The Owner's Manual for the Brain*. 1994. Austin, TX: Leornian Press.

Dhong, H. J.; S. K. Chung; R. L. Doty. 1999. Estrogen protects against 3-methylindole-induced olfactory loss. *Brain Research*. Apr; 824(2): 312-5.

Ehrlichman, H.; S. Brown; J. Zhu; S. Warrenburg. 1995. Startle reflex modulation during exposure to pleasant and unpleasant odors. *Psychophysiology*. 32: 150-4.

Kallan, C. 1991. Probing the power of common scents. *Prevention*. Oct; 43(10): 39-43.

Laurent, G. 1997. Olfactory processing: maps, times, and codes. *Current Opinion in Neurobiology*. Aug; 7(4): 547-53.

Pauli, P.; L.E. Bourne; H. Diekmann; N. Birbaumer. 1999. Cross-modality priming between odors and odor-congruent words. *American Journal of Psychology*. 112(2):175.

Schnaubelt, K. 1999. *Advanced Aromatherapy: Healing with Essential Oils*. Berkeley, CA: Frog.

van Toller, S. 1988. Odors and the brain. In *Perfumery: The Psychology and Biology of Fragrance*. S. van Toller and G. Dodd (Eds), London: Chapman & Hall. p. 121-46.

Color and Cognition

Scientists are just beginning to understand what advertisers have suspected all along: Color can enhance moods, emotions, and behaviors, and possibly cognition, as well. Why the brain responds more positively to one color over another is still not fully understood. However it is a process likely begun during infancy when exposure to color, especially bright color, plays an important role in stimulating and strengthening immature neural connections in the brain's occipital lobe or primary visual cortex.

Exposure to color is also known to play a key role in the maturation and stimulation of other areas throughout the brain. These include the parietal lobes (touch and spatial understanding), the limbic system (emotional message encoding), the temporal lobes (hearing and language), and the frontal lobes (body movement, decision-making, attention, reasoning, and memory). As such, it is not surprising that full color multi-media images in study conditions produced significantly better recall than black-and-white visuals in complex learning situations (Farley & Grant 1976). College students taking midterm exams printed on blue paper outperformed students taking the identical exam on red paper (Sinclair, et al. 1998). The color blue has been found to produce a calming effect conducive to deep thinking and concentration, while red is useful for creative thinking and short-term high energy (Birren 1978).

Color can also enhance memory of text when the colors are used in close proximity to words, and in groupings of shapes and forms (Wallace, et al. 1998). However, when color groupings were compared solely with figure-shape elements to test description recall among 286 college psychology students in a seven-trial experiment, figure-shaped elements elicited significantly more functional descriptions than did colors (Harris &

Amundson 1998). This suggests that figures can also act as important mnemonic devices.

A study conducted by Boyatziz and Varghese (1994) found that young children responded overwhelming better to bright colors such as red, pink, and blue over dark colors, such as brown, black, and gray. In addition, the study found that children's emotional reactions to bright colors became increasingly positive with age, and girls in particular showed a preference for brighter colors and a stronger dislike of darker colors than boys. Read and colleagues (1999) demonstrated that preschool children exposed to visually appealing wall colors, ceiling designs, and other physical environment changes exhibited more cooperative behavior after such exposure than before. Hephill (1996) notes that our preference for bright colors seems to continue into adulthood, with women responding more positively than men.

For instance, researchers Shaie and Heiss noted as early as 1964 that regardless of age or cultural background, short-wavelength colors—what we commonly call the warm colors (red, orange and yellow)—are highly arousing, although not necessarily pleasing. Conversely, longer wavelength hues—what we commonly call the cool colors (blues and greens)—have a calming, relaxing effect. The majority of people, the researchers noted, identify cool colors as the most pleasant.

Robson (1999) reported that people who were exposed to a red environment perceived their time spent there to be shorter than those exposed to a blue environment, even though the actual time was the same in both instances. This finding concurs with past studies, which found that short-wavelength colors, when compared to their cool counterparts, elicit a higher degree of stimulation and tension in subjects.

Colors are also being used with success as stress reducers, especially in health-care facility design. Along with lighting, signage, noise control, and other design elements, appropriate use of color has been found to have a profound influence on patient and family well-being (Frasca-Beaulieu 1999).

Action Steps

✳ Classrooms and Office Spaces: Best color is sky-blue tinged with red. This combination is conducive to thoughtful study, but also to alertness.

✳ Cafeterias: Best color is purple, which is known in the restaurant industry as a tranquilizing color that is good for the appetite.

✳ Gym or Sales Offices: Best colors are yellow, orange, and coral, which represent the energizing hues.

✳ Production Areas: Best color is green, which is known in factories to enhance production and performance.

✳ Encourage learners and employees to add color to reports, presentations, and visual displays for better recall.

Sources:

Birren, Faber. 1978. *Color and Human Response*. New York: Van Norstrand Reinhold.

Boyatzis, C.J. and R. Varghese. 1994. Children's emotional associations with colors. *Journal of Genetic Psychology*. Mar; 155(1): 77-85.

Farley, Frank and A.P. Grant. 1976. Arousal and cognition: Memory for color vs. black and white multimedia presentation. *Journal of Psychology*. Sep; 94(1): 147-50.

Frasca-Beaulieu, K. 1999. Interior design for ambulatory care facilities: How to reduce stress and anxiety in patients and families. *Journal of Ambulatory Care Management*. Jan; 22(1): 67-73.

Harris, L.J. and J.C. Amundson. 1998. Human classical conditioning of visual compound stimuli in paired-associate tasks. *Perceptual & Motor Skills*. Aug; 87(1): 227-41.

Hemphill, M. 1996. A note on adults' color-emotion associations. *Journal of Genetic Psychology*. Sept; 157(3): 275-80.

Read, Marilyn; A. Sugawara; J. Brandt. 1999. Impact of space and color in the physical environment on preschool children's cooperative behavior. *Environment and Behavior*. May 31(3): 413-4.

Robson, Stephani. 1999. Turning the tables: The psychology of design for high-volume restaurants. *Cornell University Hotel & Restaurant Administration Quarterly*. June; 40(3): 56-65.

Shaie, K.W. and R. Heiss. 1964. *Color and Personality*. Bern, Switzerland: Hans Huber. p. 75.

Sinclair, Robert C.; A.S. Soldat; Melvin M. Mark. 1998. Affective cues and processing strategy: Color-coded examination forms influence performance. *Teaching of Psychology*. 25(2): 130-2.

Wallace, David S.; S.W. West; A. Ware; D.F. Dansereau. 1998. The effect of knowledge maps that incorporate gestalt principles on learning. *Journal of Experimental Education*. Fall; 67(1): 5-16.

Formaldehyde and Indoor Air Quality: You Are What You Breathe

How safe is the air inside your building? And how can poor air quality affect cognition? Most of us are familiar with the negative impact of outdoor air pollutants, such as motor vehicle exhaust, pollen, exterior plumbing vents, and building exhausts, but what are the health risks of indoor pollutants and where do they come from?

A recent finding by the Environmental Protection Agency (1999) indicates that most indoor air pollution actually comes from sources already inside the building. These sources of pollution include carpets, upholstery, manufactured wood products, draperies, copy machines, pesticides, and cleaning agents—all of which can emit volatile organic compounds, namely formaldehyde. The World Health Organization estimates that up to 30 percent of new and remodeled buildings worldwide may be subject to health complaints connected to formaldehyde emissions.

Formaldehyde is a colorless, pungent, and irritating gas used chiefly as a disinfectant or preservative in chemical synthesis. Its effects on human health and cognition (decreased motor activity, poor concentration, headache, stress, and allergy-like symptoms) are well documented.

For example, Wantke and colleagues (1996) investigated the health complaints of 62 children (aged 8) exposed to formaldehyde concentrations (emanating from wood paneling) in classrooms. Their symptoms included poor concentration, headache, burning sensation in the eyes and nasal cavity, coughing, fatigue, rhinitis, and nose bleeding. Symptoms ceased when the children were transferred to a school building with no wood paneling. And among adults, Konopinski (1985) noted that formaldehyde toxicity levels from wood paneling are twice as high in warm weather as in cold temperatures.

Formaldehyde exposure produces mental stress, which triggers the release of adrenaline, and in-turn increases levels of formaldehyde circulation in the blood (Yu, et al. 1997). Other researchers (Boja, et al. 1985) noted that even a low level of the chemical slows motor activity by producing neurochemical changes in dopamine—a critical neurotransmitter.

Chronic exposure to formaldehyde vapors and other toxic substances endangers immune system health and blood cell interaction (Baj, et al. 1994). Thrasher and colleagues (1989) also noted that formaldehyde exposure can adversely affect the central nervous system. Cognitive impairment worsens significantly when mild head-injury patients are exposed to chronic low-levels of formaldehyde (Cripe & Dodrill 1988). And in an extensive study of workers exposed to formaldehyde, Blair and colleagues (1990) found a heightened irritating effect on the nasal cavity that may contribute to cancer of the nasopharynx and nasal cavities.

Once used primarily in medical circles, formaldehyde is used today in commercial endeavors, primarily as a resin in the production of building materials such as particleboard and urea-formaldehyde foam insulation, exposing large numbers of people to its properties. Consumer products such as cosmetics and cigarettes (nicotine) also contain formaldehyde as do automobile exhaust and combustion from gas cooking.

Other indoor pollutants, namely biological air contaminants, can also affect building occupants. Biological air contaminants, such as bacteria, mold, pollen, and viruses, can breed in stagnant water that has accumulated in ducts, humidifiers, and drain pans, or where water has collected on ceiling tiles, carpeting, or insulation, warns the Environmental Protection Agency. Sometimes even insects and bird droppings can be a source of biological contamination. Physical symptoms related to biological contamination include cough, chest tightness, fever, chills, muscle aches, and allergic responses.

The World Health Organization estimates that up to 30 percent of new and remodeled buildings worldwide may be subject to health complaints connected to formaldehyde emissions.

Action Steps

* If students or employees regularly complain of headache, poor concentration, and allergy-like symptoms, consult the school nurse, company physician, and/or your local health department immediately.
* Determine whether your building has formaldehyde resin-based wood paneling or urea-formaldehyde foam insulation. Refrain from purchasing such materials.
* Make sure that your building remains in compliance with air quality control regulations set force by the Occupational Safety and Health Administration (OSHA). If you have questions on the status of air quality at your building, contact your local OSHA representative.
* Encourage your building maintenance/custodial staff to clean ventilation ducts and vents regularly and to refrain from using formaldehyde-based cleaners and pesticides in concentrated amounts.
* Emphasize to students the importance of air quality and have them list and investigate the various indoor and outdoor air contaminants that can affect people.

Sources:

Baj, Z.; E. Majewska; K. Zeman; L. Pokoca; D. Dworniak; M. Paradowski; H. Tchorzewski. 1994. The effect of chronic exposure to formaldehyde, phenol, and organic chlorohydrocarbons on peripheral blood cells and the immune systems in humans. *Journal of Investigative Allergy and Clinical Immunology.* Jul-Aug; 4(4): 186-91.

Blair, A.; R. Saracci; P.A. Stewart; R.B. Hays; C. Shy. 1990. Epidemiologic evidence on the relationship between formaldehyde exposure and cancer. *Scandinavian Journal of Work Environmental Health.* Dec; 16(16): 381-93.

Boja, J.W.; J.A. Nielson; E. Foldvary; E. Truitt. 1985. Acute low-level formaldehyde behavioral and neurochemical toxicity in the rat. *Progress in Neuro-Psychopharmacology & Biological Psychiatry.* 9 (5-6): 671-4.

Cripe, Lloyd and C. Dodrill. 1988. Neuropsychological test performances with chronic low-level formaldehyde exposure. *Clinical Neuropsychologist.* Jan; 2(1): 41-8.

Environmental Protection Agency (with the Indoor Air Quality Information Clearinghouse). 1999. Fact Sheet: Indoor Air Facts (Revised, No. 4).

Konopinski, V.J. 1985. Seasonal formaldehyde concentrations in an office building. *American Industrial Hygiene Association Journal.* Feb; 46(2): 56-68.

Thrasher, J. D.; R. Madison; A. Broughton; Z. Gard. 1989. Building-related illness and antibodies to albumin conjugates of formaldehyde, toluene, diisocyanate, and trimelltic anhydride. *American Journal Industrial Medicine.* 15(2): 187-95.

Wantke, F.; C.M. Demmer; P. Tappler; M. Gotz; R. Jarisch. 1996. Exposure to gaseous formaldehyde induces IgE-mediated sensitization to formaldehyde in school children. *Clinical Experimental Allergy.* Mar; 26(3): 276-80.

Yu, P.H.; C.T. Lai; D.M. Zu. 1997. Formation of formaldehyde from adrenaline in vivo; A potential risk factor for stress-related angiopathy. *Neurochemical Research.* May; 22(5): 615-20.

Noise and Cognition

Have you stopped to listen lately to the noise level in your classroom or work environment? If it's too loud, learning may be impeded, say researchers. Excessive environmental noise—including traffic sounds, aircraft noise, machinery, beepers, and even casual conversation—can reduce comprehension and work performance, especially in the early stages of learning a new task (Gomes, et al. 1999; Berglund, et al. 1996). Certain noise levels are also known to adversely affect cognition among students with learning deficits or hearing loss. They can also contribute to discipline problems in the classroom and interfere with the recovery time of hospital patients (Berg, et al. 1996; Moore, et al. 1998). In a comprehensive study of Japanese factory workers, Umemura and colleagues (1992) found that the end-result of noise-impeded learning is stress, which further exacerbates the situation.

Our brain processes sound basically like this: After being channeled by the auditory nerve in the brain's medulla region, auditory information flows via the thalamus to the temporal gyrus, the part of the cerebral cortex involved in receiving and perceiving sound. There, an intense selection process occurs among neurons. Some neurons respond only to a small range of frequencies; others react to a wide range; some react only to the beginning of a sound; and others only respond to the end. Speech sounds, however, are processed less selectively. When these signals reach the primary auditory cortex in the temporal lobe of the brain, they are funneled to the left hemisphere for processing in language centers.

Our hearing system is capable of responding to a wide range of sound levels, from a soft whisper (approximately 20 decibels) to the dangerously high volume of a stereo at full blast (approximately 120 decibels—enough to cause auditory pain and damage). The Environmental Protection Agency recommends that noise levels in most situations (including classroom environments) not exceed an average of 45 decibels in the daytime, and 35 decibels at night. Ambient, or environmental noise, in many urban areas of the United States, however, exceeds these levels regularly, often ranging from 50 to 70 decibels during the day, and 45 to 65 decibels at night. Urban hospitals are no exception (Grumet 1993).

Scientists know that loud noise causes a series of immediate stress responses in the nervous system and the voluntary muscular reflex system, including the release of the neurotransmitters epinephrine and norepinephrine, increased heart rate, grimacing, and sudden muscle flexion. In persons with anxiety, hypertension, and heart problems, loud noise is known to also increase blood pressure, cortisol levels, serum cholesterol, and triglyceride levels (ibid).

In one study, Berg and colleagues (1996) noted that reverberation levels inside and outside the learning area were exacerbated by poor classroom acoustics, which negatively impacted learners' ability to understand speech. Students with learning deficits and second language learners were also impacted by the ambient noise, and more discipline problems surfaced, as well. Pekkarinen and Wiljanen (1990) reported dramatic improvement in students' speech discrimination after refitting classrooms with sound-absorbing material that reduced ambient noise.

In work settings, excessive noise was also found to interfere with learning new tasks (Gomes, et. al. 1999; Kiger 1989). The researchers suggest that noise blocks early processing of information and higher-order thinking. But is all environmental noise bad? Some studies indicate that so-called "white noise"—the low-pitched, sustained, and low-volume hum of some sounds such as the sound of a film projector or overhead fan—may help to mask all other noises, thereby aiding working memory and cognition (Carlson, et al. 1997).

Excessive environmental noise can reduce comprehension and work performance, especially in the early stages of learning a new task.

Action Steps

* If you suspect a significant problem with ambient noise, consult an acoustical engineer on the most efficient way to eliminate the distractions.
* When important mental tasks are required, close classroom/office doors and windows.
* Be especially aware of the effect that high noise levels can have on beginning students, learning disabled students, and persons with existing health problems.
* Make appropriate use of "white noise" (such as fish tanks, desktop waterfalls, background music, and environmental CDs) to mask other noises.

Sources:

Berg, Frederick; J. Blair; P. Benson. 1996. Classroom acoustics: The problem, impact, and solution. *Praxis der Kinderpsychologie and Kinderpsychiatric*. Dec; 45(10): 1620.

Berglund, B; P. Hassmen; R.F. Job. 1996. Sources and effects of low-frequency noise. *Journal of the Acoustic Society of America*. May; 99(5): 2985-3002.

Carlson, S; P. Rama; D. Artchakov; I. Linnankoski. 1997. Effects of music and white noise on working memory performance in monkeys. *Neuroreport*. Sept 8; 8(13): 2853-6.

Gomes, L; P. Martinho; A. Pimenta; N. Castelo Branco. 1999. Effects of occupational exposure to low-frequency noise on cognition. *Aviation, Space & Environmental Medicine*. 70(3, Suppl): A115-18.

Grumet, Gerald. 1993. Pandemonium in the modern hospital. *The New England Journal of Medicine*. Feb 11; 6(328).

Kiger, Derrick. 1989. Effects of music information load on a reading comprehension task. *Perceptual & Motor Skills*. Oct; 69(2): 531-4.

Moore, M.M.; D. Nguyen; S.P. Nolan; S.P. Robinson. 1998. Intervention to reduce decibel levels on patient care units. *American Surgeon*. Sept; 64(9): 894-9.

Pekkarinen, Eeva and V. Wiljanen. 1990. Effect of sound-absorbing treatment on speech discrimination in rooms. *Audiology*. Jul-Aug; 29(4): 219-27.

Umemura, M; K. Honda; Y. Kikuchi. 1992. Influence of noise on heart rate and quantity in mental work. *Annals of Physiology and Anthropology*. Sept; 11(5): 523-32.

Ergonomics and Cognition

How might the design of your students' desks play a role in their cognition? More than you think, says Galen Cranz, professor of architecture at the University of California, Berkeley (1998). Dr. Cranz calls for a more pragmatic and posture-friendly approach to the way we design and use chairs, from the boardroom to the classroom.

We spend two-thirds of our life in a chair or bed, Cranz maintains; and if one of these is not right, our health and productivity suffer. The traditional classroom desk, which carries the sitter's weight straight down and increases lower-back pressure, forces the student to sit "on" the chair instead of "in" it. Warning against equating cushiness with comfort, Cranz says a good classroom desk should keep the shoulders back and the chin up, as well as provide arm rests to minimize strain on the upper body. A good chair should have as much adjustability as possible and be easy to modify. The seat should not be so long that it digs into the back of the legs, and the chair's height should be adjusted so that the feet can touch the floor without dangling. According to Cranz, learning environments and offices should be designed like exercise par courses, offering postural variety and more freedom for workers to move around and alternate tasks.

Research suggests that the chair can be a crucial factor in preventing adverse health and cognitive effects. An effectively designed chair can also help improve learner and employee performance. Conversely, scientists know that ill-supportive chairs prevent the nervous system and the disks inbetween the vertebrae from receiving direct blood supply. This causes fatigue and eventual back pain or discomfort, which impede cognition (Linton, et al. 1994; Mark, et al. 1991).

The need for more ergonomically enhanced classroom seating is even more important as students (from elementary school on) spend increasing amounts of time at the computer in chairs with little or no support. As a result, more and more students are developing back problems in their 20s, Linton and colleagues (1994) report. Linton's 1994 study involving three classes of fourth graders found that the introduction of ergonomically designed school furniture resulted in a significant reduction in musculoskeletal symptoms among students. Back pain is second only to the common cold as a reason for missing work, costing industry an estimated $70 billion annually (Cranz 1998).

Action Steps

* When long periods of sitting are necessary, take regular breaks to "wake up" the brain and nervous systems with stretching, breathing, and other movement activities.
* Encourage your school or office to investigate the possibility of acquiring ergonomically enhanced chairs, desks, and computer stations for your students and workers.
* Encourage learners and workers not to slump while sitting, even in a chair with lumbar support. It over stretches the muscles and ligaments and puts undue stress on the back. In addition, poor posture shifts the body out of balance and forces a few muscles and joints to do all the work.
* Poor physical conditioning also plays a role in back pain and fatigue. When appropriate, encourage learners and workers to incorporate movement and exercise into their daily routine.

Sources:
Cranz, Galen. 1998. *The Chair: Rethinking Culture, Body, and Design*. New York, NY: Norton.
Linton, Steven; Anna-Lisa Hellsing; T. Halme; K. Akerstedt. 1994. The effects of ergonomically designed school furniture on pupils' attitudes, symptoms and behavior. *Applied Ergonomics*. Oct; 25(5): 299-304.
Mark, Leornard S.; Marvin Dainoff; R. Moritz; D. Vogele. 1991. *Cognition and the Symbolic Processes: Applied and Ecological Perspectives*. Hilldale, NJ: Lawrence Erlbaum Associates.

Lead Poisoning: Cognitive Impediments Lurk in Older School Buildings and Homes

Researchers report that childhood lead poisoning, although highly preventable, is one of the most common pediatric health problems, with infants and young children being the most susceptible (Banks, et al. 1997; Mendelsohn, et al. 1999). Continuous exposure to low to moderately high levels of lead (at least 10 micrograms of lead per deciliter of blood) can result in learning disabilities, decreases in IQ and attention span, hyperactivity, hearing and speech impediments, and anti-social behavior.

Higher levels of exposure can cause more serious health problems, including comma, convulsions, and death. Ingestion of lead-based paint (usually paint chips) and exposure to lead-contaminated dust are the main causes of childhood lead poisoning. And while children of all backgrounds are at risk, low-income children are often most likely affected. In fact, low-income children are more than three times as likely to have at-risk blood levels of lead exposure than middle-income children, likely due to a higher incidence of older dwellings in poor neighborhoods where deteriorating paint is common (Yiin 2000).

Yiin also reported that blood lead concentrations in exposed children tend to be highest in hot summer months. He noted that lead interferes with the brain's transmission of a powerful and common neurotransmitter called dopamine, which is primarily involved in producing positive moods and feelings and coordinated body movements. Lead is also known to inhibit activity in the hippocampus, a key memory formation area of the brain.

Minder and colleagues (1994) found in a study of 43 boys that children with higher rates of lead concentration in their hair follicles performed significantly poorer on simple reaction-time tasks. And research conducted by Shen and colleagues (1992) examined 128 Chinese preschool children living in a lead-polluted area of Shanghai and concluded that lead toxicity was directly related to the children's impairment in intelligence development.

Can schools and classrooms be sites for lead contamination? Indeed, older buildings can, especially those constructed before 1940 or painted before 1978, when the use of lead in residential and commercial paint was severely reduced by the Consumer Product Safety Commission. The California Department of Health Services estimated in 1995 that 37 percent of public schools in the state had deteriorating lead-containing paint. The amount was significant enough to present a potential health hazard. In addition, 18 percent of public schools had lead levels in drinking water that exceeded federal guidelines, and 6 percent had lead levels in soil above federally recommended levels.

The California Department of Health Services also warns that the children at greatest risk for lead poisoning are those not yet in school. These preschool-aged youngsters often come into contact with lead paint and dust when they crawl, explore with their hands, and put fingers and objects directly in their mouths. Lead-containing paint becomes a hazard when it flakes, peels, or chalks.

Action Steps

* Inquire as to when the last lead test was conducted at your school site and what the results were.
* Many lead-poisoned children have no immediate symptoms and may go undiagnosed and untreated unless they are screened with a blood test by a medical professional.If you teach in a low-income area or have low-income children in your class, recommend that they be screened once a year for lead exposure.
* Advise parents living in older dwellings (especially built before 1940) that children may be exposed to lead through deteriorating paint and dust. And drinking water may be contaminated by lead leaking from plumbing fixtures, solder in pipes, or the original water source. If a lead problem is suspected, advise them to contact their local health department immediately.

Sources:
Banks, E.C; L.E. Ferretti; D. W. Shucard. 1997. Effects of low level lead exposure on cognitive function in children: A review of behavioral, neuropsychological and biological evidence. *Neurotoxicolgy*. 18(1): 237-81.
Mendelsohn, A.L.; B.P. Dreyer; A.H. Fierman; C.M. Rosen; L.A. Legano; H.A. Kruger; S.W. Lim; S. Barasch; L. Au; C.D. Courtlandt. 1999. Low-level lead exposure and cognitive development in early childhood. *Journal of Development and Behavioral Pediatrics*. Dec; 20(6): 425-31.
Minder, B.; E.A. Das-Smaal; E.F. Brand; J.F. Orlebeke. 1994. Exposure to lead and specific attentional problems in schoolchildren. *Journal of Learning Disabilities*. Jun-Jul; 27(6): 393-9.

Shen, X.M.; D. Guo; J.D. Xu; M.X. Wang; S.D. Tao; J.D. Zhou; X.I. Gao; H.G. Lou. 1992. The adverse effect of marginally higher lead level on intelligence development of children: A Shanghai study. *Indian Journal of Pediatrics*. Mar-Apr; 59(2): 233-8.
State of California Homepage Website: 1998. California Department of Health Services; www.dhs.cahwnet.gov/opa/prssrels/1998/24-98.htm
Yiin, Lih-Ming. 2000. Childhood lead exposure peaks in warm months. *Environmental Health Perspectives*. Feb; 108(2).

Sizing Up the Classroom

Although the issue of class size is still subject to debate (and probably will be for some time), research does suggest that smaller class size can have a significant impact on learning and teacher-student interaction. Studies reveal that smaller classes can increase individual instruction time in grades K-12, increase early learning and cognitive skills in preschoolers, and enhance reading and mathematics performance in elementary-school students, especially among educationally disadvantaged children (Betts and Shkolnik 1999; Mosteller 1995; Bosker 1997; Finn, et al. 1990).

The brain responds exceptionally well to learning environments with high levels of individualized instruction, constructive feedback, small-group interaction, and high expectations—elements that have been shown to occur more readily in smaller classrooms (Sommers 1990). Research conducted by Frank (1994) and others indicate that such enriched settings allow the brain's frontal lobe region to link thoughts and newly learned material together, thereby strengthening important neural connections to aid long-term memory, planning, and decision-making. This process is especially important in the brain development of young children.

Moreover, the cognitive benefits of small-class interaction can be lasting. In a 4-year study of class size on the short- and long-term academic performance of 6,500 elementary-school students in 330 classrooms, Mosteller (1995) found that improvements in math and reading realized earlier in the study continued for months thereafter. In fact, by the end of the study, students in 17 of the most economically disadvantaged schools had improved their standing in reading and math from well below average to above average, Mosteller reports.

Researchers suggest that the optimal class size for grades K-12 is twenty-one or fewer students. Twenty-two to twenty-seven students is considered moderately sized, and twenty-seven to thirty-four students, large. A class of more than thirty-five students is considered detrimental to academic achievement, according to studies by Bosker (1997) and Sommers (1990).

Action Steps

* Make regular use of small student groupings led by either teacher or students or a combination of both.
* Remember, large classes may generate more "safety" and "threat" concerns—a problem which can impact cognition. Large groups may also stimulate more social status groupings, which can impact serotonin levels.
* Experiment with classroom chair and desk arrangements. For example, to create a sense of space, arrange desks in a circle or along the walls with the center open for student and teacher interaction.
* A change of venue often personalizes learning. Occasionally assemble students outside (perhaps in a nearby park or grassy field) for meaningful instruction.

Sources:

Betts, Julian and Jamie Shkolnik. 1999. The behavioral effects of variations in class size: The case of math teachers. *Educational Evaluation & Policy Analysis*. Summer; 21(2): 193-213.

Bosker, R.J. 1997. The end of class struggle? Background on the discussion on class size in primary education (Dutch). *Pedagogische Studieen*. 74(3): 210-27.

Finn, Jeremy; Charles Achilles; Helen Bain; John Folger. 1990. Three years in a small class. *Teaching & Teacher Education*. 6(2): 127-36.

Frank, D.A. and M.E. Greenberg. 1994. CREB: A mediator of long-term memory from mollusks to mammals. *Cell*. 79: 5-8.

French, Nancy. 1993. Elementary teacher stress and class size. *Journal of Research & Development in Education*. Winter; 26(2): 66-73.

Mosteller, Frederick. 1995. The Tennessee study of class size in the early school grades. *Future of Children*. Summer-Fall; 5(2): 113-27.

Sommers, Mary Kay. 1990. Effect of class size on student achievement and teacher behavior in third grade. Dissertation-DAI-A 51/06 (Education, Curriculum and Instruction).

Eyestrain and Cognition in the Computer Age

In this age of cyberspace, eyestrain and musculoskeletal problems continue to be chief complaints among people working at video display terminals, research suggests (Hladky & Prochazka, 1998; Lazarus, 1996). Constant exposure to computer screen glare and the sedentary work environment that computer work generally requires is not only hard on the body, it's hard on the brain.

Research conducted by Jaschinski and colleagues (1998) suggests that computer glare can indeed impair cognition. Complaints of eyestrain, headaches, and lack of concentration were alleviated significantly after adjustments were made in computer screen height and distance from the eye. Hladky and Prochazka also found that installing antiglare screen filters on the computers of 60 fulltime computer workers reduced eyestrain and musculoskeletal complaints, and improved productivity.

And in a study of computer operators with a history of eyestrain, back pain, negative mood, and low productivity, Henning and colleagues (1997) demonstrated that having workers perform body stretching every hour as part of a 3-minute break alleviated physical and productivity problems.

Pellegrini and Bjorklund (1997) noted that primary- and elementary-school children are especially at risk during extended periods at the computer due to their immature brain and visual development.

Action Steps

* Make sure computer screens can be adjusted for illumination, height, and distance from the eye, and that antiglare screen filters are available.
* Encourage students to take a 10- to 15-minute break subsequent to every hour of computer use, and to stretch, breathe deeply, and do some exercises.
* Encourage your school administration to acquire ergonomically enhanced chairs, desks, and computer stations for learners.

Sources:

Henning, Robert; P. Jacques; G. Kissel; A. Sullivan. 1997. Frequent short breaks from computer work: Effects on productivity and well being at two field sites. *Ergonomics*. Jan; 40(1): 78-91.

Hladky, A. and B. Prochazka. 1998. Using a screen filter positively influences the physical well being of VDU operators. *Central European Journal of Public Health*. Aug; 6(3): 249-53.

Jaschinski, W.; H. Heuer; H. Kylian. 1998. Preferred position of visual displays relating to the eye: A field study of visual strain and individual differences. *Ergonomics*. July; 41(7): 1034-49.

Lazarus, S.M. 1996. The use of yoked base-up and base-in prism for reducing eyestrain at the computer. *Journal of American Optometric Association*. Apr; 67(4): 204-8.

Pellegrini, Anthony and D.F. Bjorklund. 1997. The role of recess in children's cognitive performance. *Educational Psychologist*. Winter; 32(1): 35-40.

Classroom Lighting Matters

For a number of reasons learners get too little bright light these days. Early school start times mean increasingly more time in darker environments. Lifestyle and safety concerns mean fewer children walk to school. Budget constraints sometimes mean inadequate school lighting, and lack of awareness continues the under-utilization of natural lighting. But is this really a problem? It could be, says Dr. Jacob Liberman, author of *Light: Medicine of the Future* (1991).

Liberman points out that over the past 100 years, our exposure to outdoor light has generally declined. Ultraviolet light, present only outdoors, activates the synthesis of vitamin D, which aids in the absorption of essential minerals, such as calcium (MacLaughlin, et al. 1982). In addition, Benton and Roberts (1988) report that insufficient mineral intake has been shown to be a contributing factor in nonverbal cognitive deficiency.

Even early on, a very large blind study examined the impact of environmental factors on learning problems, and reported that more than 50 percent of children developed academic or health deficiencies as a result of insufficient light at school (Harmon 1951). The study, which evaluated 160,000 school children, also reported that when lighting was improved, the problems outlined on the following page were dramatically reduced:

Complaints	Reduction with Improved Lighting
visual difficulties	65%
nutritional deficits	48%
chronic infections	43%
postural problems	26%
chronic fatigue	56%

Another more recent study investigating the relationship between lighting and human performance (Heschong 1999) included 21,000 students from three districts in three states. After reviewing school facilities, architectural plans, aerial photographs, and maintenance plans, each classroom was assigned a code indicating the amount of light it received during particular times of the day and year. Controlling for variables, the study found that students with the most daylight in their classrooms progressed 20 percent faster on math tests and 26 percent faster on reading tests compared to students with the least lighting.

Reduced exposure to light can also cause depression, a condition that can severely impair cognition. It is estimated that 5 percent of school-age children are depressed. Exposure to bright lights for extended periods, however, reduces the symptoms in some cases (Yamada, et al. 1995).

Depression resulting from light deprivation is known as seasonal affective disorder (SAD), which in severe cases can be seriously debilitating. Sometimes referred to as the winter "blahs," the condition ultimately impacts mood and cognition. Characterized by recurrent episodes of depression in the fall and winter months, the symptoms then disappear in the spring and summer.

SAD, which affects many from time to time, routinely afflicts about 15 percent of the population each fall and winter. The condition appears to be genetic and directly linked to mood-altering reactions that result from extended exposure to decreased levels of sunlight (Sher, et al. 1999; Brennan, et al. 1999; Schwartz, et al. 1998). Sher also reports that SAD symptoms can result from hypothyroidism or subtle decreases in thyroid function.

In research involving 30 patients with SAD (ages 20-56), Michalon and colleagues (1997) report that the cognitive problems associated with the disorder include deficiency in visual and verbal memory, attention, and visual-construction skills. Rosenthal (1998) reports that promising treatment for SAD patients includes light therapy, antidepressant medication, St. John's Wort, and proper nutrition.

Action Steps

* During periods of limited sunlight in the fall and winter, encourage learners to get proper exercise. Suggest, perhaps, that students go for brisk walks or jogs together and encourage more group participation.
* During periods of decreased sunshine in October through March, make sure students are exposed to as much natural sunlight as possible in the classroom by opening blinds and skylights.
* If a student appears overly depressed during fall and winter months, speak to the student's parents and encourage them to have the learner medically examined for seasonal affective disorder.

Sources:

Benton, D. and G. Roberts. 1988. Effect of vitamin and mineral supplementation of intelligence of a sample of school children. *Lancet*. Jan 23; 1(8578): 140-3.

Brennen, Tim; Monica Martinussen; Bernt Ole Hansen; Odin Hjemdal. 1999. Arctic cognition: A study of cognitive performance in summer and winter at 69 degrees N. *Applied Cognitive Psychology*. Dec; 13(6): 561-80.

Harmon, D.B. 1951. The coordinated classroom. Research paper: The American Seating Company, Grand Rapids, MI.

Heschong, Lisa. 1999. *Daylighting in Schools: An Investigation into the Relationship Between Daylighting and Human Performance*. A study performed on behalf of the California Board for Energy Efficiency for the Third Party Program administered by Pacific Gas & Electric, as part of the PG & E contract 460-000. For a copy, email Lisa Heschong at: info@h-m-g.com.

Liberman, J. 1991. *Light: Medicine of the Future*. Santa Fe, NM: Bear & Company Publishing.

MacLaughlin, J.A.; R.R. Anderson; M.F. Holic. 1982. Spectral character of sunlight modulates photosynthesis of previtamin D3 and its photo-isomers in human skin. *Science*. May; 216(4549): 1001-3.

Michalon, Max; Gail Eskes; Charles Mate-Kole. 1997. Effects of light therapy on neuropsychological function and mood in seasonal affective disorder. *Journal of Psychiatry & Neuroscience*. Jan; 22(1): 19-28.

Rosenthal, Norman. 1998. *Winter Blues: Seasonal Affective Disorder*. New York, NY: The Guilford Press.

Schwartz, Paul; Norman Rosenthal; Thomas Wehr. 1998. Serotonin 1A receptors, melatonin, and the proportional control thermostat in patients with winter depression. *Archives of Psychiatry*. Oct; 55(10): 897-903.

Sher, Leo; David Goldman; Norio Ozaki; Norman Rosenthal. 1999. The role of genetic factors in the etiology of seasonal affective disorder and seasonality. *Journal of Affective Disorders*. 53(3): 203-10.

Sher, Leo; Norman Rosenthal; Thomas Wehr. 1999. Free thyroxine and thyroid-stimulating hormone levels in patients with seasonal affective disorder and matched controls. *Journal of Affective Disorders*. 56(2-3): 195-9.

Yamada, N.; M. Martin-Iverson; K. Daimon; T. Tsujimoto; S. Takahashi. 1995. Clinical and chrono-biological effects of light therapy on nonseasonal affective disorders. *Biological Psychiatry*. June 15; 37(12): 866-73.

School Violence and Cognition

Recent studies suggest that, whether perceived or real, the threat of violence in the learning environment can have a negative impact on cognition. Test scores, absenteeism, tardiness, and attention span can be affected.

As the problem of school violence and accompanying measures to prevent it (armed security guards, security checkpoints, locked doors) become even more prevalent in the lives of many children, school officials are increasingly concerned about the effect this atmosphere is having on the learning process, Hoffman (1996) reports.

Scientists know that the learning brain does not respond well to real or imagined threats of harm. Such environments trigger the amygdala (the brain's fear and emotional response center) to release an overabundance of cortisol and adrenaline. These chemicals are released in response to stress and anxiety and put the body in a constant "fight or flight" mode in order to ward off danger. This state, when chronic, can shut down meaningful learning.

Nettles and colleagues (2000) report that students who spend their time thinking about violence and arranging their lives to avoid it are expending valuable "brain cells" on efforts that could otherwise be spent on learning. In a study involving 35 fourth graders and 39 fifth graders, the researchers (ibid) suggest that children's perceived exposure to violence has significant negative impact on test scores. It was found that such students performed significantly lower on a standardized exam of reading and mathematics compared to students who did not perceive the environment to be violent.

Citing a 1994 Roper poll, the researchers report that more than 10 percent of high-school students stayed home or skipped classes due to fear of violence. The poll also cited that 160,000 children occasionally miss school because of intimidation or fear of bodily harm. Evidence also suggests that kids who are afraid to walk home from school because of gang intimidation, drive-by shootings, and other threats may be less likely to participate in sports and other after-school activities.

Other figures cited by Smith and Feiler (1995) are equally disturbing because they indicate the problem is not just relegated to the inner city. Twenty percent of suburban high-school students surveyed in 1995 endorsed shooting someone "who stole something from you," and 8 percent believed it okay to shoot a person "who did something to offend or insult you."

Action Steps

* Discuss the threat of school violence (whether perceived or real) openly with your students. Let them air their fears and anxieties about the situation. Divide the class into small groups to discuss ways in which students might prevent school violence.
* Invite a respected community leader (or police officer) to speak to your class about positive ways in which students can reduce school violence.
* Encourage school administrators and security personnel to form supportive alliances with parents and neighborhood groups.
* Seek the advice of other professionals as needed, including the school psychologist.

Sources:
Hoffman, Allan. 1996. *Schools, Violence, and Society*. Westport, CT: Praeger Publishers/Greenwood Publishing Group, Inc.
Nettles, Sandra; Wilfridah Mucherah; Dana Jones. 2000. Understanding resiliences: The role of social resources. *Journal of Education for Students Placed at Risk*. 5(1,2): 47-60.
Smith, M. Dwayne and Stephen Feiler. 1995. Absolute and relative involvement in homicide offending: Contemporary youth and the baby boom cohorts. *Violence & Victims*. Winter; 10(4): 327-33.

School Facilities and Cognition

Research indicates that learning environments with quality facilities and equipment, inviting atmospheres, high learner expectations, and small-group interaction reinforce the frontal lobe's ability to link thoughts with learned materials. These strengthened neural connections, especially important in the brain development of young children, aid long-term memory, planning, and motivation, note researchers Frank and Greenberg (1994).

Conversely, schools with shattered windows, broken-down restrooms, leaky roofs, insufficient lighting, and classes held in hallways and gymnasiums have a significant negative impact on cognition (Cash, et al. 1997). Such conditions are frequently found in many of our nation's schools, and, unfortunately, far too many children, especially those in poor urban areas, attend schools with substandard facilities. According to Cash's comprehensive study covering 325 public schools in three school districts, the adverse effect of these conditions on academic performance is significant.

Deteriorating facilities affect the morale and performance of students, teachers, and administrators alike. Betts and Shkolnik (1999) and Heschong (1999) have demonstrated that such factors as overcrowding and poor lighting distract the brain from deep learning. Similar findings were reported in less comprehensive studies by Hines (1996) and Edwards (1992).

Approximately one-third of all public schools in the United States are in need of extensive repair or outright replacement, according to a 1996 report by the General Accounting Office. The cost of bringing these schools up to par is estimated at $112 billion (Cash, et al. 1997). Ultimately, the condition of a school building rests upon the financial ability of the school board to make the needed repairs. And in most cases, school districts must rely on taxpayers' ability or willingness to help meet capital expenses.

Overcrowding and poor lighting distract the brain from deep learning.

Action Steps

* Take stock of building conditions at your school. Are the walls in need of paint? Are restroom facilities adequate and functioning? Are the ventilation, heating, and cooling systems up to par? These and other factors can affect students' ability to concentrate and learn.

* Work with your school administration and PTA to positively influence the condition of school facilities. Ask PTA members to exert pressure on local officials to obtain funding from the city; organize volunteers to improve the environment; support a political candidate or educational measure that promises to bring about change.

* Form partnerships with area businesses to improve building conditions. For example, the Phoenix Union High School District formed a partnership with a private firm that offered the district financing and expertise in energy efficiency. The district received a substantial renovation program that included future energy savings over a 10-year period—energy savings that will pay for all the costs of renovation.

Sources:

Betts, Julian and Jamie Shkolnik. 1999. The behavioral effects of variations in class size: The case of math teachers. *Educational Evaluation & Policy Analysis*. Summer; 21(2): 193-213.

Cash, Carol; Glen Earthman; Eric Hines. 1997. Building condition tied to successful learning. *School Planning and Management* Jan; 21(1): 48-53.

Edwards, Maureen. 1992. *Building Conditions, Parental Involvement and Student Achievement in the D.C. Public School System*. Washington, D.C.: Georgetown University.

Frank, D.A. and M.E. Greenberg. 1994. CREB: A mediator of long-term memory from mollusks to mammals. *Cell*. 79: 5-8.

Heschong, Lisa. 1999. *Daylighting in Schools: An Investigation into the Relationship Between Daylighting and Human Performance*. A study performed on behalf of the California Board for Energy Efficiency for the Third Party Program administered by Pacific Gas & Electric, as part of the PG & E contract 460-000. For a copy, email Lisa Heschong at: info@h-m-g.com

Hines, Eric. 1996. *Building Condition and Student Achievement*. Blacksburg, VA: Virginia Polytechnic Institute and State University.

Chapter 3
Achievement and Test Performance

cientists over the past few decades have sought to determine what links exist between the human brain and specific performance conditions. What we've learned is that a host of variables seem to impact the brain's performance at test time. These positive performance effects, although often slight, are of extreme interest to many—especially to athletes, high-powered executives, students competing for a limited number of openings in prestigious colleges, and of course, teachers and administrators who are expected to improve student test scores. Thus, much interest has been generated around this topic in recent years. Some of the variables found to influence test performance include the following:

* Quality of original learning
* Timing of original learning
* Degree of content rehearsal
* Types of tests
* Test-taking experience and sophistication
* Test-taker's level of motivation and interest in content
* Test-taker's ability to manage stress
* Health of the test taker's brain (i.e., brain injuries, mental conditions, emotional stress, mental fitness, neurotransmitter levels)
* Physical health (i.e., diet, nutrition, exercise, sleep, illnesses, etc.)

Educators who understand these factors can influence learners to a significant advantage. While there is a practical level to the amount of resources we can corral in any given school or district to increase test scores and learning, it's reassuring to know that we, as parents, educators, and/or managers, influence (consciously or unconsciously) so many learning variables every day. The articles in this chapter explore these influences and suggest how we can help learners prepare for and achieve peak-performance learning and higher test scores.

Better Measures: What, When, and Where?

Take-Home vs. In-Class Exams

When considering whether to give your students a traditional in-class exam or a take-home test, examine what some research suggests. Take-home exams tend to work best when students know the subject matter reasonably well, have a good rapport with the teacher, and when the test entails theoretical, objective, and higher-order thinking.

Although in-class tests can require more studying, written take-home exams, when given under the right conditions, allow the learner ample time to reflect, explore, and analyze the subject matter in more depth, report Andrada and Linden (1993), and Haynie (1991). In addition, Zoller and Ben-Chaim (1990) found that take-home exams significantly reduced test anxiety among men and women.

Frank and Greenberg (1994) noted that the brain responds well to mental processing when it is allowed to reflect and analyze with minimal stress after meaningful learning, especially learning that requires abstract thinking. Reflection time allows the brain's frontal lobe region to filter information, link thoughts to prior learning, and draw associations—processing tasks that aid memory, planning, and decision-making.

In a study of 290 college students in a basic educational psychology course, half were given an in-class exam requiring higher-order thinking and the other half were given the same test at home. The researchers concluded that the take-home students performed as well as the in-class group (Andrada & Linden 1993).

Haynie noted the same results in a study involving more than 100 undergraduate technology education students. And in one of the earliest comprehensive studies on take-home and in-class examinations, Weber (1983) found that scores on knowledge test items were higher on take-homes, anxiety was lower, and cheating was not a problem.

Multiple-Choice vs. Essay Tests

While essay and multiple choice tests represent two different types of cognitive measures, both tend to produce the same range of academic scores, even though essays are often seen by students as more valid indicators of cognition (Bridgeman & Morgan 1996; Bridgeman & Lewis 1994; Burke 1992).

Across different subject areas, including American and European history, English composition, and biology, essays produce scores that are essentially equivalent to multiple choice scores, suggest Bridgeman and Morgan, and Bridgeman and Lewis. The studies matched college freshman grades in test samples involving more than 8,000 students from 36 colleges nationwide.

In addition, Braswell and Kupin (1993) noted that in the testing of mathematical ability, multiple-choice questions are reliable indicators of student cognition, but that other complementary testing formats, such as essay and short-answer questions, should also be considered.

Hambleton and Murphy (1992) noted the following differences between the brain's processing of essay and multiple-choice modes: Essays tend to require higher-order thinking skills, drawing on the brain's short- and long-term memory capability and the frontal lobes (planning and critical thinking). Conversely, multiple choice tests set the brain up to view matters in a right or wrong mentality—also an aspect of critical thinking, but with multiple responses often serving as cues to trigger the brain's recall. The researchers call for continued research on the strengths and weaknesses of both forms of testing.

In other studies, Gellman and Berkowitz (1993) and Burke (1992) found that, while students preferred multiple-choice and essay testing over true-false, matching, and short-answer formats, they often viewed essays as more valid indicators of cognitive measurement. In addition, Gellman and Berkowitz reported that females overwhelmingly preferred essays. And Burke indicated that students, after taking both essay and multiple choice tests, were significantly better able to predict their score on the essay exam than on the multiple-choice format.

Interestingly, after following 113 undergraduates over two semesters, Landrum and colleagues (1993) found that students performed significantly better on multiple choice tests with three-answer options than with four-answer options (corrected for chance guessing).

Action Steps

* Assign take-home tests selectively, first making sure that students have a good command of the subject matter and that you have established a constructive relationship with the class.
* Take-home exams yield the best results when the subject matter requires objective, higher-order thinking skills, such as required by historical, scientific, and literary analysis.
* After a take-home test, follow up with an analysis of your own. Survey students on what they liked or didn't like about the take-home exam compared to an in-class examination.
* Consider combining multiple modes of testing in a single exam.
* Use essay and multiple-choice testing interchangeably.
* When creating a multiple-choice test, limit the number of answer options to three.

Sources:

Andrada, Gilbert and Kathryn Linden. 1993. Effects of two testing conditions on classroom achievement: Traditional in-class vs. experimental take-home conditions. Paper presented at the Annual Meeting of the American Educational Research Association (Atlanta, GA, April 12-16).

Braswell, James and Jane Kupin. 1993. Item formats for assessment in mathematics. In: Bennett, Randy (Ed). *Construction vs. Choice in Cognitive Measurement: Issues in Constructed Response, Performance Testing, and Portfolio Assessment.* Hillsdale, NJ: Lawrence Erlbaum Associates.

Bridgeman, Brent and Charles Lewis. 1994. The relationship of essay and multiple-choice scores with grades in college courses. *Journal of Educational Measurement.* Spring; 31(1): 37-50.

Bridgeman, Brent and Rick Morgan. 1996. Success in college for students with discrepancies between performance on multiple-choice and essay tests. *Journal of Educational Psychology.* June; 88(2): 333-40.

Burke, Tracie. 1992. *An Investigation of Exam Type Preference, Performance Attribution, and Exam Choice Outcome (essay exams, multiple choice exams).* Dissertation Abstracts International. Oct; 53(4): 1095.

Frank, D.A. and M.E. Greenberg. 1994. CREB: A mediator of long-term memory from mollusks to mammals. *Cell.* 79: pp. 5-8.

Gellman, Estelle and Mina Berkowitz. 1993. Test-item type: What students prefer and why. *College Student Journal.* March; 27(1): 17-26.

Hambleton, Ronald and Edward Murphy. 1992. A psychometric perspective on authentic measurement. *Applied Measurement in Education.* 5(1): 1-16.

Haynie, W.J. 1991. Effects of take-home and in-class tests on delayed retention learning acquired via individualization, self-paced instructional texts. *Journal of Industrial Teacher Education.* 28(4).

Landrum, R.E.; Jeffrey Cashin; Kristina Theis. 1993. More evidence in favor of three-option multiple-choice tests. *Educational & Psychological Measurement.* Fall; 53(3): 771-8.

Weber, Larry. 1983. Take home tests: An experimental study. *Research in Higher Education.* 18(4).

Zoller, Uri and David Ben-Chaim: 1990. Gender differences in examination-type preferences, test anxiety, and academic achievements in college science education. *Science Education.* Nov; 74(6): 597-608.

Pop Quizzes Can Improve Exam Scores

Do unannounced quizzes ultimately improve exam scores? Research on the effectiveness of quizzes is limited, but a recent study by Graham (1999) confirms the findings of earlier research on the subject. Pop quizzes, although moderately stressful to some students, tend to enhance exam scores and increase motivation to study assigned material.

The study collected test scores from four college psychology classes over two semesters and found that test scores following quizzes averaged half a letter grade higher than scores from classes without quizzes. Students with average grades benefited the most, with 84 percent of C students gaining a better letter grade. Approximately 10 unannounced quizzes were given per semester, and attitude surveys following the courses revealed a high level of student acceptance for the quizzes as positive motivators.

Scientists know that moderate stress levels (like those produced by unannounced quizzes) can stimulate the application of knowledge and skill. Moderate levels of stress trigger the brain's hypothalamus to release two primary stress hormones, cortisol and adrenaline, which stimulate arousal, motivation, action, and long-term memory. Earlier studies by Mawhinney and colleagues (1971) and Solomon (1979) found that surprise quizzes also decreased incidences of cramming before tests by encouraging a more even distribution of studying.

In a survey conducted on participating students following the Graham's study, it was found that, despite any anxiety resulting from pop quizzes, more than 85 percent of participants felt that the quizzes were a good idea and provided a major motivation to study.

Action Steps

✱ Use pop quizzes regularly throughout the course as a learning motivator, announcing to the students at the outset how many quizzes to expect per week.

✱ It is usually best to schedule quizzes in manageable intervals, like at the end of an important chapter or sizeable chunk of learning.

✱ Unannounced quizzes motivate students to study on a more regular basis, reduce last-minute cramming, and enhance grades on final exams.

Sources:

Graham, Robert. 1999. Unannounced quizzes raise test scores selectively for mid-range students. *Teaching of Psychology*. 26(4): 271-3.

Mawhinney, V.; D. Bostow; D. Law. 1971. A comparison of students' studying behavior produced by daily, weekly, and three-week testing schedules. *Journal of Applied Behavior Analysis*. 4: 257-64.

Solomon, P.R. 1979. The two-point system: A method for encouraging students to read assigned material before class. *Teaching of Psychology*. 6: 77-80.

Cramming Can Undermine Long-Term Learning

All of us can likely remember such a scenario: A big exam is scheduled for the next morning, and we haven't studied for it yet. So, what do we do? Spend all night cramming. But how effective is cramming? And what brings on such procrastination?

Although research on these questions is limited, studies do indicate that cramming can be useful for short-term memory recall, but often fails in creating long-term lasting meaning (Kovach, et al. 1998; Fulkerson & Martin 1981). In addition, chronic bouts of cramming point to poor study habits and time management skills, often leading to stress and anxiety, which can stifle deeper learning (Kovach, et al. 1998; Sommer 1990).

We know that in order for new information to be stored, it must make sense to us and be meaningful. At the heart of this process is the hippocampus, located at the base of cerebrum. The hippocampus plays a major role in consolidating learning and converting information from working or short-term memory to long-term storage—a process that may take weeks before real meaning is formed. Although essential to solidifying meaning, the hippocampus has limited storage ability and must first process and "index" the learning before sending it to the cortex. Thus, if the hippocampus is overloaded, the information stagnates, is not processed, and long-term memory formation suffers.

Because sense and meaning are independent of each other, it is quite possible for us to remember an item for hours after cramming if the information seems to make sense or sounds reasonable, but we will most likely forget it by the following day if it lacks meaning. This is especially true if the information comes from textbooks and lengthy notes, suggests Sommer (1968).

The notion that cramming may be helpful when done close to test time is borne out in research conducted by Vacha and McBride (1993) and Crew (1969). Crew, in a controlled study of 133 undergraduates, found that those students who crammed for 2 hours the day before taking a multiple-choice test, scored significantly higher than those individuals who did not. And after analyzing the final exam grades of self-professed undergraduate crammers, Vacha and colleagues found that their results were as good or better than those who employed other strategies. Sommer (1968) reported that cramming was more prevalent in college courses that required memorization rather than creativity.

But habitual cramming can cause stress and anxiety, which can also hinder the cognitive process, reported Kovach and colleagues (1998) and Sommer (1990), in studies involving post-secondary and college students. Kovach's work reported significant reduction of cramming behavior after measures were taken to deal with poor time management and procrastination behaviors—habits that often extend into adult working life if not addressed.

Psychological studies of chronic crammers and other procrastinators show a strong tendency towards thrill or sensation seeking, buck-passing, lack of planning structure, low self-esteem as decision makers, and boredom (Sarmany-Schuler 1999; Vodanovich & Rupp 1999).

Action Steps

* Advise learners to take inventory of their projected goals, time-management skills, and study habits and to reorganize them appropriately. Students who give their academic concerns top priority and allow ample time for studying (including exam preparation), often perform best (Yaworski 1998).

* If help is needed in establishing a personal study schedule, or if chronic procrastination persists, encourage learners to seek the advice of a guidance counselor or related professional.

* Provide learners with short quizzes that ultimately lead up to the final exam. Research by Tuckman (1998) reported that students (rated as procrastinators) performed 12 percent better on final examinations when quizzed subsequent to completing each text chapter. In fact, the known procrastinators outperformed non-procrastinating students who were asked to only outline each text chapter as a home work assignment.

* Encourage learners to take extra steps during note-taking. For example, ask them to integrate notes from a reading assignment with notes from a related lecture. This step decreases the chances of forgetting or distorting the information. Recall and meaning are also enhanced by such techniques as role playing, mental practice, rehearsal, repetition, and feedback.

Sources:

Crew, J.C. 1969. The effect of study strategies on the retention of college text material. *Journal of Reading Behavior*. Spring; 1(2): 45-52.

Fulkerson, F.E. and G. Martin. 1981. Effects of exam frequency on student performance, evaluations of instructor, and test anxiety. *Teaching of Psychology*. April; 8(2): 90-3.

Kovach, K.; L.R. Wilgosh; L.L. Stewin. 1998. Dealing with test anxiety and underachievement in post-secondary students with learning disabilities. *Developmental Disabilities Bulletin*. 26(2): 63-76.

Sarmany-Schuller, I. 1999. Procrastination, need for cognition and sensation seeking. *Studia Psychologica*. 41(1): 73-85.

Sommer, R. 1968. The social psychology of cramming. *Personnel & Guidance Journal*. 47(2): 104-9.

Sommer, W.G. 1990. Procrastination and cramming: How adept students ace the system. *Journal of American College Health*. July; 39(1): 5-10.

Tuckman, B.W. 1998. Using tests as an incentive to motivate procrastinators to study. *Journal of Experimental Education*. Winter; 66(2): 141-7.

Vacha, Edward F. and Michael J. McBride. 1993. Cramming: A barrier to student success, a way to beat the system, or an effective learning strategy? *College Student Journal*. Mar; 27(1): 2-11.

Voaanovich, S.J. and E. Rupp. 1999. Are procrastinators prone to boredom? *Social Behavior & Personality*. 27(1): 11-6.

Yaworkski, Joann. 1998. Why do students succeed or fail: A case study comparative. *Journal of College Reading and Learning*. Fall; 29(1): 57-8.

The Biology of Cheating

From boardrooms to classrooms around the world, cheating remains a persistent weakness and a potential threat to the integrity of education, business, and government. We've all heard about the scandals that seemingly pervade the halls of corporate America and academia. But while research confirms that dishonest attempts to advance oneself still occur at all echelons of society, no conclusions have been drawn about the seeming increased prevalence of it.

Recent research does, however, indicate that there are lower incidents of cheating at institutions (notably colleges) where such behavior is explicitly deemed socially unacceptable (McCabe & Trevino 1993). Educational psychologist Fred Schab suggested in 1991 that much of our attitudes toward cheating may be shaped by various factors including our parents, home environment, role models, and cultural values. But what are the biological mechanisms and factors that influence a person's decision to cheat?

We know that the prefrontal cortex, which integrates emotions (values) with cognition and sensations, is the brain's primary decision-maker. We also know that this area can be underdeveloped in children who have experienced neglect, severe trauma, or abuse in their first year of life. As a result, an over-pruning of synapses may occur, which is believed to influence inappropriate decision-making later in life.

Our values are essentially emotional states influenced by a complex interaction of brain chemicals such as norepinephrine, serotonin, and dopamine that ultimately impact our decisions. LeDoux (1996) reports that during emotional states, such as value-based decision making, these neurotransmitters are triggered and travel along a "superhighway" of the middle brain to the amygdala—a critical sensory processing area that plays an important role in emotionally-laden memories. Our mind (and body) are thus inextricably linked to the decisions we make. In other words, if your value is honesty, you feel bad when you are dishonest.

In addition, McCabe and Bowers (1994) found that students and other learners functioning under stress (such as pressure to maintain high GPAs or pressure from parents or superiors) are more likely to cheat. Another reason is that to many learners, the "rush" or thrill of beating the system, and not getting caught, stimulates the brain's pleasure chemicals. Learners who have under active dopamine and noradrenaline circuitry may find cheating especially attractive.

Conversely, cheating is less of a problem, McCabe and Trevino report (1996), when students are made to feel part of the campus community, when they believe the faculty are committed to their courses, and when they are aware of the institution's policy toward dishonesty.

This seems to explain the success of honor codes at universities that employ them since these approaches foster feelings of support, community, peer review, and accountability—environments in which the learning brain responds well, the researchers (ibid) suggest. Students at these institutions talk about how cheating would be "socially unacceptable," about how dishonesty would "violate the trust" of the school and other students, and how "embarrassed" one would feel.

Action Steps

* To encourage feelings of trust and well-being in learning and business settings, establish honesty policies that students and employees can buy into.
* Experiment with self-marked exams and use peer-conduct review committees, when appropriate, in disciplinary action.
* Create or allow legitimate opportunities for "thrill seekers" to get their kicks elsewhere such as through highly competitive athletics or the company's skydiving club.

Sources:

LeDoux, Joseph. 1996. *The Emotional Brain*. New York: Simon and Schuster.

McCabe, Donald and Linda Trevino. 1996. What we know about cheating in college. *Change*. Jan-Feb; 28(1): 28-33.

McCabe, Donald and Linda Trevino. 1993. Academic dishonesty: Honor codes and other contextual influences. *Journal of Higher Education*. 64(5): 538-52.

McCabe, Donald and W.J. Bowers. 1994. Academic Dishonesty among male college students: A thirty-year perspective. *Journal of College Student Development*. 35(1): 3-10.

Schab, F. 1991. Schooling without learning: Thirty years of cheating in high school. *Adolescence*. Winter; 26(104): 840-6.

Good Study Habits Yield High Academic Results

Do good study habits really translate to higher academic performance? The answer may be yes, according to results of two separate studies begun in 1994 by the National Assessment of Educational Progress (NAEP) and published in 1997 (Vanneman 1997).

The research examined the performance of hundreds of fourth-, eighth-, and twelfth-grade geography

and history students across the country. Results suggest a positive correlation between high test results and good study habits—"good" being a judgment of time spent on homework, frequency of home discussions held about studies, and quantity of daily reading engaged in at school and home.

Perhaps even more significant, the study indicated that successful students tended to view homework assignments as highly relevant to the subject being studied. We know that the brain responds positively to cognitive reinforcement (such as homework) that is relevant and specific. This enhances meaning, which in-turn stimulates long-term memory and learning.

Meaning is processed in various parts of the brain. For instance, when something is meaningful emotionally, there tends to be increased activity in the frontal, occipital, and mid-brain areas; whereas, if something is meaningful during reading, there's usually more activity in the left frontal, temporal, or parietal lobe (Damasio 1994).

Relevance, however, happens on a simple cellular level in the brain. An already existing neuron simply connects with a nearby neuron. The greater the number of links and associations that your brain creates, the more neural territory will be involved and the more firmly the information will be neurologically embedded. Remember, every thought you think increases your chances of thinking that thought again.

The NAEP study found that the better students perform academically, the more likely they are to (1) discuss their studies at home every day with a parent or other family member, friend, or study partner; (2) spend more than one hour per day on homework; and (3) read more than 20 pages per day in school and for homework. These findings held true, in most cases, for all three grade levels tested, especially those students performing in the 90th percentile of tests administered in geography and history.

The study concludes that although more definitive research in the relationship between academic performance and good study habits is needed, a useful basis has been established for further examination on the subject.

Action Steps

* Encourage in-class discussion of homework assignments immediately after homework is turned in. This encourages student interaction on the subject and allows for discussion on problems encountered during the completion of the assignment, possible solutions, and knowledge obtained.
* Make sure homework assignments are relevant and specific to the subject or lesson being studied.
* Encourage students' parents to take an active role in supporting good study habits. Encourage parents to discuss assignments with their children; make sure children adhere to a scheduled time period each day to complete school assignments; and keep abreast of student progress through the teacher.

Sources:
Damasio, Antonio. 1994. *Descartes' Error*. New York: Putnam and Sons.
Vanneman, Alan. 1997. *Good Study Habits and Academic Performance: Findings From the NAEP 1994 History and Geography Assessments*. NAEP Publications; Aug 2(4).

Gender Differences and Learning Performance

How much of a difference is there between the sexes when it comes to learning? The answer, it turns out, it quite complex. Although there are some statistically significant differences between how males and females learn and their respective proclivities, many of the studies that have examined gender differences in learning have reported contradictory conclusions.

Let's start, however, with examining some of the physiological differences, since measuring these pose fewer problems to researchers. Males in general have a 10 to 15 percent larger brain than females. When a control is set up for body size, studies still indicate that male brains average 100 grams heavier (Ankey 1992). In addition, men have about four billion more cortical neurons than women (Pakenberg & Gundersen 1997). Other areas of the brain are different, too. In the hypothalamus, some areas are smaller in women (INAH region) and others are larger (SCN), the former area plays a key role in sexuality, the latter a role in biological rhythms. The hippocampus is larger in male rats, but at this point, there's no human evidence of such a difference.

The corpus collosum was originally thought to be much thicker in females than in males. Recent research has debunked the earlier studies, however, and now they are thought to be of similar size (Driesen & Raz 1995). Another, lesser known bundle of interhemispheric fibers, however, called the anterior commissure is clearly larger in female brains (Allen & Gorski 1991). This advantage may allow females to tie together verbal and nonverbal information more efficiently. Other areas of the brain, including a cortical region called the planum parietale, show some differences but are closely tied with other traits, so the correlations are weak.

We know there are some physical differences in the brain, but what effects might these differences have on cognition?

Females generally outperform males on the following skills/tasks:

* Fine motor skills—ability to move fingers rapidly in unison
* Computation tests
* Multi-tasking
* Recalling the position of objects in an array
* Spelling
* Fluency of word generation
* Skills that require being sensitive to external stimuli (except visual stimuli)
* Remembering landmarks along a route
* Use of verbal memory
* Appreciation of depth and perceptual speed
* Reading body language and facial expressions

Males generally outperform females on the following skills/tasks:

* Targeting skills
* Working vocabulary
* Extended focus and concentration
* Mathematical reasoning and problem-solving aptitude
* Navigation with geometric properties of space
* Higher verbal intelligence
* Habit formation and maintenance
* Most spatial tasks, especially imaginal ones

Although some of these findings show a variance in results, all of them are statistically significant (Kimura 1999).

But what does this tell us about learning? While some parents and administrators have opted for same-sex schools to better meet their child's needs, the effectiveness of such an intervention on cognition and social skills is unknown.

We should not confuse equality of opportunity with equality of outcome. Often the most objective criteria for a standardized test (like an SAT or LSAT) may result in higher male or higher female scores due to general differences. Some advocate altering aptitude tests so that scores don't waver widely across genders, calling that the true "unbiased" measure. The PSAT adopted a policy which, instead of weighting the math and verbal scores evenly, used an index called "two times the verbal score plus the math" to try to raise girl's scores. Adding a writing skills subtest to the PSAT has also been tried. These alterations, however, have still not offset boys' generally higher scores in math (Arenson 1998).

Although we can acknowledge the physiological differences between the genders and note performance differences overall, additional research is necessary before we can draw more definitive conclusions. Meanwhile, becoming familiar with gender differences and their potential impact on learners is a good way to move towards meeting the gender-specific needs of all learners.

Action Steps

* Be aware of how gender differences may impact learners.
* Be patient with learners who may not show the same brain development that others do (especially with boys who usually learn language skills 1 to 2 years later than girls; or girls who are not as skilled in spatial or physical tasks as early as boys).
* Respect differences and appreciate each learner's uniqueness. Use differences as an opportunity to teach about respecting our own and others developmental timelines.

Sources:
Allen, L.S. and R.A. Gorski. 1991. Sexual dimorphism of the anterior commissure and massa intermedia of the human brain. *Journal of Comparative Neurology*. 312: 97-104.
Ankey, C.D. 1992. Sex differences in relative brain size: The mismeasure of woman, too? *Intelligence*. 16: 329-36.
Arenson, K. 1998. Test gap between sexes narrows. *Toronto Globe and Mail*. 15 January: A-15.
Driesen, N.R. and N. Raz. 1995. The influence of sex, age, and handedness on corpus collosum morphology: A meta-analysis. *Psychobiology*. 23: 240-7.

Kimura, D. 1999. *Sex and Cognition*. A Bradford Book. Boston, MA: MIT Press.
Pakenberg, B. and H.J.G. Gundersen. 1997. Neocortical neuron number in humans: Effect of sex and age. *Journal of Comparative Neurology*. 384: 312-20.

Increase Learner Participation: Allow Sufficient Answer Time

How long should a teacher wait for a response from a student after calling on him or her in class? One study found that many high-school teachers wait an average of just over one second, and that elementary-school teachers wait an average of three seconds.

In both cases, Rowe (1974, 1978) found this was hardly enough time for students, especially slower retrievers, to transfer the answer from long-term memory in the brain's hippocampus to short-term (or working) memory. Rowe found that when teachers extend the wait time to 5 or more seconds, the length and quality of student responses increased; slower learners participated more often; students used more evidence to support inferences; and higher-order responses increased. These results occurred at all grade levels and in all subjects.

In addition, Rowe found that teachers who consistently provided longer wait times used higher-order questioning more often and demonstrated greater flexibility in evaluating responses.

When teachers extend the wait time to 5 or more seconds, the length and quality of student responses increases.

Action Steps

✱ Wait at least five seconds for a response from a student before calling on someone else. This allows the student to retrieve the information from memory and to form a response.

✱ If a student is still not sure of the answer, coax the answer from the student by giving him or her hints or key words. This priming can also serve as memory cues for future retrieval.

✱ To promote cooperative or group learning try the following strategy: Ask your students to think about a certain question (i.e., What were the major factors that influenced the end of the Cold War?) After adequate wait time, have the students form pairs and exchange the results of their thinking. Then, have each group share their ideas with the entire class.

Sources:
Rowe, M.B. 1978. Wait, wait, wait...*School Science and Mathematics*. 78: 207-16.
———— 1974. Wait-time and rewards as instructional variables: Their influence on language, logic and fate control. *Journal of Research on Science Teaching*. 2: 81-94.

Excessive Parental Pressure Can Curtail Academic Achievement

Research consistently shows that gifted children and adolescents have the capacity for intensified thinking and feeling, as well as high academic achievement (Schuler 1999). However, behavioral scientists also note that these laudable traits can be dramatically reversed when parents exert undue pressure on their gifted kids in hopes of achieving academic "perfection," according to a study by Ablard and Parker (1997).

Constant parental pressure on children for top grades, advanced grade-level work, career commitments, and other performance goals creates an atmosphere of anxiety that can turn high-achievers into under-achievers, the Ablard and Parker study concludes.

Stress and anxiety are known to seriously impede cognition. During such emotional duress, our adrenal glands release a peptide called cortisol, which in high amounts can kill brain cells in the hippocampus, a region critical to explicit memory. Prolonged exposure to stress can result in depression, low self-esteem, self-imposed isolation, and anger (Schuler 1999; Schmitz & Galbraith 1985; Dirkes 1983). When a child feels as if he/she is "not good enough," they may intentionally "downplay" their academic abilities by adopting poor study habits and failing tests (Silverman, 1987).

In a study of 127 sets of parents and their sixth-grade academically-talented children, Ablard and Parker found that children of parents who strongly emphasized performance goals were more likely to exhibit dysfunctional perfectionism than children whose parents emphasized learning goals. Ablard and Parker also concluded that parents' achievement goals can help predict which students might be at risk for adjustment problems and future underachievement.

Action Steps

* Major warning signs of at-risk gifted children include excessive sadness, difficulty with social relationships, low frustration tolerance level, resistance to authority, lack of sufficient challenge in schoolwork, gradual or sudden drop in grades, self- imposed isolation from others, thoughts and expressions of suicide, and substance abuse.
* Discuss the matter with the student's parents immediately, and if necessary, urge the parents and student to seek family counseling as soon as possible.
* If your school or educational service currently lacks appropriate counseling and support mechanisms to address the needs of gifted individuals, work with administrators to get them in place.
* Be aware of how home and school can be stressful places for bright kids.

Sources:

Ablard, Karen E. and Wayne D. Parker. 1997. Parents' achievement goals and perfectionism in their academically-talented children. *Journal of Youth and Adolescence*; Dec., 26(6): 651-67.

Dirkes, M.A. 1983. Anxiety in the gifted: Pluses and minuses. *Roeper Review*; 6(2): 68-70.

Schmitz, C.C. and J. Galbraith. 1985. *Managing the Social and Emotional Needs of the Gifted: A Teacher's Survival Guide*. Minneapolis, MN: Free Spirit.

Schuler, Pat. 1999. Gifted kids at risk: Who's listening? Advocacy for Gifted and Talented Education in New York (AGATE). Website: www.agateny.org

Silverman, L.K. 1987. Applying knowledge about social development to the counseling process with gifted adolescents. In: *Understanding Gifted and Talented Adolescents.* Buescher, T.M. (Ed). Evanston, IL: The Center for Talent Development.

Chapter 4

The Musical, Visual, and Performing Arts

esearchers are finding that the arts, in all their varied forms, contribute significantly to the development of critical neural and biological systems, including cognition, emotion, perceptual-motor skills, immunity, and circulation. The fusion of dance, drama, music, role playing, painting, and design with the more traditional subjects of math, science, and writing takes learners several steps closer to success. Howard Gardner (1993) refers to the skills derived from artistic activities as "bodily-kinesthetic intelligences" and "musical intelligences." Others refer to them as the "kinetic arts." Whatever their name, they provide a powerful vehicle to enhance learning with no downside risk. The arts deserve a strong, daily place in the curriculum of every K-12 student.

Movement activates the majority of the brain's systems, creating a state of arousal that invigorates the mind and improves learning. Recent research supports the fundamental value of the arts as an integral aspect of the academic curriculum. It should no longer be called a cultural add-on. Musical, visual, and kinetic arts enhance the important and distinct neurological systems that drive attention, emotion, perception, motivation, motor coordination, learning, and memory.

The latest politically-correct juggernaut is called "higher standards." Some believe that higher standards will ensure that all learners do better in school. This may or may not be true. But to reach this Holy Grail, many short-sighted policy-makers are eliminating arts programs. That's a mistake. The accumulation of art-related brain research strongly suggests the opposite; we need the arts to achieve better learning.

Making the arts a core part of the curriculum and thoughtfully integrating them into every subject may not elicit an immediate increase in test scores. But it may create a classroom full of engaged, motivated, and attentive learners—students who will develop a heightened sense of confidence, creativity, cultural awareness, and an increased love of learning. With these elements in place, higher test scores ultimately happen.

The 'Mozart Effect'™ Under Fire: Where Do We Go From Here?

Last summer was a contentious time indeed for the 'Mozart Effect.' A study led by Chabris (1999) suggested that listening to Mozart's music does little, if anything, to enhance IQ or spatial-temporal processing abilities. A similar study by Steele and colleagues (1999) also tried but failed to confirm the findings of an earlier study by Rauscher and colleagues (1993), which reported an increase in spatial-reasoning scores among participants after listening to the first movement of Mozart's Sonata k. 448. The Rauscher finding sparked considerable interest, not only in the world of cognitive science, but also among educators and the general public.

With the initial results of the Mozart Effect contested, where do we go from here? The obvious answer would be to conduct more research. The overall, positive effects of music on learning, such as activation and stimulation of the brain's limbic system, stress reduction, and increased molecular energy—all of which affect cognition and creativity—are well-documented. But further examination of the Mozart Effect is warranted.

Findings by Nantais and Schellenberg (1999) added to the controversy. Their study suggests that Mozart's music does indeed increase spatial-reasoning skills. The researchers were able not only to replicate, but also to *extend* the Mozart Effect findings of Rauscher's earlier study. In the media hoopla surrounding the contradictory evidence, however, the study has not gained prominence. Nantais and Schellenberg's study of 56 college students found that spatial-temporal abilities were enhanced after listening to music composed by Mozart or Schubert, rather than after sitting in silence or listening to a narration of the learner's choice.

Moreover, in responding to the Chabris findings, which put the Mozart Effect into doubt, Rauscher and Shaw suggested that failure to produce the effect could arise from carryover by-products of a spatial reasoning pre-test, which may interfere with the cognitive impact of listening to Mozart. They cite an unpublished study in which a verbal distracter was inserted between the pre-test and actual listening test, with the manipulation producing a recovery of a Mozart Effect. Rauscher adds that the Steele study has "methodological problems" and largely fails to follow the original experimental design.

Sources:
Chabris, Christopher; Kenneth Steele; S. Bella; Isabelle Peretz, et al. 1999. Prelude or requiem for the "Mozart Effect." *Nature.* Aug; 400(6747): 826-8.
Gardner, Howard. 1993. *Multiple Intelligences: The Theory in Practice.* New York, NY: Basic Books.
Nantais, Kristin M. and E. Glenn Schellenberg. 1999. "The Mozart Effect:" An artifact of preference. *Psychological Science.* Jul 10(4): 370-3.
Rauscher, F.H.; Gordon Shaw; L.J. Levine; K.N. Ky; E.L. Wright. 1993. Music and spatial task performance. *Nature.* 365: 611.
Steele, Kenneth; Karen Bass; M. Crook. 1999. The mystery of the "Mozart Effect:" Failure to replicate. *Psychological Science.* July 10(4): 366-9.
Steele, Kenneth; Joshua Brown; J. Stoecker. 1999. Failure to confirm the Rauscher and Shaw description of recovery of the "Mozart Effect." *Perceptual & Motor Skills.* Jun 88(3, Pt 1): 843-8.

Does Viewing Art Enhance Brain Power?

Some researchers say yes! And they speculate that abstract art may be especially potent. Because of its hidden meanings and atypical shapes and contours, abstract art, like abstract thinking, requires the viewer to "step out of reality" and make use of more cognitive regions—a process that Rose (1991) calls "tension and release." The process calls for the viewer to take in the art as a whole, then visually and mentally dissect it, and finally put it back together to gain meaning. This stimulates the brain's occipital lobe (which controls vision and spatial and geometric functions), the temporal lobe (non-verbal pattern recognition), and the cerebrum (sensory interpretation, thinking and memory). Because more brain areas are stimulated and used than in routine observation, the brain gets a heightened mental workout which can enhance perception and learning, states Rose.

Deregowski and colleagues (1996) found that preschool children as early as age four can improve their ability to recognize and discriminate between typical shapes and contours of objects and non-typical ones, and to encode them perceptually. And in a study of abstract features in Paleolithic art, Halverson (1992) concluded that recognition of the various forms induced the cognitive functions of conceptual and analytical thinking, operational thought, and synthesis.

What benefits might be derived of the required visual exertion? Zangenmeister and colleagues (1995) studied the eye movements and blink rates of both professional and non-experienced art viewers as they gazed at pieces of abstract and realistic art. He found that the professional viewers demonstrated increased visual effort when viewing abstract art over realistic art, while non-professional viewers showed no significant visual exertion when observing either art mode.

Additional findings regarding the viewing of abstract art follow:

* When abstract pieces are accompanied with titles, meaningful interpretation increases (Russell & Milne 1997).
* Elementary- and high-school-age children tend to respond better to smaller reproductions of moderately complex abstract art rather than full-sized original abstract pieces of high complexity (Farley & Weinstock 1980).
* Abstract images produced by psychiatric patients often give mental health professionals important clues about the troubled psyche of such patients. For example, Dickman and colleagues (1996) found that chemical-dependency patients using at least 66 percent of abstract or geometric configurations (and other elements) in their art therapy drawings stood a significant chance of relapsing three months after treatment. And an examination in 1996 of the drawings of Ukrainian school-age children and adolescents who survived the 1986 Chernobyl nuclear disaster indicated that the survivors were still traumatized: Their abstract-like images depicted hysteria, terror, depression, paranoia, and other manifestations (Batov 1997).
* Intuitive individuals are more apt to like abstract art than non-intuitive persons (Van Rooij 1996), and younger adults tend to conceptualize abstract structures more easily than older adults (Hess & Wallsten 1987). However, regardless of age, abstract art can be appreciated and perceived aesthetically by persons unfamiliar with art (Clemmer & Leitner 1984).

Action Steps

* Dot the walls of your classroom, hallways, and break areas with appropriate art work. Ask an art consultant or art teacher for advice on selection and procurement.
* Have students view and compare selected pieces of realistic and abstract art. Ask questions such as, "Why do you prefer one type over another?" Break into discussion groups to dialogue about individual and collective meanings. Then have teams present their thinking to the rest of the class.
* Make a class visit to a local art gallery.
* Create an art show from student work and encourage families to view it together.

Sources:

Batov, Vitaliy I. 1997. Psychological analysis of children's drawings about the Chernobyl nuclear disaster. *Voprosy Psikhologii*. 1: 26-33.

Clemmer, Edward and Amy Leitner. 1984. The affective re-cognition of abstract art: Language and aesthetics. *Visual Arts Research*. Fall; 10(2): 58-65.

Deregowski, J.B.; D.M. Parker; S. Dziurawiec. 1996. The role of typical contours in object processing by children. *British Journal of Developmental Psychology*. Nov; 14(4): 425-40.

Dickman, Sara B.; J.E. Dunn; A.W. Wolf. 1996. The use of art therapy as a predictor of relapse in chemical dependency treatment. *Art Therapy*. 13(4): 232-7.

Farley, Frank H. and C.A. Weinstock. 1980. Experimental Aesthetics: Children's complexity preference in original art and photo reproductions. *Bulletin of the Psychonomic Society*. Mar; 15(3): 194-6.

Halverson, John. 1992. Paleolithic art and cognition. *Journal of Psychology*. May; 126(3): 221-36.

Hess, Thomas M. and S.M. Wallsten. 1987. Adult age differences in the perception and learning of artistic style categories. *Psychology & Aging*. Sept, 2(3): 243-53.

Rose, G.J. 1991. Abstract art and emotion: Expressive form and the sense of wholeness. *Journal of American Psychoanalysis Association*. 39(1): 131-56.

Russell, P.A. and S. Milne. 1997. Meaningfulness and hedonic value of paintings: Effects of titles. *Empirical Studies of the Arts*. 15(1): 61-73.

Van Rooij, Jan. 1996. The Jungian psychological functions sensing and intuition and the preferences for art. *Psychological Reports*. Dec, 79(3, Pt. 2): 1216-18.

Zangemeister, W.H.; K. Sherman; L. Stark. 1995. Evidence for a global scanpath strategy in viewing abstract compared with realistic images. *Neuropsychologia*. Aug; 33(8): 1009-25.

Acting and Drama: "Getting Inside Another Person's Head" Can Pay Cognitive Dividends

Helping your students write and stage a dramatic play of their own can turn your class into a more active and exciting learning environment, according to Slade (1998) and Sturkie and Cassidy (1990). Student participation in dramatic performances—especially character drama that compels one to think, feel, and act in specific situations—helps cement learning, enhances critical thinking, and reinforces positive social values, suggests recent research.

Slade suggests that encouraging students to "get inside another person's head" via character acting helps strengthen neural connections that are formed while learning, thereby aiding in the conversion of information from short- to long-term memory. Scientists have long known that the most effective way to learn is not necessarily by reading or listening, but by actually doing. Sturkie and others also suggest that acting out a situation stimulates the brain's frontal lobe region, which is known to control such functions as critical thinking, planning, and decision-making.

In addition, it is known that acting out intense emotions can stimulate the amygdala, an area of the brain involved in long-term memory. And, when the body is engaged physically, the cerebellum (which contains 40 percent of the brain's neurons) is stimulated, ultimately strengthening memory.

Moreover, social values can be reinforced through acting. In a study involving 7 prison inmates convicted of domestic violence, Cogan and Paulson (1998) found that inmates' attitudes and feelings about their crimes were significantly altered after participation in a 17-week drama in which they reenacted their violence and then later played the role of the victim.

Sturkie and Cassidy (1990) reported that teenagers are more likely to talk about difficult subjects (i.e., abortion, suicide, child abuse, drugs, parental divorce) by participating in dramatic plays on these topics. And Slade found that play acting can be an effective way to put negative social behavior, such as violence and declining moral attitudes, into proper perspective and provide an important link between home and school learning.

Action Steps

* To cement classroom learning and critical thinking skills, encourage students to write and act in their own dramatic plays.
* Use play acting to encourage dialog about intense subjects such as dating, physical abuse, death from AIDS, depression, teenage pregnancy, and race relations.
* Hold a class discussion after the production to debrief and assess the experience and to provide constructive feedback.

Sources:
Cogan, Karen and Barbara Paulson. 1998. Picking up the pieces: Brief report on inmates' experiences of a family violence drama project. *Arts in Psychotherapy*. 25(1): 37-43.
Slade, Peter. 1998. High-school dramatic play and social value learning. *Child Psychology & Psychiatric Review*. 3(3): 110-2.
Sturkie, Joan and M. Cassidy. 1990. *Acting It Out: Seventy-Four Short Plays for Starting Discussions with Teenagers*. San Jose, CA: Resource Publications.

Heavy Metal: A Link to Learned Helplessness

The effects of heavy metal music—its loud penetrating bass and dissonant lyrics—have long been the source of discussion among psychologists, researchers, parents, public officials, and others concerned about adolescent behavior. Researchers suggest that heavy metal's prominent themes of alienation, loneliness, and chaos feed into and reinforce the brain's learned helplessness response, report Stack (1994, 1998) and Arnett (1991, 1992). At the heart of learned helplessness is a sense of fear and threat about the world around us. This creates stress, which can lead to emotions ranging from depression to anger, suggests Peterson (1993).

When we feel stressed, our adrenal glands release a peptide called cortisol. Chronically high cortisol levels can kill brain cells in the hippocampus—a brain mechanism critical to explicit memory formation. Further, the moment our brain detects fear or threat, it jumps into high gear. The amygdala, which triggers the release of adrenaline, vasopressin, and cortisol in response to threat, puts our body on alert to cope with a potential emergency. This response alters the way we think, feel, and act (LeDoux, 1996).

Prominent questions asked about heavy metal, such as whether it can lead to suicide and aberrant behavior, cannot be answered conclusively at this time; however, research does suggest that the music may nurture suicidal tendencies already present in the subculture of chronic, hard-core fans (Stack 1994). The disturbing telltale signs among frequent heavy-metal listeners can include alienation, defensiveness, tendency toward risky or aggressive behavior, extreme pessimism, suicidal acceptance, and hopelessness, studies by Stack indicate.

Riding the undercurrent of suicidal tendencies is a phenomenon scientists are discovering more about—learned helplessness. Researcher Martin Seligman, in his book *Learned Optimism*, describes how both rats and humans learn to be helpless. When either rats or humans determine that they have no control over their environment, they give up trying to exert it. Learned helplessness is reflected in comments such as "I'm stupid, so why bother?" or "Don't count on me; I'm bad luck;" and, probably most heard, "I don't care." In most cases of learned helplessness, subjects are haunted by traumatic experiences (verbal, physical, or psychological) over which they felt, or later decided, they had no control (Peterson & Seligman 1993).

How does learned helplessness relate to die-hard heavy-metal fans? Research suggests that the alienation and hopelessness experienced by many heavy-metal fans is driven by the negative feelings they have toward themselves and their circumstances. Metal fans, especially chronic (or "trash") metal types, are disproportionately from poor working-class backgrounds, a part of American society that was hurt worst and never fully recovered from the economic stagnation and de-industrialization that began in the 1970s (ironically when heavy metal music became popular). Tied to this is the fact that many young fans come from broken or abusive families. Waas and colleagues (1989) found, in fact, that family disorganization contributes to metal fans' basic attraction to the music.

Other research (Arnett, 1991, 1992) has closely linked frequent metal listening to discipline problems at school and to a higher tendency towards reckless behavior involving automobile driving, substance abuse, and sexual behavior compared to adolescents who preferred acoustic pop or mainstream rock. More disturbing is that metal fans tend to be drawn from social groups at higher-than-average risk of suicide: white males driven by hopelessness and a strong male identity, reports Stack (1994, 1998).

As long as this music continues to have meaning and purpose to so many individuals, it deserves our continued examination and attention. If you have heavy-metal fans in your classroom or at home, make a point to listen to their music, especially the more popular groups like Metallica, Judas Priest, or Ozzy Osborne. Discuss with the learner why he or she finds the music appealing. If overt or extreme feelings of hopelessness and alienation are detected, discuss these feelings further with the teen to determine how prevalent they are. In any case, seeking the advice of a trained mental health professional is advisable.

Sources:

Arnett, J. 1992. The soundtrack of recklessness: Musical preferences and reckless behavior among adolescents. *Journal of Adolescent Research*. 7(3): 313-31.

———1991. Heavy metal music and reckless behavior among adolescents. *Journal of Youth and Adolescence*. 20(6): 573-592.

LeDoux, Joseph. 1996. *The Emotional Brain*, New York: Simon and Schuster.

Peterson, C.; S. Maier; and M.E.P. Seligman. 1993. *Learned Helplessness*, New York: Oxford University Press.

Seligman, M.E.P. 1991. *Learned Optimism*. New York: Knopf.

Stack, Steven. 1998. Heavy metal, religiosity, and suicide acceptability. *Suicide and Life-Threatening Behavior*. Winter: 284(4): 389-394.

———1994. The heavy metal subculture and suicide. *Suicide and Life-Threatening Behavior*. Spring: 24(1): 15-23.

Waas, H.; M.D. Miller; and R.G. Stevenson. 1989. Factors affecting adolescents' behavior and attitudes toward destructive rock lyrics. *Death Studies*. 13, 287-301.

Artwork Displays May Increase Motivation of Young Learners

Research conducted by Creekmore (1987) suggests that classroom displays of student art, well-done homework assignments, and other student work give young students the recognition among peers and adults that they seek, thereby motivating them towards higher levels of creativity and achievement. Scientists know that recognition and achievement enhance learning, triggering the release of "feel good" endorphins in the brain and freeing up the cerebral cortex for stress-free activity.

Jones and Villarino (1994) found that art displays created by the children themselves motivated them to think divergently and create their own unique depictions of their experiences. Students were able to incorporate other learning experiences into their artwork as well, using the various thoughts, drawings, and writings experienced earlier in class and at home. Students benefit from then being able to "show off" these learning pieces to others.

Action Steps

* Designate a certain portion of the classroom specifically for student art and other student displays. It is important that students come to think of this as their "space."
* Avoid displaying only the "best" art. Recognize all students by displaying their work. It is okay, however, to recognize the efforts of individual students with a gold star or other special recognition.
* Display student art and other work during parent visitation nights so that parents and students can view together.

Sources:
Creekmore, W.N. 1987. Effective use of classroom walls. *Academic Therapy*. Mar; 22(4): 341-8.
Jones, Elizabeth and Georgina Villarino. 1994. What goes up on the classroom walls—and why? *Young Children*. Jan; 49(2): 38-40.

What's in a Song?

What do daydreaming and singing in the shower have in common? Both are forms of subconscious thought that can reduce stress, according to research conducted by Kaser (1993). Kaser notes that many of the same brain areas activated by singing and music—including the right hemisphere, which controls fantasy, creativity, and intuition—are also directly affected by daydreaming.

And like daydreaming, singing (especially singing for pleasure), gives the brain a welcome respite from mundane, everyday problems and concerns, while triggering a battery of "feel good" stress-reducing endorphins, including serotonin and noradrenaline, Kaser reports. Adding to the pleasure is the singer's personal identification with the song's melody and lyrics. It is of little wonder that singing therapy is often a mainstay in psychiatric treatment settings, elder care centers, and other therapeutic environments.

In a study examining the effect of singing on psychotically aggressive patients, Kaser found that singing during therapy sessions significantly improved mood and attitude. And in a face-recognition study involving seven elderly patients with Alzheimer's disease, senile dementia, and stroke, Carruth (1997) determined that singing therapy accounted for improved memory recognition in the majority of the patients.

Action Steps

* Make singing with your kids a regular ritual.
* Include singing as a component of your music curriculum in which students can sing contemporary songs, as well as learn traditional and classic songs.
* Encourage participation in the school glee club or chorus.

Sources:
Carruth, Ellen. 1997. The effects of singing and the spaced retrieval technique on improving face-name recognition in nursing home residents with memory loss. *Journal of Music Therapy*. Fall; 34(3): 165-81.

Kaser, Vaughn. 1993. Musical expressions of subconscious feelings: A clinical perspective. *Music Therapy Perspectives*. 11(1): 16-23.

Storytelling Enhances Creativity, Imagination, and Learning

Anyone who has children or deals directly with them can appreciate the blissful look of amazement on their faces as they listen with rapt attention to a vivid children's story told by an adult. However, even more significant are the cognitive benefits of enhanced creativity and imagination that youngsters reap from such encounters. Studies indicate that listening to stories rich in imagery encourages children to temporarily suspend reality and enter an imaginary world, while the right hemisphere of the brain gets a workout.

So engrossed is the child's imagination during periods of storytelling that Sturm (1999) and Tart (1975) have literally dubbed the phenomenon "the storytelling trance," which they describe as an altered state of consciousness. The attention that good storytelling elicits in young children engages them profoundly in the learning process, including stimulating their interest in reading, Goetz and Sadowski (1996) found.

Sturm (1999) also suggests that listening and reasoning skills are enhanced since children have to follow the twists and turns of the story's plot to obtain meaning and comprehension, an activity that involves the auditory and frontal lobes. In addition, the mental picture painted in the child's mind by the story's colorful characters activates the visual cortex and the hippocampus to help store the episode and its moral lesson in long-term memory (Farah 1995).

Storytelling has enjoyed a renaissance in the past 20 years, Sturm observes. Professional storytellers are making careers out of performing at festivals, libraries, schools, and conferences throughout the nation. Books on storytelling fill bookstore shelves, and the leading national journal of storytelling, *Storytelling Magazine*, is also flourishing.

The attention that good storytelling elicits in children engages them profoundly in the learning process, including stimulating their interest in reading.

Action Steps

* Remember, good storytelling engages all major regions of the brain, enhancing visual/auditory skills, reasoning, memory, and reading skills.
* Immerse your learners in imagery-rich texts, videos, and other learning aids.
* Use storytelling as a well-deserved break after intensive learning. Doing so helps the brain "relax" and solidify newly learned material.
* For more information and ideas on storytelling, contact *Storytelling Magazine* at www.storynet.org

Sources:

Farah, Martha. 1995. The neural basis of mental imagery. In: *The Cognitive Neurosciences* (pp. 963-75); Cambridge, MA: MIT Press.

Goetz, Ernest and Mark Sadowski. 1996. *Empirical Approaches to Literature and Aesthetics.* Norwood, NJ: Ablex Publishing Corporation.

Sturm, Brian. 1999. The enhanced imagination: Storytelling? Power to entrance listeners. *Storytelling.* 2(2).

Tart, Charles. 1975. *States of consciousness.* New York: Dutton.

Background Music? Not While I'm Concentrating

Many students claim to study better with rock, jazz, instrumental, or even heavy-metal music playing simultaneously; but does the research support this? Some researchers say yes; other researchers say no. Some studies have extolled the benefits of instrumental music played during learning, but other research suggests that neither music nor significant noise should be present when careful mental work is required (Nittono 1997; Carlson, et al. 1997). Based on the hypothesis that the brain cannot adequately concentrate on more than one stimulus at a time, the studies indicate that music (no matter how benign) forces the brain to alternate and compete between multiple stimuli, increasing the potential for errors in thinking and writing.

To illustrate stimuli overload, Kosslyn (1992) and Hobson (1994) noted the various brain areas that are activated during problem solving:

* **The frontal lobes**—a vital part of the cerebrum controlling verbal expression, willpower, planning and other functions.
* **The thalamus**—a key sensory-perception area in the midbrain.
* **The occipital lobe**—controls vision from its location in the upper brain.
* **The reticular formation**—regulates attention, arousal, and consciousness from its location atop the brainstem.

Now consider additional brain areas activated by music listening:

* The auditory cortex
* The left hemisphere (which controls rhythm)
* The right hemisphere (which controls beat)

In other words, listening to relaxing or invigorating forms of music *before* a test may be valuable, but listening *during* a test or while doing homework (when so many brain sites are activated) may be distracting.

Conversely, in environments where routine tasks and activities are performed (i.e., elevators, retail stores, and some manufacturing assembly situations) background music was found to foster improved moods (Sousou, 1997). Studies by Chlan (1995) and Magill-Levreault (1993), in fact, report that such music may also prove beneficial in patient care and therapy situations by lowering heart and respiratory rates, decreasing pain perception, and promoting relaxation.

Some studies have extolled the benefits of instrumental music played during learning, but other research suggests that neither music nor significant noise should be present when careful mental work is required.

Action Steps

* When intense mental work is required, reduce all ambient noises (including music) as much as possible.
* Use background music as an adjunct to routine tasks when mental activity is minimal, or during periods of relaxation *before* or *after* high mental activity.
* Higher pitches may result in quicker positive effects, while slower, minor keys may foster both cortical and limbic alertness.
* Fast tempos in major keys often result in better moods.
* Also recommended are jazz (if it is not improvisational or too dissident) and predictable mood-setting music (i.e., Steven Halpern).

Sources:

Carlson, S.; P. Rama; D. Artchakov; I. Linnankoski. 1997. Effects of music and white noise on working memory performance in monkeys. *Neuroreport*. Sept 8; 8(13): 2853-6.

Chlan, L. L. 1995. Psychophysiologic responses of mechanically ventilated patients to music: A pilot study. *American Journal of Critical Care*. May; 4(3): 233-8.

Hobson, J. A. 1994. *Chemistry of Conscious States*. Boston, MA: Little Brown and Company.

Kosslyn, S. 1992. *Wet Mind*. New York: Simon and Schuster.

Magill-Levreault, L. 1993. Music therapy in pain and symptom management. *Journal of Palliative Care*. Winter; 9(4): 42-8.

Nittono, H. 1997. Background instrumental music and serial recall. *Perceptual & Motor Skills*. June 1984; (3 Pt; 2): 1307-13.

Sousou, S. D. 1997. Effects of melody and lyrics on mood and memory. *Perceptual & Motor Skills*. Aug; 85(1): 31-40.

Teach Kids Good Planning Skills Early: Draw

Encouraging children to draw simple pictures in an organized supervised art class goes a long way toward enhancing their overall planning skills, according to studies by Jing and colleagues (1999), Stiles and colleagues (1997), and Sayil (1993).

Jing, Stiles, and Sayil indicate that drawing rough pictures of objects, human figures, and buildings encourages children to use their conscious and unconscious thought processes to visualize and plan their sketches. This process is enhanced when children are allowed to draw what they wish, Sayil noted.

Stiles and Sayil found that voluntary, supervised drawing impacts planning and spatial configuration development in children—skills that directly affect the brain's frontal lobe region. Jing noted a direct correlation between human figure drawings and verbal IQ in learning disabled children.

And a study of artistic behavior by Gnezda-Smith (1994) notes that it is an artist's conscious and unconscious pre-planning of a work that is often the most essential step in the artistic process, again suggesting the important role the frontal lobe region of the brain plays in art creation.

Action Steps

✽ Set aside time at least twice a week for learners to draw both assigned and unassigned pictures. Provide feedback on their work, and give recognition by displaying the art in a visible area.
✽ Encourage the drawing of objects, human figures, buildings, and other things that enhance spatial configuration development.

Sources:

Gnezda-Smith, Nicole. 1994. The internal forces of creativity: When the heart starts to flutter. *Roeper Review*. Dec; 17(2): 138-43.

Jing, Jin; C. Yuan; J. Liu. 1999. Study of human figure drawings in learning disabilities. *Chinese Mental Health Journal*. May; 13(3): 133-4.

Sayil, Melike. 1993. Relationship between children's general planning skills and planning of drawings. *Teurk Psikoloji Dergisi*. June; 8(29): 38-45.

Stiles, Joan; Doris Trauner; M. Engel; R. Nass. 1997. The development of drawing in children with congenital focal brain injury: Evidence for limited functional recovery. *Neuropsychologia*. Mar; 35(3): 299-312.

Can Music Reduce Aggressive Behavior?

Research continues to support music therapy's healing and relaxing effects and its positive implications for reducing behavioral problems in the classroom, including behavior associated with learning disabilities and emotional disorders. Specifically, music is frequently used as a viable therapy for reducing aggressive behavior and learning problems brought on by autism, mental retardation, attention-deficit disorder, emotional trauma, and other related conditions.

Positive results with meditative, sedative music to lessen anxiety and disruptive behavior have been noted by Susan Ford (1999), Tony Wigram (1993), and Iwanaga and Moroki (1999). Moreover, the discretionary use of music, especially the combination of meditative music with fast-paced rhythms, can help emotionally disturbed and learning-disabled children channel anger, frustration, and aggression into creativity and self-mastery, according to research by Durand (1998), Montello and Coons (1998), Lehtonen and Shaughnessy (1997), and Cripe (1986).

In a study of 20 male patients with Alzheimer's disease, Kumar and colleagues (1999) found that meditative/classical music tends to produce high levels of melatonin, a neurotransmitter that plays a key role in relaxation, sleep onset, heart rate, and blood pressure. Fast music with an intense beat, on the other hand, increases levels of norepinephrine and epinephrine (two neurotransmitters linked to emotional arousal) and is effective in increasing attention span and motivation, Kumar noted. In a study comparing the effects of techno and classical music listening on 18 psychologically healthy 18- and 19-year-olds, Gerra and colleagues (1998) found that techno music was associated with increased heart rate and systolic blood pressure.

While classical and meditative music tends to produce calming, sedative reactions, energizing music tends to have more positive long-term effects on aggressive individuals, allowing their feelings to be vented and directed in constructive directions (Montello & Coons 1998). Ideally, meditative music combined with energizing beats may be a viable approach for reducing aberrant, angry behavior (Gunter 1993).

Action Steps

* Classical and meditative music selections (i.e., Gustav Mahler, Ravi Shankar, Johann Strauss) in controlled learning environments help calm and sedate anxious learners so that aggression/anger can be better managed.

* Energizing beats (i.e., rock, hip-hop, techno) produce emotional arousal, which in controlled situations, allows angry learners to vent their frustrations so that such feelings can be better identified, harnessed, and directed in positive directions.

* Use both modes of music to better address the emotional and learning needs of students.

* Combine music listening with other cognition-enhancing activities such as art, dance, and physical exercise.

* Consult a music therapy professional to learn more about music's benefits and uses.

* After an intense period of mental concentration and learning (or right before such a session), lessen student anxiety by playing relaxing, meditative music in the classroom.

* For periods when you want students to feel energized (before the big game or group competition), play upbeat music with an intense beat.

* Allow students to choose music from a library of selected recordings.

Sources:

Cripe, Frances. 1986. Rock music as therapy for children with attention-deficit disorder: An explanatory study. *Journal of Music Therapy*. Spr; 23(1): 30-7.

Durand, Mark. 1998. Influence of mood-inducing music on challenging behavior. *American Journal on Mental Retardation*. Jan; 102(4): 367-78.

Ford, Suzanne. 1999. The effect of music on the self-injurious behavior of an adult female with severe developmental disabilities. *Journal of Music Therapy*. Winter; 36(4): 293-313.

Gerra, G.; A. Zaimovic; D. Franchini; M. Palladino. 1998. Neuroendocrine responses of healthy volunteers to techno-music: Relationships with personality traits and emotional state. *International Journal of Psychophysiology*. Jan; 28(1): 99-111.

Gunter, Philip. 1993. A case study of the reduction of aberrant, repetitive responses of an adolescent with autism. *Education and Treatment of Children*. May; 16(2): 187-97.

Iwanaga, Makoto and Y. Moroki. 1999. Subjective and physiological responses to music stimuli controlled over activity and preference. *Journal of Music Therapy*. Spr; 36(1): 26-38.

Kumar, A.M.; F. Tims; D.G. Cruess; M.J. Mintzer. 1999. Music therapy increases serum melatonin levels in patients with Alzheimer's disease. *Alternative Therapy in Health and Medicine*. Nov; 5(6): 49-57.

Lehtonen, Kimmo and Michael Shaughnessy. 1997. Music as a treatment channel of adolescent destructivity. *International Journal of Adolescent & Youth*. 7(1): 55-65.

Montello, Louise; Edgar Coons. 1998. Effects of active vs. passive group music therapy on pre-adolescents with emotional, learning, and behavioral disorders. *Journal of Music Therapy*. Spr; 35(1): 49-67.

Wigram, Tony. 1993. The feeling of sound: The effect of music and low frequency sound in reducing anxiety and challenging behavior in clients with leaning difficulties. In: *Handbook of Inquiry in the Arts Therapies: One River, Many Currents*. Helen Payne (Ed). London, England: Jessica Kingsley Publishers, Ltd. pp. 177-96.

Mock Trials Add Cognitive Spark to Learning

Mock trials, replete with witnesses, prosecutors, and defenders, stimulate learning when opposing viewpoints and issues are apparent. Such methods have been used successfully with children as young as 6 years of age and are known to sharpen recall and use of newly acquired information and training.

Why are mock trials effective? In short, behavior in one environment tends to transfer to other environments that are similar (Beck 1999; Hersch & Viscusi 1998). The researchers investigated the usefulness of mock trials and debates conducted in the classroom and found that this transfer effect creates meaning and relevance in the brain, which in turn, facilitates long-term memory and learning.

Scientists know that meaning can originate in various parts of the brain, making it a complex process to understand. For example, when something is emotionally meaningful, there may be increased activity in the frontal, occipital, and midbrain areas. Damasio (1994) suggests that if something is meaningful during speaking or reading, there is usually more activity in the left frontal, temporal, or parietal lobes. Intense emotions are also known to impact the amygdala, a brain area associated with emotionally laden memory.

Relevance happens on a simple cellular level in the brain. An already existing neuron simply connects with a nearby neuron. The greater number of links and associations that your brain creates and the more neural territory involved, the more firmly the information is embedded.

This link-association transfer was borne out in a study by Hersch and Viscusi (1998). Staging mock trials in an economics class to instruct students in various economic principles, the researchers found that the trials were not only significant in helping students apply economic analysis to real-life situations, but also in enhancing such valuable skills as listening, questioning, group deliberation, and oral expression.

Action Steps

* Organize your mock trial session around the particular subject matter you are covering. For example, if you are teaching about sexual harassment, develop a scenario in which an employee or student is accused of harassment.

* Any controversial subject can be explored through this means. For first graders, the subject of your mock trial might be "Who hit whom at recess?" For eighth graders it might be a trial on "Does downloading music off the Internet constitute stealing?" For high-school seniors, a controversial world event might be stimulating. Roles to be assigned to learners include defendant, defense attorney, judge, prosecution, defense witnesses, and prosecuting attorney.

* Have the defendant and defense attorney and the plaintiff and prosecutor (along with the witnesses) meet separately as a group to determine strategies and to prepare their testimony.

* Have the rest of the students serve as the jury.

* Have each group, using the principles of the subject learned in class, make a commitment to reaching a fair and equitable decision.

Sources:

Beck, Charles R. 1999. Conducting mock trials and debates in the classroom. *Social Studies*. March-April; 90(2): 78-85.

Damasio, Antonio. 1994. *Descartes' Error*. New York, Putnam and Sons.

Hersch, Joni and W.K. Viscusi. 1998. The courtroom comes to the classroom: Estimating economic damages as an instructional device. *Journal of Economic Education*. Fall; 29(4): 301-12.

Music May Benefit the Cognitive-Social Skills of Preschoolers

The cognitive benefits of music therapy with adults are well documented, but how does music affect the social-cognitive adjustment skills of preschoolers? Research conducted by Ulfarsdottir and Erwin (1999) indicates that positive results among young children may take time to develop, but they do occur, often with long-lasting impact.

In a study involving 76 preschoolers, Ulfarsdottir and Erwin examined the effects of vocal nursery rhymes and background classical music therapy among three groups of children. The separate groups included 27 children who received a short-term but intensive, daily exposure to music; 16 who had recently begun attending a musically enriched preschool; and 33 who received no musical exposure. Several weeks later, all the children completed the Preschool Interpersonal Problem-Solving Test, which measures alternative solutions thinking and consequential thinking—two critical cognitive-social adjustment measures. No significant differences were immediately noticed in test results among the three groups.

However, a seven month follow-up showed significant differences after all of the children retook the tests. Preschoolers who had participated in the short-term musical therapy program scored significantly higher on all tests than before and outperformed children in the non-exposed control group. In addition, children already enrolled in musically enriched preschool substantially outscored both groups.

Additionally, research conducted by Nantais and colleagues (1999) and others has reported on music's ability to stimulate the brain's right frontal lobe area (the site of verbal functioning, verbal skills, planning, and social conduct) and other important cognitive regions.

Evidence suggests that musical arts are central to learning. The systems they nourish are in fact, the driving force behind all learning.

Action Steps

✳ Use interactive, sing-along nursery rhymes to teach and reinforce verbal skills and other behaviors.

✳ Use background music (such as classical selections by Mozart and Beethoven) during restful, low-mental activities.

✳ Encourage children to make up their own personal songs and other creations from what they learned during the week.

Sources:

Jensen, Eric. 2000. *Music with the Brain in Mind*. San Diego, CA: The Brain Store.

Nantais, Kristin; Schellenber; E. Glenn. 1999. The Mozart Effect: An artifact of preference. *Psychological Science*. Jul; 10(4): 370-3.

Ulfardottir, Lilja and Philip Erwin. 1999. The influence of music on social-cognitive skills. *Arts in Psychotherapy*. 26(2): 81-4.

Learning Is Enhanced When We Play the Role

Techniques such as role playing, mock trials, and practice situations are excellent ways to affect the positive transfer of new knowledge and skills from present to future application. Such methods have long been used by political candidates, law students, emergency professionals, and others to sharpen recall and facilitate employment of newly acquired information.

Why are these knowledge/skill transfer techniques effective? In short, behavior in one environment tends to transfer to other environments that are similar. This, in turn, creates meaningfulness and relevance for the brain, stimulating long-term memory and learning.

Meaning originates in various parts of the brain, making it a complex process to understand. For example, when emotional meaning is triggered, increased activity in the frontal, occipital, and midbrain areas can usually be observed, found researcher Damasio (1994). But, if something is found meaningful during reading, specifically, more activity in the left frontal, temporal, or parietal lobe is usually observed.

Quite simply, relevance happens at the cellular level when an existing neuron connects with a nearby neuron. The greater number of links and associations made among neurons, the more firmly the new information is woven into the brain. Remember, every thought you think increases the chances of you thinking that thought again. Commercial jet pilots, for example, are first trained in flight simulators before they fly their actual aircraft. All the training they acquire in the simulator (an exact replica) transfers well to the real flying situation. This positive transfer helps the pilot get accustomed quickly to the actual plane and results in reduced errors and increased confidence. Teachers use the same approach when conducting fire, earthquake, or other disaster drills with their students.

Called "simulation games" or "hugging" by some neuroscience professionals, these techniques can result in an almost automatic response on the part of the learner when the new situation is encountered, depending upon the knowledge or skill being transferred. Park (1996) found, in a study involving 44 schizophrenic adult patients and 20 normal adults, that role playing of appropriate adult behavior significantly improved the actions and attitudes of patients in various hospital situations. And Hew and colleagues (1997) used mock situations and role playing to sensitize and educate reluctant paramedics in the performance of mouth-to-mouth resuscitation techniques in hospital and community settings.

Action Steps

* Before making that big presentation to your client, hold a mock presentation with a member or members of your staff. Take turns playing the role of the client and others involved. Explore all possible questions, issues, and challenges that may occur.
* To bring home to students how our court and jury system works, hold a mock criminal or civil trial with your students. Get students acquainted with the system first with textbook and lecture information, then role play the various people in the setting: judge, lawyers, witnesses, and jury.

Sources:

Damasio, Anthony. 1994. *Descartes' Error*. New York: Putnam and Sons.

Hew, P.; B. Brenner; J. Kaufman. 1997. Reluctance of paramedics and emergency medical technicians to perform mouth-to-mouth resuscitation. *Journal of Emergency Medicine*. May-June; 15(3): 279-84.

Park, S.G. 1996. Investigation of social appropriateness and impaired perspective of schizophrenics through role-playing. *Korean Journal of Clinical Psychology*. Dec: 15(1): 91-101.

Music Training May Improve Math Skills

New evidence has emerged supporting the theory that music education at an early age improves students' math skills. Participation in musical training, especially keyboard training, has a positive effect on the right brain hemisphere—an area that controls relational and mathematical operations, spatial-temporal reasoning, and music recognition. Studies further suggest that the quick and constant mental calculations and coordination required in reading and playing music may contribute to exercising and sharpening this portion of the brain (Graziano, et al. 1999; Cochena, et al. 2000).

Graziano and colleagues (1999) found that, when 237 preschool children were given 6 months of piano training, they improved dramatically in spatial-temporal reasoning over children in a control group who did not receive music training. Later in the study, it was found that, when the piano-trained children were given instruction on an unrelated math video game, they scored significantly higher on the task compared to children who did not receive the piano training.

National SAT scores during the years 1990 through 1995 also support the theory that music, coupled with the arts in general, has a positive effect on math and verbal skills (The College Board). In 1995 alone, those students who had studied the arts four or more years scored 59 points higher and 44 points higher on the verbal and math portions of the SAT, respectively, compared to students with no coursework or experience in the arts. In the same year, students with training in music scored 51 points higher on the verbal portion of the SAT and 39 points higher on the math portion compared to students with no experience in music.

In an analysis of the math test results of eighth graders taking the Iowa Test of Basic Skills (ITBS), Cheek and Smith (1999) found that those who had received private music lessons for two years, in addition to in-school music instruction, performed significantly better on the composite mathematics portion of the test than those who did not take private lessons. The research also noted that students who received lessons on the keyboard had significantly higher ITBS math scores compared to children who did not receive keyboard training.

Action Steps

❊ Support music education programs at your school and encourage students to participate in school concerts, the marching band, the choir, the glee club, or other activities that emphasize music reading and performance.

❊ Study the growing body of research that suggests music training has a direct impact on students' mathematical and spatial reasoning abilities.

❊ Encourage students to supplement their in-school musical training with private lessons.

Sources:

Cheek, J.M. and L.R. Smith. 1999. Music training and mathematical achievement. *Adolescence.* Winter; 34(136): 759-61.

Cochena, L.; S. Dehaeneb; F. Chochona; S. Lehericyc; L. Naccacheb. 2000. *Neuropsychologia.* Sept; 38(10): 1426-40.

(The) College Board: Profile of SAT and Achievement Test Takers for 1990-1995. For more information, contact Gail Crum, Music Educators National Conference Information Services, (800) 336-3768.

Graziano, A.B.; M. Peterson; G.L. Shaw. 1999. Enhanced learning of proportional math through music training and spatial-temporal training. *Neurological Research.* Mar; 21(2): 139-52.

Chapter 5
Memory Solutions

emory is both the process of encoding information and the act of retrieving it. Our memories are stored in bits and pieces in various parts of our brain, then reassembled through associative cues at the time of need. We have different types of memory and they are classified in a variety of ways. For example, there is explicit memory (facts and figures / semantic / episodic) and implicit memory (reflexive / procedural). Explicit memories are more malleable over time; whereas, implicit memories are more fixed. If you've tried to change a long-standing habit, you know first hand the power of implicit memory and the hold is has in our lives. Explicit memory, though more malleable, can also be forgotten easily.

New memories are formed when neurons make connections at the synapse. Signals from the sending neuron travel down the axon and are transmitted across the synapse using messenger RNAs (proteins). Another protein called CREB acts as a switch in the receiving dendrite to say either "keep this connection" (memory) or "let it go" (forget). Thus, there's a manipulation in the synaptic strengths by proteins that will either encode or erase a potential memory. This process alters the probability of future neuronal connectivity (memories triggered). Our more complex memories (those that involve all our senses, over various periods of time) require the binding together of many properties (spatial, factual, temporal, and emotional) in a single memory network. Ultimately, memory is the probability that a particular neuronal connection will be reactivated.

Our memories are prioritized because nature has learned what kinds of memory are most important to the preservation of the species. When trauma is induced, for example, we tend to remember it. We also remember

The Brain and Memory

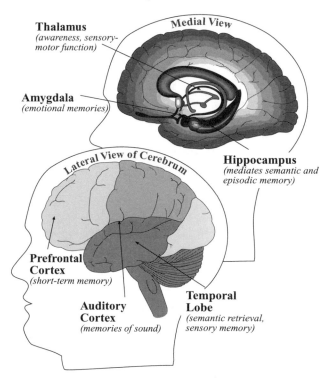

Thalamus
(awareness, sensory-motor function)

Medial View

Amygdala
(emotional memories)

Lateral View of Cerebrum

Hippocampus
(mediates semantic and episodic memory)

Prefrontal Cortex
(short-term memory)

Auditory Cortex
(memories of sound)

Temporal Lobe
(semantic retrieval, sensory memory)

places and situations of great pleasure and pain. We know where to find food and water. We remember the most important numbers, while struggling to remember the less critical ones. And we retain motor learning, such as walking, talking, eating, and other activities we engage in daily. When we understand that humans remember that which is most important to our survival, we can begin to appreciate the importance of meaning in the learning process. To remember the tangential facts imparted in last week's chemistry lecture, we must study hard and make personal meaning out of the facts.

Teaching, in the traditional sense, was conceived as an act of imparting facts to others with a heavy reliance on semantic or explicit memory. A significant amount of our learning, however, is stored implicitly. And, the modern brain-based approach capitalizes on this principle. By engaging active and emotional pathways (the "how" and the "wow"), we supply an additional "hook" for learning. Both the element of movement—the "how" pathway—and the emotive "binder" of shock, fear, surprise, curiosity, or excitement—the "wow" pathway—enhance our recall by engaging more of the brain. The integrated approach rejects extended seatwork as advocated by the teacher training programs of old. If you want your learners to remember more of what they're learning, there are a multitude of strategies you can use to arouse multiple memory pathways. This chapter presents both the research that explains the memory process and some related applications for immediate use in your learning community.

Mnemonics: How to Cement Recall with Rhymes and Acronyms

Mnemonics is a term meaning to assist memory. It refers to an assortment of mental tools and strategies used for remembering unrelated information, patterns, or rules. You can probably still recall, in fact, some mnemonics learned in childhood. For example, "In 1492 Columbus sailed the ocean blue"; or "I before e, except after c"; and "Thirty days hath September..."

We know that rhyming and other memory techniques increase our ability to recall information (Aldridge 1999; Brooks, et al. 1999). One reason may be that mnemonics help stimulate the creation of stronger neuro-links that are stored in the hippocampus—the memory-regulating center of the brain, which is crucial to both short- and long-term memory. To get a better idea of how this stimulation occurs, consider that how, when reciting a rhyme from memory, you must first recall the initial rhyming word or line, which in turn prompts additional recall and propels the cycle.

In addition to rhyming, another effective mnemonic device is called reduction mnemonics (Pinkofsky & Reeves 1998). In this scheme, you reduce a large body of information to a shorter form and use a letter to represent each shortened piece. For example, as an elementary student you may have learned that the first letter of each of the five Great Lakes when combined (Huron, Ontario, Michigan, Erie, and Superior) spells HOMES. And the sentence, "My Very Earnest Mother Just Served Us Nine Pizzas," is a useful device for remembering the order and names of the nine planets that make up our solar system: Mercury, Venus, Earth, Mars, Jupiter, Saturn, Uranus, Neptune, and Pluto.

Research shows that mnemonics can be effective in numerous settings, including education, law enforcement, medical training, and geriatric environments. Aldridge (1999) reported that mnemonics enhance the ability of children who are victims or witnesses to crimes to recall valuable details. A study by Brooks and colleagues (1999) found that the technique is also useful in helping the elderly recall words and proper names, while Fulk and colleagues (1997) reported that first-grade students with special needs were helped significantly by integrated picture mnemonics in acquiring letter-sound skills and letter recognition. Follow-up by Fulk at 2-week and 4-week delay intervals demonstrated that results were maintained over time. In addition, research by Pinkofsky and Reeves (1998) found that psychiatric care professionals were aided by acronym mnemonics (like the HOMES example above) in recalling various diagnostic criteria.

Action Steps

* When employing mnemonics, make them as job- or task-specific as possible. For example, a math teacher might use the following mnemonic reduction sentence to help students remember the order for solving algebraic equations: **P**lease **E**xcuse **M**y **D**ear **A**unt **S**ally to remember **P**arenthesis, **E**xponents, **M**ultiplication, **D**ivision, **A**ddition, and **S**ubtraction. And a history teacher might use the following rhyme to help students remember the period of the Spanish Armada: The Spanish Armada met its fate in fifteen hundred and eighty-eight.
* Encourage learners to create their own mnemonics for recalling important information.

Sources:

Aldridge, N.C. 1999. Enhancing children's memory through cognitive interviewing: An assessment technique for social work practice. *Child and Adolescent Social Work Journal*. April; 16(2): 101-26.

Brooks, J.O., III; L. Friedman; A.M. Pearman; C. Gray; J.A. Yesavage. 1999. Mnemonic training in older adults: Effects of age, length of training, and type of cognitive pretraining. *International Psychogeriatrics*. March; 11(1): 75-84.

Fulk, B.M.; D. Lohman; P.J. Belfiore. 1997. Effects of integrated picture mnemonics on the letter recognition and letter-sound acquisition of transitional first-grade students with special needs. *Learning Disability Quarterly*. Winter; 20(1): 33-42.

Pinkofsky, H.B. and R.R. Reeves. 1998. Mnemonics for DSM-IV substance-related disorders. *General Hospital Psychiatry*. Nov; (206): 368-70.

Getting the Most from Drill and Practice

Drill and practice is a learning technique that facilitates the storage of facts into short-term memory. But how is information transferred from *short-term* memory to *long-term* memory? Research suggests that the process is facilitated by applying new information expediently to real-life situations and experiences (Goodwin, et al. 1998). And, when practical applications of a new skill are followed by immediate and frequent feedback, recall is further enhanced (Alcade, et al. 1998; Goodwin, et al. 1998; Kudo 1994).

In a memory-retention study of 80 undergraduates, Goodwin found that retention was significantly improved when students applied their new knowledge and skills within two hours of learning (drill and practice), and when the tasks were carried out in varied performance situations followed by regular feedback.

While the physical and verbal repetitiveness of drill and practice demands little cognitive effort, gaining understanding of how a skill relates to practical, everyday situations requires greater cognitive effort and is important to long-term memory storage and recall.

"Drill and practice by itself can facilitate the learning of subject matter like basic math and reading skills" says Goodwin. "But getting students to think about why they are learning these skills is also essential to a meaningful education." This is why applying skills in the real world is important.

Action Steps

* Use drill and practice for acquiring fundamental skills in math, reading, and writing, but have students apply those new skills immediately following any drill and practice exercise.
* Provide immediate and regular feedback during both drill and practice sessions and when new skills are being applied. Reduce the frequency of feedback appropriately as learning is mastered.
* Explore the use of computer-assisted drill and practice methods, especially those related to mathematics, reading, and writing.

Sources:

Alcade, C.; J. Navarro; E. Marchena. 1998. Acquisition of basic concepts by children with intellectual disabilities using a computer-assisted learning approach. *Psychological Reports*. Jun; 82(3 Pt 1): 1051-6.

Goodwin, J.E.; C.R. Grimes; J.M. Erickson. 1998. *Perception and Motor Skills*. Aug; 87(1): 147-51.

Kudo, K. 1994. Locus of the retention benefits of variable practice in motor learning. *Shinrigaku Kenkyu*. Jun; 65(2): 103-11

Noteworthy Note-Taking

As every good student knows, effective note-taking primes the brain to store and recall information for future use. At the heart of this process is the hippocampus, located at the base of the cerebrum. The hippocampus plays a major role in the consolidation of learning and in converting information from working (or short-term) memory to long-term storage.

Research suggests that note-taking enhances both immediate and long-term recall by providing a written record for later review (Hadwin, et al. 1999; Hegarty & Steinhoff 1997; Maqsud 1980). What's more, the shorter more concise notes tend to aid recall better than long rambling notes. And reviewing personal lecture notes together with the teacher's notes or handouts facilitates even greater recall, reports Maqsud.

The very act of writing down information, observations, and thoughts helps the brain organize and make sense of complex, multi-faceted bits of information. A timely review of these details further increases the probability that it will be retained by the brain for long-term storage (Hadwin, et al. 1999; Stahl 1985; Einstein, et al. 1985).

When you consider that 70 to 90 percent of new learning is normally forgotten 18 to 24 hours after a lesson (Stahl 1985), the enhanced recall derived from note-taking is considerable. Reviewing new material within the 18- to 24-hour "forget zone" definitely helps solidify details in long-term storage.

While all of us can benefit from effective note-taking, research indicates that some learners benefit more than others. Hadwin and colleagues (1999) found in a study of 82 first year university students that those with average or low-level working memories were helped more by both listening to lectures and taking notes than students with higher-level working memories. Students with higher-level working memories tend to be above-average readers who effectively combine lecture-listening skills with light note-taking and knowledge of text information (Hadwin, et al. 1999; Haenggi & Perfetti 1992).

Kraker (1993) reported that learning-disabled children were more tentative in the use of notation than normally achieving children—a difference most likely due to deficits in symbol/sound recognition, attention, and memory in some learning-disabled children.

A study by Oakhill and colleagues (1991) reported that expectations of the type of test or exam to be administered on class material can impact the quality of student note-taking. Students expecting to undergo a free-recall test, for example, took better notes after listening to a short prose passage than those anticipating a multiple-choice test after listening to the same passage, the study reported.

Action Steps

* Encourage students to rewrite and integrate class notes with text notes within 24 hours of the learning session. Rewriting the day's information in the student's own words reduces the chance for distorting details.
* Make concise instructor notes or outlines available for students to integrate with their own notes.
* For improved visual recognition and semantic retention, encourage students to underline key words and concepts with colored marking pens.

Sources:
Einstein, Gilles; Joy Morris; Susan Smith. 1985. Note-taking, individual differences, and memory for lecture information. *Journal of Educational Psychology*. Oct; 77(5): 522-32.

Hadwin, Allyson F; J.R. Kirby; R.A. Woodhouse. 1999. Individual differences in note-taking, summarization and learning from lectures. *Alberta Journal of Educational Research*. Spring; 45(1): 1-17.

Haenggi, Dieter and C.A. Perfetti. 1992. Individual differences in reprocessing of text. *Journal of Educational Psychology*. Jun; 84(2): 182-92.

Hegarty, Mary and Kathryn Steinhoff. 1997. Individual differences in use of diagrams as external memory in mechanical reasoning. *Learning & Individual Differences*. 9(1): 19-42.

Kraker, Myra. 1993. Learning to write: Children's use of notation. *Reading Research & Instruction*. Winter; 32(2): 55-75.

Maqsud, Muhammed. 1980. Effects of personal lecture notes and teacher notes on recall of university students. *British Journal of Educational Psychology*. Nov; 50(30): 289-94.

Oakhill, Jane and Anne-Marie Davies. 1991. The effects of test expectancy on quality of note-taking and recall of text at different times of day. *British Journal of Psychology*. May; 82(2): 179-89.

Stahl, R.J. 1985. Cognitive Information Processes and Processing within a Uniprocess Superstructure/Microstructure Framework: A Practical Information-Based Model. Unpublished manuscript, University of Arizona, Tucson.

Keeping Memory Intact During Stage Fright

Have you ever noticed how a moment of fear or anxiety can cause your "cognitive juices" to temoprarily drain from your brain? Perhaps no other phenomenon demonstrates this better than episodes of stage fright. It's a common classroom occurrence: Students are asked to speak or perform before a group (sometimes even on short notice), and suddenly, an overwhelming feeling of dread consumes them. They lose their ability to concentrate; their heart races; their blood pressure soars; and sometimes they sweat and tremble profusely. No doubt, this scenario has happened to most of us. Many professionals still harbor a fear of public speaking as a result.

Stage fright is the body's reaction to fear. Even though the body is in no physical danger, it acts as if it is by releasing a mass of hormones and neurotransmitters (including cortisol and epinephrine) into the bloodstream, which puts the body in the classic "fight or flight" mode. Acute and long-term periods of stress cause the hypothalamus (a brain region critical to basic metabolic regulation and sympathetic arousal) to release higher concentrations of cortisol than normal. Higher hormone levels trigger changes in the hippocampus (the brain area important to learning and memory), and over time can kill brain cells and inhibit recall.

Frederickson and Gunnarsson (1992) found in a study of 19 musicians that stage fright increases levels of cortisol, epinephrine, heart rate, and other distress indicators that negatively impact public performance. In research involving 178 adult drama students, Steptoe and colleagues (1995) found that stage fright also triggered thoughts of physical collapse, severe panic, and loss of control, in addition to increased irritability, poor appetite, and skin rashes.

Looking deeper into the psyche of chronic sufferers of stage fright, Gabbard (1997) and Bose (1992) determined that the problem is a chronic form of self-consciousness based on shame and fear—including the fear of envy that may be stirred up in the audience, and personal fears of failure or success.

Scientists know that low or moderate levels of stress are actually good for daily motivation, arousal, action, and long-term memory, but to help your learners avoid the high stress level that accompanies stage fright, teach stress-reduction techniques such as deep breathing and visualization.

Action Steps

＊ Have your students close their eyes and visualize a situation that has caused fear of speaking in public. Ask them to think of what might cause the fear. Now, have them visualize themselves handling the situation coolly and confidently. Have them imagine that people around them are admiring their grace under pressure and that everyone is clapping enthusiastically for them. They're a great success.

＊ Have students over-practice their presentation or performance. Confidence comes from a thorough understanding and knowledge of the material, as well as a desensitization to a new and novel experience. Encourage them to practice in front of a mirror, on video, or in front of a friend or supportive family member. Show them how to solicit helpful feedback.

＊ Encourage students to back up their memory with a hard copy. There is nothing wrong with using visual cues. Have them outline main points on index cards or a sheet of paper.

＊ Teach students how to use humor appropriately. Show them how making fun of themselves, especially if they make a mistake during their presentation, can ease the stress.

＊ Suggest that students share notes, thoughts, and observations about each other's presentations in group-study sessions.

Sources:

Bose, Joerg. 1992. The difficult patient or the difficult dyad? Stage fright in psychotherapy. *Contemporary Psychoanalysis*. Jul; 28(3): 503-12.

Frederickson, Mats and R. Gunnarsson. 1992. Psychobiology of stage fright: The effect of public performance on neuroendocrine, cardiovascular and subjective reactions. *Biological Psychology*. May; 33(1): 51-61.

Gabbard, Glen O: 1997. The vicissitudes of shame in stage fright. In: *Work and Its Inhibitions: Psychoanalytic Essays*. Charles W. Socarides; Selma Kramer, et al. (Eds). Madison, CT: International Universities Press, Inc.

Steptoe, Andrew; Farida Malik; C. Pay; P. Pearson. 1995. The impact of stage fright on student actors. *British Journal of Psychology*. Feb; 86(1): 27-39.

Text Is Better Recalled as a Song

Have you ever considered incorporating hard-to-remember facts and phrases into a song for your students? Recent research indicates that text information is often better recalled if heard in a song rather than as speech, provided that the music and words repeat themselves (Nittono 1997; Wallace 1994).

Musical structure can assist in learning, in retrieving information, and if necessary, in reconstructing a text. Music is a rich structure that segments words and phrases, identifies stress patterns, adds emphasis, and focuses listeners' attention on these characteristics, reports Wallace (1994).

Suggesting that music's repetition and rhyme also have positive cognitive effects, Nittono (1997) demonstrated that music often increases our ability to recall information by stimulating the creation of stronger neuro links to be stored in the hippocampus—the memory-regulating center of the brain that is crucial to both short-term and long-term memory. For example, when reciting or recalling the words to a popular tune, one must first recall the initial rhyming word or line, which in turn spurs the memory to recall the next part of the series, which in turn links us to the next and remaining parts. Each time we repeat the exercise, a deeper "groove" or neuro pathway forms to aid recall in the future. Some grooves become so deep that remembering the words is virtually effortless, such as remembering the words to the Star Spangled Banner or to your favorite advertising jingle.

In a study examining the recall ability of 64 undergraduates, Wallace (1994) found that the majority of the subjects performed better when they heard three verses of a text sung to a well-known melody, versus when it was spoken. In addition, she determined, that sung verses have better verbatim recall than do rhythmically spoken verses. Explaining the study's results, Wallace postulates that perhaps the sheer repetition of the songs established a strong, stable memory. Or, "it could be that the text and melody in combination make the memory more unique and connected and, therefore, more easily accessible," the researcher adds.

Action Steps

* Recall the power of nursery rhymes and songs as teaching tools.
* Make rhymes and songs as task-specific as possible. For instance, elementary school English teachers might find the tried-and-true rhyme "i before e, except after c," to be helpful, and history teachers might use variations of "In 1492 Columbus sailed the ocean blue," to enhance recall of important dates.
* Encourage learners to create their own rhymes, raps, cheers, or songs to remember important information.

Sources:

Nittono, H. 1997. Background music and serial recall. *Perception & Motor Skills*. June; 84(3 Pt 2): 1307-13.

Wallace, Wanda. 1994. Memory for music: Effect of melody on recall of text. *Journal of Experimental Psychology: Learning, Memory and Cognition*. 20(6): 1471-85.

Mental Imagery Adds Life to Recall

Have you noticed that almost anything seems possible when you imagine it or see it in your mind's eye? This says much about the power of mental imagery and visualization.

Studies suggest that visualization is a potent tool in enhancing recall and problem solving, especially when it is used soon after task-learning and immediately before and during new-task application (Antonietti, et al. 1994; Antonietti 1999).

Our ability to paint pictures and images in our mind involves the same cognitive areas used in visual perception (Gleissner, et al. 1998; Farah 1995; Sakai & Miyashita 1994). These brain regions include spatially mapped areas of the occipital cortex, which controls vision, and the right hippocampus, which regulates visual memory, visuoconstruction, and spatial visualization.

Researchers report that the more colorful imagery we are exposed to when we first learn a task, the better primed we are to employ similar images when we later mentally reconstruct the learning situation for recall. For example, Goetz and Sadoski (1996) found that young readers exposed to reading material rich in illustrations and word imagery became more involved and engaged in the learning experience and were more apt to "relive" their favorite literary scenes away from class. Similar results in recall and comprehension were noted by Gambrell and Jawitz (1993).

In a study of 60 university students on the effects of mental visualization on mathematical, geometric, and instrumental problem solving, Antonietti (1999) demonstrated that visualization works best when employed after studying the problem (following a short "daydreaming" break) and before testing the solution. The researcher also found that the more task-similar images the students elicited, the more creative the solutions. Another study by Abbate and Di Nuovo (1999) demonstrated that visualization of numbers and digits, particularly for the mental addition of column numbers, often proves more difficult than visualizing concepts, words, and real-life images and scenes.

Action Steps

* Immerse young learners in imagery-rich texts, videos, and other learning aids.
* Do not minimize the effectiveness of "daydreaming" and other non-directive thinking as a trigger for recall and imaginative problem-solving.
* Visualization tends to work best following new-task learning and immediately before or during task application.
* Continue visual and mental rehearsal of the task until learning confidence is obtained.

Sources:

Abbate, C.S.; Santo F. DiNuovo. 1999. Attentional memory and visualization strategies in mental addictions. *Perceptual and Motor Skills*. Dec; 87(3, pt1): 955-62.

Antonietti, Alessandro. 1999. Can students predict when imagery will allow them to discover the problem solution? *European Journal of Cognitive Psychology*. Sept; 11(3): 407-28.

Antonietti, Alessandro; P. Cerana; L. Scafidi. 1994. Mental visualization before and after problem presentation: A comparison. *Perceptual & Motor Skills*. Feb; 78(1): 179-89.

Farah, Martha. 1995. The neural basis of mental imagery. In: *The Cognitive Neurosciences*. Cambridge, MA: MIT Press.

Gambrell, Linda and Paula Jawitz. 1993. Mental imagery, text illustrations, and children's story comprehension and recall. *Reading Quarterly*. Jul-Sept; 28(3): 264-76.

Gleissner, U.; C. Helmstaedter; C.E. Elger. 1998. Right hippocampal contribution to memory: A presurgical and postsurgical study in patients with temporal lobe epilepsy. *Journal of Neurology, Neurosurgery, and Psychology*. Nov; 65(s): 665-9.

Goetz, Ernest and Mark Sadoski. 1996. *Empirical Approaches to Literature and Aesthetics: Advances in Discourse Processes*. Norwood, NJ: Ablex Publishing. Corp.

Sakai, K. and Y. Miyashita. 1994. Visual imagery: An interaction between memory retrieval and focal attention. *Trends in Neuroscience*. 17(7): 287-9.

Scaffidi, Abbate S. and Santo Di Nuovo. 1998. Attentional memory and visualization strategies in mental addition. *Perceptual and Motor Skills*. 87: 955-62.

Simplify Recall of Complex Information: Use Chunking

The recall of abstract data and long strings of information (credit card numbers, mathematical formulas, and phone numbers) can be a daunting task until the data is broken down into manageable segments—an associative memory technique called chunking.

Scientists know that when we manipulate information or experiment with it, or are asked to solve a problem related to it, the data gets encoded along multiple memory pathways—including visual, auditory, and kinesthetic ones—increasing the chance for retrieval. Wickelgren (1999) confirmed previous studies which found that these associations are stored in the cerebral cortex in "webs," or innate neuron assemblies. These assemblies become linked with chunking or when new idea associations are formed. In fact, for long-term memory, the brain actually stores templates of these linkages, report Gobet and Simon (1998).

We know the conscious brain can only process about five bits of information at one time, but this amount varies depending upon the learner's age and prior learning, report Halford and colleagues (1998), who also found that children's ability to process complex chunking associations increases as they get older. Generally, children ages 3 to 7 can recall up to two chunks (or steps in instructions); kids ages 8 to 16 can retain up to three chunks; and those older than 16 can usually manage four or more chunks (Markowitz & Jensen 1999).

Replicating the findings of previous researchers, Gobet and Simon reported in a study of 26 chess players of various skill levels (ages 18-49) that players' ability to copy and recall chess positions was attributable to their storage of thousands of chunks (patterned clusters of chess pieces) in long-term memory.

To demonstrate chunking, try memorizing the following list of numbers:

149217761812

This can be accomplished by connecting the smaller chunks of data to each other with visual images or associations. For example, you might associate the first four digits—1492—with the famous date in history (which is when "Columbus sailed the ocean blue"); then link it to the next meaningful number sequence with another related image (in this case, the signing of the Declaration of Independence), and so on.

Lists of letters, such as SRMDBRNDEC can be recalled quickly with the following chunking grouping: The senior doctor (SRMD) was born in December (BRNDEC).

Action Steps

✻ Begin using chunking techniques with children as early as age 3 to strengthen neural connections and to help form important verbal and visual associations. Chunking is a great way to help young children remember their telephone numbers, birth dates, and addresses, especially when incorporated with rhyme and music.

✻ Increase complexity of chunking exercises as children get older, to help students remember important historical dates, geographic data, mathematical formulas, and other information.

✻ New chunks of learning should be practiced frequently at first so that they are quickly consolidated into long-term storage.

Sources:

Gobet, Fernand and Herbert Simon. 1998. Expert chess memory: Revisiting the chunking hypothesis. *Memory*. May; 6(3): 225-55.

Halford, Graeme; William Wilson; Steven Phillips. 1998. Processing capacity defined by relational complexity: Implications for comparative, developmental, and cognitive psychology. *Behavioral & Brain Sciences*. Dec; 21(6): 803-64.

Markowitz, Karen and Eric Jensen. 1999. *The Great Memory Book*. San Diego, CA: The Brain Store.

Wickelgren, Wayne. 1999. Webs, cell assemblies, and chunking in neural nets: Introduction. *Canadian Journal of Experimental Psychology*. Mar; 53(1): 118-31.

Using Common Scents to Enhance Memory

Scientists now recognize that our sense of smell is one of our least understood senses, but research has revealed that the information our nose brings to our brain has some important implications for learning (Baron 1997; Biella & de Curtis 2000; Hofland & Dieter 1999).

Smell is a powerful trigger of memory. While odors in and of themselves don't help people recall more, particular odors invoke memories that are emotionally laden, which helps further spur our brain's memory mechanisms, report Baron and Hofland and Dieter.

How does the brain process our sense of smell? After odor molecules dissolve in the mucus lining of the roof of the nose, the odor travels to its first way station in the brain, the olfactory bulb. This structure, about the size of two blueberries, is made up of lumps of cortex from which neurons extend through the skull into the nose. Smell molecules, those wafting off a cinnamon bun for example, bind to these olfactory neurons, which fire off their signals first to the olfactory bulb and then to the limbic system—the seat of sexual drive, emotions, and emotional memory. That is why certain smells, such as a perfume or freshly baked cookies, can almost immediately trigger memories and emotions from our past.

Biella and de Curtis note that a mid-brain structure known as the medial entorhinal cortex also plays an important role (via the hippocampus, a major memory center of the brain) in assisting the limbic system in responding to olfactory input. Baron and others have noted that scent cues can be effective in enhancing memory recall, especially when they are subtle and constant.

As testament to the important role that odor plays in human behavior, Schab (1990) noted that a baby recognizes its mother by her odor soon after birth, and that a woman's scent—genetically determined—changes in pregnancy to reflect a combination of her odor and that of her fetus.

As interest in olfactory research is increasing, so is that of aromatherapy—a term coined by French chemist Rene M. Gattefosse in the 1920s that refers to the practice of using fragrances from essential oils in flowers and roots to enhance mental and emotional health. In an article in *Scientific American*, Holloway (1999) reports that aromas are increasingly being used in corporate and commercial settings to enhance mood and well-being:

* Some Japanese companies pipe the scent of lemon into factories via air ducts to increase productivity and encourage the consumption of peppermint tea during breaks to energize workers.
* Disney World's Magic House at Epcot Center uses the scent of freshly baked chocolate chip cookies to promote relaxation and comfort.
* Some American hospitals are using chamomile to reduce patients' anxiety before MRI testing.
* Many shoe stores find that more shoes are sold when there is the scent of leather or flowers in the shops.

Does scientific research bear out the effectiveness of aromatherapy? Although continued study is warranted, research does confirm some validity to using aroma to affect mood and learning:

* In a study of 33 undergraduate psychology majors, Baron (1997) noted that food-associated smells such as vanilla and chocolate have a strong influence on people's willingness to help or volunteer.
* Sullivan and colleagues (1998) reported that brain injury patients performed equally well compared to healthy control participants in a vigilance test after receiving periodic whiffs of peppermint.
* Engen (1991), in a study of college undergraduates, found that lemon extract fragrances improved concentration and attention.
* Significant improvement in word association and word naming tests were realized among university undergraduates after being exposed to background odors of lavender and vanilla, according to a study by Schnabelt (1999).
* Heliotropine, a vanilla-almond fragrance, was found to dramatically relieve stress and anxiety among patients at Memorial Sloan-Kettering Cancer Center in New York (Kallan 1991).

Action Steps

* Use lemon, peppermint, or mint as background aromas in the learning environment to increase alertness, reduce errors, and boost productivity.
* Use chamomile, heliotropine, rose, jasmine, lavender, or vanilla scents to reduce stress.
* Use peppermint, thyme, or rosemary to energize a group.
* Unpleasant odors are known to inhibit learning, so be sensitive to others' complaints about bothersome smells. Be aware that some people may be allergic to specific odors. Inquire before using.
* Aromas such as peppermint, lemon, and jasmine are also available as tea-bags. Consider making them available in break/lunch areas as an alternative to soft drinks and coffee.
* Aromatherapy scents and oils are available at most bath and body shops, health food stores, and/or online.

Sources:

Baron, R.A. 1997. The sweet smell of helping: Effects of pleasant ambient fragrance on prosocial behavior in shopping malls. *Journal of Personality and Social Psychology*. 23(5): 498-503.

Biella, G. and M. de Curtis. 2000. Olfactory inputs activate the medial entorhinal cortex via the hippocampus. *Journal of Neurophysiology*. Apr; 83(4): 1924-31.

Hofland, Stephanie and Rebekah Dieter. 1999. *Psychology Education*. 1: 256-62.

Engen, T. 1991. *Odor Sensation and Memory*. New York, NY: Praeger.

Holloway, Marguerite. 1999. The ascent of scent. *Scientific American*. Nov.

Kallan, C. 1991. Probing the power of common scents. *Prevention*. Oct; 43(10): 39-43.

Schab, F.R. 1990. Odors and the remembrance of things past. *Journal of Experimental Psychology: Learning, Memory and Cognition*. 16: 648-55.

Schnaubelt, K. 1999. *Medical Aromatheraphy: Healing with Essential Oils*. Berkeley, CA: Frog; Enfield: Airlift.

Sullivan, T.E.; B.K. Schefft; J.S. Warm; W.N. Dember. 1998. Effects of olfactory stimulation on the vigilance performance of individuals with brain injury. *Journal of Clinical and Experimental Neuropsychology*. Apr; 20(2): 227-36.

Journaling, Memory, and Cognition

Research suggests that writing down our thoughts (especially complex or emotional ones) on a consistent basis can serve as a tool for reflection and contemplation, allowing us to sift through a problem more clearly. The process also helps us recall recent events more clearly and helps us relate them to our present situation.

Stone (1998) reported that journaling and other forms of note-taking enhance both immediate and long-term recall by providing a written record for later review. The act of writing down information itself helps the brain organize and make sense out of complex, multi-faceted pieces of information. And a timely review of these notes further increases the probability that they will be retained in the brain's long-term storage.

Effective journaling, noted Nielsen (1999), engages the mind and the senses in a creative process of "personal storytelling." But she adds that this process does not come immediately; it requires practice. Stone reports that "writing our way through a problem" not only encourages viable solutions to come to the surface naturally, it also helps us to trust and take advantage of our inner thoughts. Journaling is the same process that writers use to develop characters and plot, as well as to overcome "writer's block," Nielsen notes.

In a 12-week study of 702 fifth graders, Hudelson (1997) demonstrated that journaling enhances both the motivation to read and reading comprehension. Patton and colleagues (1997) found that nursing students who made journal entries on a daily basis improved their critical thinking, observation, and empathy.

Audet and colleagues (1996) reported that online journaling helped high-school students in advanced physics interact more closely with fellow students, improving their ability to share thoughts and observations, defend viewpoints, and negotiate consensus about their thinking.

Action Steps

* When students encounter difficulties in the learning process, encourage them to document their thoughts, feelings, and actions in a journal. The act of writing their problems down often serves as a welcome catharsis, and later as a form of contemplation to explore viable solutions.
* Offer to discuss journal entries with the student each week to provide feedback and further insight. However, if the individual would prefer to keep their journal entries private, respect that desire.
* When more than one student or a group of students are encountering the same problem, encourage all of them to keep a journal and to meet at least once a week to discuss progress and potential solutions.

Sources:
Audet, Richard; Paul Hickman; G. Dobrynina. 1996. Learning logs: A classroom practice for enhancing scientific sense making. *Journal of Research in Science Teaching.* 33(2): 205-22.

Hudelson, Judith. 1997. *Metacognition and Journaling in Process Reading: Their Relationship to Reading Comprehension and Motivation to Read.* Dissertation Abstracts International, Section A: Humanities and Social Sciences. Sep; 58(3-A).

Nielsen, Bonnie Ann. 1999. *The Red Studio: An Exploration of the Perceptual/Cognitive Workings of the 'Enactive' Mind.* Contextual essay. Dissertation Abstracts International, Section A: Humanities and Social Sciences. Aug; 60(2-A).

Patton, J.G.; S.J. Woods; T. Agarenzo. 1997. Enhancing the clinical practicum experience through journal writing. *Journal of Nursing Education.* 36(5): 238-40.

Stone, Mark. 1998. Journaling with clients. *Journal of Individual Psychology.* 54(4): 535-45.

Autobiographical Memory: A Powerful Learning Tool

Events and activities that occur between the ages of 10 and 30 years are recalled more often (or better) and judged to be more important than events from other age periods, especially among older individuals, according to a comprehensive study by Rubin and colleagues (1998). The study is among

the first to identify just how important this stage of our life may be to emotional memory formation.

Called autobiographical memory, this type of recall usually originates from the period in a subject's life that is most influential—when their favorite films, music, and books were discovered, for example; and by their judgment, when the most important world events occurred, report researchers (ibid). Tying these memorable events to current learning topics or experiences, especially when dealing with more seasoned learners, is an effective way to stimulate cognition.

Researchers know that pleasant memories (such as the smell of freshly baked cookies or bread, a favorite tune, or a certain geographical location) stimulate the amygdala, the almond-shaped structure in the brain's limbic system that encodes emotional messages to long-term storage. The amygdala then releases certain neurotransmitters, most notably serotonin, which produce a calming, relaxing effect—a condition conducive to meaningful learning.

Rubin suggests that when significant, pleasant, or uplifting memories are combined or linked to appropriate learning experiences (such as tying Martin Luther King's tenacity in overcoming racial barriers to lessons in the benefits of quiet but determined resolve for discouraged middle-aged minority learners), the two are said to be associated or bonded in a positive way. This prompts meaningful learning transfer, Rubin reports.

The Rubin study is significant in that it quizzed older adults (aged 66 to 72) about their most pleasant memories, such as their favorite movies, songs, events from the past and then retested them again a decade later on the same subjects. When compared to younger adults the seniors' responses were more accurate and consistent, and they viewed the age period of 10 to 30 years old as more significant.

Action Steps

* Remember older learners are probably more apt to benefit from autobiographical memory techniques and to recall or view events occurring between the ages of 10 and 30 as more significant.
* When tying current learning to nostalgic movies, songs, or events be as task-specific as possible. For example, a class on how to remain mentally and physically active might feature publicized exercise tips from such period actors as Cary Grant, Sophia Loren, or Dick Clark.

Sources:
Rubin, David; Tamara Rahhal; L. Poon. 1998. Things learned in early adulthood are remembered best. *Memory & Cognition*. Jan; 26(1): 3-19.

Memory is Best at the Beginning of a Learning Session

It is a simple fact, but often-forgotten: During a learning episode, we remember best the information that comes first; then we remember second best that which comes last; and finally, we remember least that which comes just past the middle, suggests a study by Henson (1999).

This proven theory (called the primacy-recency effect) has important implications for teachers and trainers as they plan their learning presentations. In a standard 40-minute presentation, the most essential information or skills ought to be taught first (usually in the first 15 minutes) while the attention bias is high and the material is uncontaminated, Henson suggests.

New learning ought to be followed (within 10 minutes) by a processing period devoted to feedback, practice, or review, according to Thomas (1972). This helps the learner organize the information for further processing, enhancing his or her ability to digest the learning, and to then get it right.

The next 10 to 15 minutes ought to be devoted to your closing. This is the second most remembered part of the presentation and an important opportunity for the learner to determine sense and meaning. Once the material has been presented, it is time to solidify and embed it in long-term memory.

Action Steps

* Teach the most important material first—the time of greatest attentional bias.
* Avoid using precious prime-time for classroom management tasks (such as taking attendance). Rather, accomplish such tasks during down-time periods (or in the middle of your presentation).
* Use the conclusion of your presentation to embed the information and to help learners attach sense and meaning to it. Memory devices, games, music, or drama can help encode the learning.

Sources:
Henson, Richard. 1999. Positional information in short-term memory: Relative or absolute? *Memory and Cognition.* 27(5): 915-27.
Thomas, E.J. 1972. The variation of memory with time for information appearing during a lecture. *Studies in Adult Education.* Apr; 57-62.

Complex Problem Got You Stumped?
Try Mind-Mapping

Got a complex subject that you need broken down into simple terms for future recall and comprehension? Research suggests that a mnemonic technique, known as mind mapping, may help solve your problem. Mind mapping is a process that encourages visualization of complex subjects or problems into fundamental elements depicted by pictures and symbols with bright colors denoting relationships. This visual outline aids the brain in understanding the situation, devising potential solutions, and storing the critical components in long-term memory for future recall.

Research conducted by Truscott and colleagues (1999), McClure and colleagues (1999), and Vidal-Abarca and Gilabert (1995) suggests that mind-mapping can enhance thinking. Truscott found that the technique encouraged higher-order thinking. And Vidal-Abarca, in a study of 60 middle-school students, who mind-mapped text chapters, concluded that participants' recall and comprehension increased significantly.

The graphic component is important for effective recall reports Hadwin and colleagues (1999). When text is combined with meaningful graphics in note-taking (as it is in mind mapping), information is better retained.

Karen Markowitz and Eric Jensen, co-authors of *The Great Memory Book* (1999), explain in four easy steps how to create a simple mind-map:

1. Gather a large sheet of paper and some colored marking pens.
2. Write or draw the central topic or problem on your paper.
3. Add lines or branches radiating out from the main concept and sub-branches, depicting key ideas, perceptions, and relationships.
4. Personalize with colorful details—doodles, illustrations, and symbols—all which help fix concepts in the brain for later recall.

Action Steps

*   Use mind-maps to devise lesson plans or to explain complex theoretical concepts to students.
*   Encourage your students to employ mind-mapping when outlining text chapters or when encountering difficult multifaceted problems.
*   Personalize mind-maps with colorful and elaborate details.

Sources:
Hadwin, Allyson; F. Kirby; J.W. Woodhouse. 1999. Individual differences in note-taking, summarization and learning from lectures. *Alberta Journal of Educational Research*. Spring; 45(1): 1-17.
Markowitz, Karen; Eric Jensen. 1999. *The Great Memory Book*. San Diego, CA: The Brain Store.
McClure, John; Brian Sonak; Hoi Suen. 1999. Concept map assessment of classroom learning: Reliability, validity, and logistical practicality. *Journal of Research in Science Training*. Apr; 36(4): 475-92.
Truscott, Derek; Barbara Paulson; Robin Everall. 1999. Studying participants' experiences using concept mapping. *Alberta Journal of Educational Research*. Fall; 45(3): 320-3.
Vidal-Abarca, Eduardo and Ramiro Gilabert. 1995. Teaching strategies to create visual representations of key ideas in content and text materials: A long-term intervention inserted in school curriculum. *European Journal of Psychology of Education*. Dec; 10(4): 433-47.

Chapter 6

The Mind/Body Connection

he potential of the human brain is staggering, although much of it goes untapped. When the brain is faced with learning massive amounts of new information, it handles the challenge most effectively with the support of the entire mind/body system. It's hard to understand, therefore, why the bulk of education in America divides the mind, body, and emotions. If a reliance on multiple pathways increases our cognitive capacity, shouldn't we be using an integrated approach in every classroom across the country?

This fused approach employs active, kinesthetic, and emotional elements that facilitate implicit learning. Instead of acquiring information explicitly—through lecture, text, and pictures—we learn it by doing, experiencing, discovering, feeling, and moving. This includes the "wow" responses, like instant emotions and reflexive behaviors, and the more measured "how" responses, like procedural, skill-based, operational, and tactile behaviors. Implicit learning, *combined* with the traditional explicit, represents the whole—which is what smarter learning is all about. This active, mind/body approach provides the following 10 distinctions and advantages:

✳ **Robustness:** The effects are stronger and last longer.
✳ **Age independent:** It is effective for all learners, regardless of age.
✳ **Ease of learning:** It utilizes user-friendly approaches such as role-modeling, real-life learning, trial and error, experimentation, and peer demonstrations.
✳ **Cross-cultural:** It applies to a range of human experience and diverse cultures.

* **Multiple intelligences:** There are various types of intelligence, and the mind/body approach encourages them all.
* **Efficiency:** It takes place outside of conscious awareness and requires few attentional resources.
* **Value:** Virtually all complex behaviors are implicitly learned.
* **Integrity:** Mind/body learning is less susceptible to brain insults.
* **Transfer:** There is evidence of considerable transfer and recall with a mind/body approach.
* **Integrative:** Such learning builds a powerfully effective bridge between the body and the mind.

This chapter not only presents the research that supports integrated, implicit/explicit teaching and learning, it also describes many of the ways to achieve it.

Why Some Learners Thrive on Stress

Most of us are familiar with the cognitive damage that high-level mental stress can cause. But recent research sheds light on how low- to moderately-high levels of stress can enhance cognition by acting as a cognitive motivator.

Key to thriving under stress and making stressors work for, rather than against, you is an intense feeling of self-confidence to cope with the task at hand, combined with a healthy dose of self-esteem (Bar-Tal, et al. 1999). When these keys are in place, positive pressure can enhance decision-making, information processing, and new learning applications. Previous studies by Bar-Tal (1994) and others found that when we feel secure with ourselves and our surroundings, we tend to view potential stressful situations as less so, and even look upon them as learning experiences and challenges.

Scientists know that when we perceive a situation as non-threatening, the proper stage is set in our brain for alterations in neural networks to occur; thus aiding our ability to think, plan, and remember. To help us do this, our brain releases such cognitive-enhancing neurotransmitters as acetylcholine, interferon, and interleukins. The brain also maintains a moderate level of cortisol and adrenaline, allowing us to react enthusiastically and logically to challenges. However, when we perceive a situation as threatening, abnormally high levels of cortisol and adrenaline are released, decreasing semantic learning and recall.

Stress and the Brain

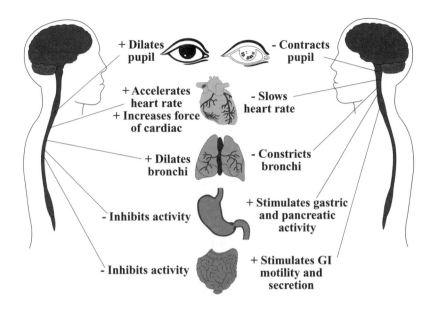

Bar-Tal's 1999 study measured stress reactions and stress levels in 90 new mothers as they adjusted to the birth of their child (48 of them were first-time mothers). Experienced mothers, the four-part study found, made stressful decisions more quickly, with more confidence, and less anxiety than first-time moms, adding credence to the fact that experience breeds self-assuredness.

In other studies, high stress levels in children have been found to produce disruptive behavior (especially in children from poor backgrounds). Research conducted by Masten and colleagues (1988) with more than 200 children and young adult subjects demonstrated that under high stress, disadvantaged students were more likely to exhibit hostile behavior than advantaged children, suggesting that both a self-esteem and family background factor may exist.

When we perceive a situation as threatening, abnormally high levels of cortisol and adrenaline are released, decreasing semantic learning and recall.

Action Steps

* Teach learners about the various levels of stress and how moderate stress can be motivational.
* Make sure that learners demonstrate a competence at basic or fundamental learning levels before advancing to the next level, And, along the way, take the time to build confidence levels with such techniques as role playing, group study, and positive feedback.
* Increase the difficulty level of tasks in gradual, manageable increments.
* Encourage learners to learn from their mistakes; to notice how high stress may be impacting them; and to remember that the keys to mastering such situations are self-confidence and preparation.

Sources:

Bar-Tal, Yoram. 1994. The effect of need and ability to achieve cognitive structure on mundane decision-making. *European Journal of Personality*. 8: 45-58.

Bar-Tal, Yoram; Amiram Raviv; Ada Spitzer. 1999. The need and ability to achieve cognitive structuring: Individual differences that moderate the effect of stress on information processing. *Journal of Personality & Social Psychology*. Jul; 77(1): 35-51.

Masten, Ann; N. Garmezy; A. Tellegen; D. Pellegrini. 1988. Competence and stress in school children: The moderating effects of individual and family qualities. *Journal of Child Psychology & Psychiatry & Allied Disciplines*. Nov; 29(6): 745-64.

Does Physical Exercise Lessen Aggression?

The positive effects of regular physical exercise on psychological health are well documented, but can exercise actually reduce aggression and hostility? Recent research suggests that it can, especially when conducted alone in a non-competitive atmosphere (Widmeyer & McGuire 1997; Wagner 1997; Nouri & Beer 1989).

For example, Widmeyer and McGuire report that during competitive physical activity such as team athletics, testosterone levels and aggression increase more rapidly than when physical exercise is done alone. In a study of professional ice hockey players, the researchers found that aggression levels increased the more athletes competed with another individual or team.

Conversely, Nouri and Beer found in a study of 100 males with varying degrees of aggression and anxiety that a regular regimen of non-competitive aerobic exercise, such as jogging, significantly lessened aggressive behavior. And Wagner (1997) found in a study of adult male prison inmates that weight lifting and other non-competitive activities of choice, reduced verbal aggression, hostility, and anger. Similar results were noted by Mosseri (1998) in a study examining the effects of movement therapy on aggressive adolescent boys in a long-term psychiatric facility.

Scientists know that exercise, especially aerobic exercise, enhances the release of endorphins (the neurotransmitters that relax us into a state of cortical alertness) and reduce the symptoms of stress and depression. Exercise also tends to positively affect levels of neurotransmitters such as glucose, serotonin, noradrenaline, and dopamine—all of which stimulate cognition. In studying aggression and stress in rats, Tanaka (1999) noted that dramatic increases in noradrenaline in the hypothalamus and amygdala regions of the brain occurred during aggressive behavior.

Action Steps

* Always attempt to ascertain the source of a learner's aggression first, even recommending psychological counseling if necessary.
* As an outlet for aggression, encourage learners to engage in non-competitive, individual physical workouts such as jogging, cycling, skating, and brisk walking. Team-related physical activity tends to increase aggression in aggressive individuals.
* Encourage such stress-reducing activities as meditation, journaling, and music.

Sources:

Mosseri, Rami. 1998. Changing the culture of violence: A seven-day admission to a secure unit provides a powerful norm in residential care. *Residential Treatment for Children & Youth.* 16(1): 1-9.

Nouri, Shawn and John Beer. 1989. Relations of moderate physical exercise to scores on hostility, aggression, and trait-anxiety. *Perceptual and Motor Skills.* 68: 1191-4.

Tanaka, M. 1999. Emotional stress and characteristics of brain noradrenaline release in the rat. *Industrial Health.* Apr; 37(2): 143-56.

Wagner, Matthew. 1997. *The Effects of Isotonic Resistance Exercise on Aggression Variable in Adult Male Inmates in the Texas Department of Criminal Justice.* Texas A & M University; UMI Order Number AAM9701731 Dissertation Abstracts International Section A: Humanities & Social Sciences; Feb; p57(8-A): 3442.

Widmeyer, W. Neil and Edward McGuire. 1997. Frequency of competition and aggression in professional ice hockey. *International Journal of Sport Psychology.* Jan-Mar; 28(1): 57-66.

Run and Read a Book

Researchers have found that brain activity is most enhanced after running and other strenuous exercise, and that cognitive reading skills in humans are most affected. Physical exercise invigorates existing brain cells, and may even stimulate the growth of new ones—most notably in the hippocampus, the brain area critical to learning and memory formation (van Praag, et al. 1999; Hogervorst, et al. 1996; Ryman, et al. 1985).

Hogervorst and colleagues (1996) noted that 15 endurance-trained athletes performed significantly better on complex word tests and improved their scores on a battery of psychomotor examinations after a bicycle ergometer endurance test. And in 1985, Ryman noted that Marine Corp enlistees remembered sentences using the active voice better than sentences using the passive voice after the initial phases of strenuous exercise. However, as exercise was prolonged over three days, reading comprehension decreased.

In a month-long study of adult mice, van Praag and colleagues (1999) found that voluntary running doubled the number of surviving brain cells in the newborn rodents' hippocampus region. And caffeine lovers will be glad to hear that consumption of carbohydrate-electrolyte sports drinks (containing low to medium amounts of caffeine) before or immediately after strenuous exercise, adds to cognitive improvements in reading (Hogervorst 1999).

Action Steps

✳ To aid recall and comprehension, encourage learners to take short aerobic exercise breaks (brisk runs, walks, jumping jacks) after significant reading and learning.

✳ Schedule physical education classes as much as possible in the late morning or early afternoon after mental activity has taken place.

✳ For added support (and a healthy dose of competition), encourage students to exercise with other students or friends.

Sources:

Hogervorst, E.; W. Riedel; A. Jeukendrup; J. Jolles. 1996. Cognitive performance after strenuous physical exercise. *Perceptual & Motor Skills*. Oct; 83(2): 478-88.

Hogervorst, E; W. Riedel; E. Kovacs; F. Brouns; J. Jolles. 1999. Caffeine improves cognitive performance after strenuous physical exercise. *International Journal of Sports Medicine*. Aug; 20(6): 354-61.

Ryman, David; P. Naitoh; Carl Englund. 1985. Decrements in logical reasoning performance under conditions of sleep loss and physical exercise: The factor of sentence complexity. *Perceptual & Motor Skills*. Dec; 61(3, Pt 2): 1179-88.

van Praag, Henriette; B. Christie; T. Sejnowski; F. Gage. 1999. Running enhances neurogenesis, learning, and long-term potentiation in mice. *Neurobiology*. Nov. 9; 96(23).

Proper Breathing Relaxes the Body and Fuels the Brain

Have you ever noticed how taking a deep breath directly from the diaphragm and ribs relieves and relaxes you, immediately altering your mind and mood? This occurs because oxygen is a vital, natural nourishment for the brain, muscles, and other organs.

Research suggests that normal breathing patterns can be interrupted by mental stress and anxiety—robbing the brain and body of adequate oxygen and impacting learning (Bernardi, et al. 2000; Sloan, et al. 1991). Conversely, studies indicate that proper breathing exercises can enhance oxygen flow, thereby reducing heart rate and anxiety (Bernardi et al. 2000; van Dixhoorn 1998).

We know that oxygen is essential for learning. Proper breathing provides sufficient oxygen for the correct and efficient functioning of brain cells. Without sufficient oxygen, cells cannot metabolize food properly or rid themselves of all the noxious by-products of metabolism, especially carbon dioxide. Scientists also know that brain cells have an especially high rate of metabolism, so the brain requires much more oxygen than any other organ of the body. Although the brain makes up only one-fiftieth of the body's weight, it uses an amazing one-fifth of the body's oxygen. A lack of oxygen to the brain results in disorientation, confusion, fatigue, sluggishness, concentration, and memory problems.

Action Steps

❋ One of the most common remedies for stress is to take a series of deep breaths followed by a series of slow exhalations (ridding the body of harmful carbon dioxide).

❋ Deep breathing can have a significant influence on health and mood. When breathing is full and deep, the diaphragm moves downward to massage the liver, stomach, and other organs and upward to massage the heart. This motion also serves to detoxify our organs, including the brain. Deep breathing also increases blood flow.

❋ Deep breathing combined with stretching "wakes up" the brain and the rest of the central nervous system by increasing the flow of cerebrospinal fluid to critical tension areas such as the neck and shoulders. It also produces relaxation and stimulates key sensory areas such as vision and hearing.

Sources:

Bernardi, L.; J. Wdowczyk-Szulc; C. Valenti. 2000. Effects of controlled breathing, mental activity and mental stress with or without verbalization on heart rate variability. *Journal of American College of Cardiology.* May; 35(6): 1462-9.

Sloan, R.P.; J. Korten; M. Myers. 1991. Components of heart rate reactivity during mental arithmetic with and without speaking. *Physiological Behavior.* Nov; 50(5): 1039-45.

van Dixhoorn, J. 1998. Cardiorespiratory effects of breathing and relaxation instruction in myocardial infarction patients. *Biological Psychology.* Sep; 49S(1): 123-35.

Obesity and Cognition

Obese individuals may be at greater risk of chronic stress, which not only has long-term detrimental effects on learning and memory, but also increases susceptibility to such conditions as heart disease and hypertension, reports Raber (1998). Obese persons are also at greater risk for learned helplessness, which can contribute to a passive, defeatist attitude towards new learning and physical activity (Johnson, et al. 1997).

In research confirming the findings of previous studies, Raber found that obesity tends to stimulate the over-production of a complex set of stress hormones called glucocorticoids, activated by the brain's hypothalamus and secreted by the adrenal and pituitary glands as cortisol. Glucocorticoids affect the metabolism of glucose (a major source of energy) and can be released with epinephrine, another stress hormone, in response to prolonged physical stress. Raber noted that overexposure to glucocorticoids not only damages and destroys neurons in the brain's hippocampus (a region crucial to memory and learning) but, like elevated levels of epinephrine, can also contribute to chronic hypertension, diabetes, heart disease, and to the suppression of major bodily systems.

Other conditions known to cause an over-production of glucocorticoids are Alzheimer's disease, AIDS, dementia, and depression. The damaging effect of glucocorticoids on the hippocampus may be the reason why below-average cognitive results were noted in studies of persons with obesity, diabetes, and heart disease, speculate Kilander and colleagues (1997) and Nolan and Blass (1992).

Obesity has also been linked to a high risk of obstructive sleep apnea, which affects up to 100,000 snorers annually in the United States. The condition involves the temporary closure of the upper airway, which can occur up to ten times an hour during sleep. Sleep apnea in obese persons occurs because of a greater-than-average amount of fat around the neck, which does not allow the airway to remain sufficiently open at night to allow normal breathing. Obese patients often complain of falling asleep during the day and of lapses in concentration. Rhoades and colleagues (1995) found in a study of 14 morbidly obese children with sleep apnea that they had significant deficits in memory, learning, and vocabulary, while Nolan and Blass (1992) noted similar results in obese adults with sleep apnea.

In a comprehensive study known as the Bogalusa (Louisiana) Heart Study, Johnson and colleagues examined obesity in more than 1,400 children in the Bogalusa public school system (all grade levels). A direct correlation was found between obesity and lack of academic and physical motivation, especially as it related to learned helplessness behaviors.

Action Steps

* Remember, obese students often view their physical condition as hopeless, which can lead to learned helplessness behaviors (characterized by a lack of motivation, self-confidence, physical activity, and effort in school work and other endeavors).
* Continual emotional support is important: Provide positive feedback and encouragement, as well as a highly structured learning environment with physical group activity factored in.
* If the learner seems overly tired (falls asleep in class and is sluggish), review the learner's daily sleep/study schedule to determine if ample time is devoted to homework and sleep. If a sleep apnea problem exists, encourage the parents to seek medical attention for the child.
* If a learning or memory problem exists, encourage the student to participate in a study group arrangement or tutoring. Refer the student to special education services if the problem persists.
* Encourage and support the student in following a healthful diet and exercise regimen.

Sources:

Johnson, Carolyn; L. Myers; Larry Webber; S. Hunter; S. Bonura; G. Berenson. 1997. Learned helplessness with excess weight and other cardiovascular risk factors in children. *American Journal of Health Behavior.* 21(1): 51-9.

Kilander, L.; H. Nyman; M. Bober; H. Lithell. 1997. Cognitive function, vascular risk factors and education. A cross-sectional study based on a cohort of 70-year-old men. *Journal of Internal Medicine.* Oct; 142(4): 313-21.

Nolan, K.A. and J.P. Blass. 1992. Preventing cognitive decline. *Clinical Geriatric Medicine.* Feb; 8(1): 19-34.

Raber, J. 1998. Detrimental effects of chronic hypothalmic-pituitary-adrenal axis activation: From obesity to memory deficits. *Molecular Neurobiology.* Aug; 18(1): 1-22.

Rhoades, S. K.; K.C. Shimoda; L.R. Waid; P.M. O'Neil. 1995. Neurocognitive deficits in morbidly obese children with obstructive sleep apnea. *Journal of Pediatrics.* Nov; 127(5): 741-4.

Stretching Enhances Cognitive Flow After Sitting

Intermittent periods of stretching, recent research suggests (Henning, et. al. 1997), can enhance cognition among those engaged in sedentary tasks, such as computer work. In addition, studies indicate that physical activity aids the sedentary body and the learning brain by producing increased levels of a neuro-stimulator known as brain derived neurotrophic factor (BDNF), which promotes neuron growth and protects neurons against deterioration (Kesslak, et al. 1998). BDNF is also thought to play an important role in the hippocampus, the brain structure associated with spatial memory.

Stretching in particular is known to "wake up" the brain and the rest of the central nervous system by increasing cerebrospinal fluid flow to critical tension areas such as the neck and shoulder muscles, which not only produces relaxation but also stimulates keys sensory areas such as vision and hearing. And when done with breathing exercises, stretching helps give the brain a healthy dose of oxygen to reactivate focus and provide further relief from a grueling stint at the computer or classroom desk.

In a study of computer operators with musculoskeletal pain, eye strain, negative mood, and low productivity, Henning and colleagues (1997) found that having workers perform body stretching every hour as part of a 3-minute break dramatically improved mood, productivity, and lessened eye, leg, and foot discomfort. Sifft and Khalsa (1991) reported in a study of 60 college undergraduates that "Brain Gym™" stretching activities enhanced visual cognition and alertness among male and female participants.

Body stretching every hour as part of a 3-minute break dramatically improved mood, productivity, and lessened eye, leg, and foot discomfort.

Action Steps

* If long periods of sitting are required in your sessions, have learners engage in brief energizers for several minutes each hour.
* Try this one: Place hands on the desk in front of you. Lower your chin to your chest, feeling the stretch in the back of your neck and relaxed shoulders. Taking a deep breath, scoop forward with the head, bringing it up and back and allowing the back to arch slightly, opening the rib cage. Then exhale, curving the back and bringing the chin back to rest on your chest. This stretching activity, known in Brain Gym circles as "The Energizer," activates the vestibular system, waking up the brain, relaxing the shoulders (which improves hearing) and allowing more oxygen flow to assist nervous system function.
* Stand up every 20 minutes or so to briefly stretch the whole body. Tai Chi and cross laterals are known to be very helpful, as well.

Sources:
Henning, Robert; P. Jacques; G. Kissel; A. Sullivan. 1997. Frequent short breaks from computer work: Effects on productivity and well-being at two field sites. *Ergonomics*. Jan; 40(1): 78-91.
Kesslak, J. Patrick; V. So; J. Choi; C. Cotman; F. Gomez-Pinilla. 1998. Learning upregulates brain-derived neurotrophic factor messenger ribonucleic acid: A mechanism to facilitate encoding and circuit maintenance? *Behavioral Neuroscience*. Aug; 112(4): 1012-19.
Sifft, Josie M. and G. Khalsa. 1991. Effect of educational kinesiology upon simple response times and choice response times. *Perceptual & Motor Skills*. Dec; 73(3 Pt 1): 1011-15.

Aerobic Exercise May Improve Decision-Making

Contributing to a growing quantity of research that extols the cognitive benefits of physical exercise, a recent study by Kramer and colleagues (1999) concluded that a regular regimen of aerobic exercise enhances executive control functions in adults, such as decision-making, working memory, planning, and scheduling.

Past research has suggested that aerobic exercise has at least three positive effects on mental processes: (1) speedier recall; (2) increased stimulation of endorphins (the neurotransmitters that relax us into a state of cortical alertness); and (3) reduced symptoms of depression. Research suggests that the benefit of exercise in treating depression, in particular, may be due to increased levels of a brain chemical called serotonin (Bailey 1991; Folkins & Sime 1981).

Results of the Kramer study strongly suggest that aerobic exercise, such as jogging, running in place, brisk walking, jumping rope, and chair stepping, also impacts the frontal lobe or planning and decision-making region. Additionally, aerobic activity has long been known to inhibit hunger by increasing levels of five neurotransmitters associated with appetite: glucose, serotonin, epinephrine, norepinephrine, and dopamine. Aerobic exercise also increases absorption of oxygen and has been reported to arrest, and even reverse, some of the degenerative effects of aging (Folkins & Sime, 1981).

For example, Etnier and colleagues (1999) suggest that among older patients with chronic lung disease a relationship may exist between physical fitness and maintenance of cognitive function. Chronic lung disease patients are at particular risk because of a decrease in available oxygen to the brain. The study, which examined 98 patients (ranging in age from 56 to 80) with chronic obstructive pulmonary disease, assessed each patient's lung function and measured aerobic fitness by a 6-minute walking test in which subjects were asked to cover as much ground as possible on a measured course.

Cognitive tests given in the study measured reaction time, the speed at which subjects processed information, memory span, and problem solving. The investigators found that subjects who were the most aerobically fit also had the fastest cognitive responses. Older subjects tended to respond more slowly. The researchers noted that additional studies are needed to determine the precise relationship between aerobic fitness, age, and cognition.

Action Steps

✱ Before starting a new exercise regime, consult a physician and monitor important physical parameters such as blood pressure and heart rate.

✱ To get the most positive effects from aerobic activity, it must be engaged in for at least 12 minutes nonstop, or more, if activity is stationary, such as a Life Cycle. For jogging and running, 15 minutes minimum is recommended; for brisk walking and stationary bicycling, 20 minutes is the recommendation (Bailey 1991).

✱ For maximum benefit, encourage learners to exercise after the most stressful part of the day and before a period in which mental alertness is required or desired.

✱ Don't ride when you can walk; don't sit when you can stand. If you must be sedentary for long periods, learn deep-breathing exercises (breathe in for six counts, hold for four counts, exhale for six counts).

✱ Encourage aerobic activity at appropriate times in your classroom, during physical education classes, in the workplace, and in training environments to help relieve stress and increase cognition.

Sources:

Bailey, C. 1991. *The New Fit or Fat*. Boston: Houghton Mifflin.

Etnier, J.; R. Johnston; D. Dagenbach; R.J. Pollard; W.J. Rejeski; M. Berry. 1999. The relationships among pulmonary function, aerobic fitness, and cognitive functioning in older COPD patients. *Chest*. Oct; 116(4): 953-60.

Folkins, C.H. and W.E. Sime. 1981. Physical fitness training and mental health. *American Psychologist*. 36(4): 373-89.

Kramer, Arthur; S. Hahn; N.J. Cohen; M.T. Banich; E. McAuley; C.R. Harrison; J. Chason; E. Vakil; L. Bardel; R.A. Boileau; A. Colcombe. 1999. Aging, fitness and neurocognitive function. *Nature*. July 29; 400(743): 418-9.

Can Riding a Merry-Go-Round Enhance Cognition?

Spinning, tumbling, and other stimulating body motions found in such physical activities as children's games, figure skating, and gymnastics may actually help to enhance spatial and motor control, research suggests (Sharma 1997; Dobie, et al. 1990; Secadas 1984). Novices may initially have difficulty adjusting to such "abnormal" motion; however, thanks to the plasticity of the central nervous system, problems of balance, disorientation, and motion sickness can often be reduced or overcome with practice (Reschke, et al. 1998).

The spinning and body-rotation games children play (ring-around-the-rosy, merry-go-round, airplane) and the tumbling moves children commonly perform (cartwheels, somersaults) may essentially strengthen immature brain regions that control motor and spatial functions, reports Secades. However, when performed for short periods, these acrobatic motions can cause perception and stimuli confusion in the brain's parietal lobes, which control spatial, sensory, and motor learning. The temporal lobes (hearing, balance, and memory storage) and the occipital lobes (vision), can also be affected report Prothero and colleagues (1999).

Abnormal motion can also affect levels of common neurotransmitters, such as acetylcholine, which is involved in long-term memory formation, and norepinephrine, which influences such functions as blood pressure, metabolic rate, mood, and emotions (Murray 1997). In addition, Martin and colleagues (1997) speculate that spinning and rotation can temporarily throw the pre-configured internal memory map located in the hippocampus out of whack, contributing to disorientation.

Research suggests that practice and training in activities that involve spinning—especially when external visual cues to enhance orientation are used—often help us adjust to or overcome problems of dizziness and balance. This in turn allows the motion to stimulate neural connections in affected brain areas, which may help us reap cognitive rewards in spatial and motor learning (Sharma 1997; Dobie, et. al. 1990; Collins 1966; Secadas 1984).

Collins reported as early as 1966 that professional figure skaters who attempted high-velocity spinning maneuvers with visual cues learned their routines faster and experienced fewer periods of disorientation and loss of equilibrium than those skaters who trained without visual cues.

In an aeronautics simulator study, Dobie and colleagues (1990) found that repeated exposure to active bodily spinning and rotation over days significantly improved normal walking and other motor performance—better, in fact, than exposure to simulated rotation. Bodily rotation also increased the body's tolerance for simulated rotation.

Prothero and colleagues (1999) found that the clearer and more visible the visual cue during bodily rotation the better it aided sensory perception and lessened feelings of dizziness. In addition, Woodman and Griffin (1997) noted that moving the head up as opposed to down during constant speed rotation of the body increased orientation and reduced vertigo.

Children can also benefit from periods of controlled spinning, suggests Secadas (1984). In a childhood developmental study that examined the stair climbing and descending skills of 4,706 children between the ages of 6 months and 5 years, Secadas concluded that the motor and spatial skills kids acquire through spinning exercises may be the same skills needed for stair mastery.

In another comprehensive investigation, Sharma (1997) studied 535 individuals (ages 10 to 55) and their susceptibility to motion sickness caused by spinning and other movements. He found that individuals with greater spatial and motor control—which he says is often derived from such sports as gymnastics, rowing, and football— are less likely to suffer from motion sickness. Conversely, he reported that motion sickness is significantly higher in individuals with spatial disorientation, migraines, and gastrointestinal disorders. And females are more susceptible to motion sickness than males (27.3 percent vs. 16.8 percent), the study found.

The spinning and body-rotation games children play may essentially strengthen immature brain regions that control motor and spatial functions.

Action Steps

✱ Encourage young students to participate in such games as ring-around-the-rosy and merry-go-round riding.

✱ Incorporate appropriate spinning and tumbling exercises into P.E. curriculum to strengthen balance, hand-eye coordination, motor control, and spatial learning.

✱ In sports that involve spinning and rotating actions, such as figure skating, gymnastics, and ballet, use external visual cues to stay oriented and to reduce feelings of vertigo.

✱ Note: Spinning activities are not advisable for elderly persons, individuals with acute spatial and motor-skill deficits, or persons with digestive problems, motion sickness, or other physical problems.

Sources:

Collins, William. 1966. Vestibular responses from figure skaters. *Aerospace Medicine*. 37(11): 1098-104.

Dobie, Thomas G.; James May; C. Gutierrez; S. Heller. 1990. The transfer of adaptation between actual and simulated rotary stimulation. *Aviation, Space & Environmental Medicine*. Dec; 61(12): 1085-91.

Martin, Gerald; C. Harley; A. Smith; E.S. Hoyles. 1997. Spatial disorientation blocks reliable goal location on a plus maze but does not prevent goal location in the Morris maze. *Journal of Experimental Psychology; Animal Behavior Processes*. Apr; 23(2): 183-93.

Murray, John B. 1997. Psychophysiological aspects of motion sickness. *Perceptual & Motor Skills*. Dec; 85(3, Pt 2): 1163-7.

Prothero, Jerrold D.; Mark Draper; T. Furness; D. Parker; M. Wells. 1999. The use of independent visual background to reduce simulator side-effects. *Aviation, Space & Environmental Medicine*. Mar; 70(3, Sect 1): 277-83.

Reschke, Millard F.; J. Bloomber; D. Harm; W. Paloski; C. Layne; V. McDonald. 1998. Posture, loco motion, spatial orientation, and motion sickness as a function of space flight. *Brain Research Reviews*. Nov; 28(1-2): 102-17.

Secadas, Francisco. 1984. When does the child climb the stairs? *Psicologica*. 5(3): 241-63.

Sharma, Krishan. 1997. Prevalence and correlates of susceptibility to motion sickness. *Acta Geneticae Medicae et Gemellologiae*. Twin Research; 46(2): 105-21.

Woodman, Paul D. and M.J. Griffin. 1997. Effect of direction of head movement on motion sickness caused by Coriolis stimulation. *Aviation, Space & Environmental Medicine*. Feb; 68(2): 93-8.

How Important Is Recess to Cognition?

Despite steps by some elementary schools to eliminate recess, recent research suggests that this unstructured play period not only reduces student stress and restlessness, it also enhances attention, social skills and spatial cognition (Bjorklund & Brown 1998; Rivkin 1995).

Bjorklund found that children's attempts to make their way across monkey bars, negotiate hopscotch courses, play jacks, perform tumbles and summersaults, or toss a football require intricate behaviors of balance, planning, and strength—skills that are essential to healthy development. These skills also play an important role in enhancing spatial cognition. In addition, scientists know that physical exercise and rest breaks (especially offered in a relaxed atmosphere among peers) reduce stress and anxiety and allow for important mental reflection.

When one considers that among 5- to 8-year-olds, 40 percent are increasingly susceptible to obesity, high cholesterol, and inactive lifestyles, the physical activity afforded by recess is fundamentally important, Rivkin reports. "Increasing demands on schools and on working parents have resulted in a number of children with less time to play under adult supervision," the researcher notes. "Instead, they are spending more time at home behind locked doors watching television, playing video and computer games, and growing obese."

Studies also suggest that outdoor versus indoor exercise is a more effective enhancer of cognition and mood. Exposure to natural sunlight may be the key factor responsible for this phenomenon. Natural sunlight is known to stimulate certain endorphins and neurotransmitters (including dopamine) that affect mood, arousal, and metabolism. In a clinical trial conducted by Partonen and colleagues (1998), it was found that exposure to sunlight and fresh air, when combined with the stimulating effects of exercise, can multiply resulting mental and physical benefits.

Structured physical activity, like unstructured play, also has been found to significantly improve mental focus and concentration levels in young children (Caterino & Polak 1999). The findings suggest that physical exercise, such as running, jumping, and aerobic game playing, has a definite impact on children's frontal lobe—a primary brain area for mental concentration, planning, and decision-making.

In a study involving second-, third-, and fourth-grade students, Caterino and Polak were among the first to find a definite association between exercise and mental concentration in healthy kids. The researchers conducted a standardized test of mental concentration on one group of students after the group completed structured periods of running, jumping, and aerobic games, and then tested another group after it completed non-physical classroom activity. Children who had engaged in physical activity performed significantly better on concentration and attention tasks than the control group. Results were particularly significant among fourth-graders, suggesting that older children may benefit cognitively the most. Earlier research by Ju (1985) and Porter and Omizo (1984) suggests that structured physical activities also enhance attention and concentration in hyperactive and mentally retarded children.

Action Steps

* Remember the cognitive and physical benefits of providing your young learners with at least 20 minutes of recess and rest breaks each day.
* Provide exercise breaks for students after the most stressful part of the day and before periods in which mental focus is necessary.
* If your school has eliminated recess, allow students to participate in other physical movement activities in the classroom, such as breathing and stretching exercises or running in place.
* Encourage your learners to participate in physical activity at home and with friends after school in lieu of watching television and playing video games. Suggest to students that they walk instead of ride, stand instead of sit, and to practice deep breathing during long, sedentary periods of learning.
* Provide learners with adult supervision, age-appropriate equipment, and a secure playground environment to get the most out of recess.
* Instead of always holding class inside, enhance mood and motivation by taking your class outside for stretching, group interaction, story telling, sharing, etc.

Sources:

Bjorklund, D.F. and R.D. Brown. 1998. Physical play and cognitive development: Integrating activity, cognition, and education. *Child Development*. June; 69(3): 577-98.

Caterino, M.C. and E.D. Polak. 1999. Effects of two types of activity on the performance of second, third-, and fourth-grade students on a test of concentration. *Perceptual & Motor Skills*. Aug; 89(1): 245-8.

Ju, Peili. 1985. Preliminary study of the effect of martial arts on the concentration, memory, and coordination of reading-impaired students. *Information of Psychological Sciences*. 4: 49-50.

Partonen, Timo; S. Leppaemaeki; J. Hurme. 1998. Randomized trial of physical exercise alone or combined with bright light on mood and health-related quality of life. *Psychological Medicine*. Nov; 28(6): 1359-64.

Porter, Sally and Michael Omizo. 1984. The effects of group relaxation training, large muscle exercise, and parental involvement on attention to task, impulsivity, and locus control among hyperactive boys. *Exceptional Child*. Mar; 31(1): 54-64.

Rivkin, M.S. 1995. *The Great Outdoors: Restoring Children's Right to Play Outside*. Washington, DC: National Association for the Education of Young Children.

Sarkin, M. 1997. Gender differences in physical activity during fifth-grade physical education and recess periods. *Journal of Teaching in Physical Education*. 17: 99-106.

Optimal Learning Occurs Before Lunch

We all know the feeling: After consuming lunch, especially a large or heavy one, our motivation wanes, leaving us sleepy, physically tired, and mentally sluggish as we return to the classroom or office. Called the post-lunch dip syndrome or post-prandial hypoglycemia (a naturally occurring form of low blood sugar), this phenomenon is so common that many teachers abhor having to teach immediately following lunch (Getlinger 1996; Javierre, et al. 1996).

Moreover, Getlinger found that elementary-school children obtained more physical and mental benefits from recess when it was scheduled before lunch—a strategy that may help counter the effects of post-lunch dip. In addition, Getlinger found that scheduling physical activity first tended to sharpen children's appetites.

Post-lunch dip has *less* to do with the time of day the meal is eaten and *more* to do with what is eaten, how much, and the overall effect of the digestive process on the brain, studies involving students and athletes suggest (Getlinger 1996; Javierre 1996; Smith 1993). Scientists know that several aspects of the digestive process tend to sap our energy, especially if meals precede exercise and intense mental activity. One is the metabolic process itself. Even though we get our energy from food, it takes a lot of energy for our digestive tract to process food so that our body can use it. It is estimated that our metabolism rate increases 25 to 50 percent following a meal. Moreover, Smith and McNeill (1991) found that students who ate larger lunches before performing a battery of focused attention and search tasks, made more errors than those who consumed a small- to normal-sized lunch.

In addition, the food we eat stimulates the release of insulin from the pancreas into our blood stream. There is a bit of a lag in this process, so the level of insulin may not start to peak for about 30 minutes after we begin a meal. Later, the insulin production may not shut off precisely when we need it to, so an hour or so after the meal, blood-sugar production may still be underway, leading to a lower-than-normal dip in sugar levels, thereby resulting in exhaustion and sleepiness.

Also figuring into the mix is a digestive hormone called cholecystokinin, whose role, among many others, is to signal the brain that we are full. But this hormone also tends to make us sleepy by activating areas in the brain associated with sleep. And finally, when we eat certain foods—mainly those made up of carbohydrates—the level of tryptophan, an amino acid in the blood, increases. Tryptophan is converted into serotonin in the brain. And guess what serotonin does? It makes us sleepy.

Action Steps

* If possible, allow your learners to engage in physical exercise (recess, physical education class, and sports training) before eating lunch, rather than after.
* If physical or mental exertion is required immediately after eating, encourage learners to eat a lighter lunch that contains fewer carbohydrates or to eat a piece of fruit when they begin to feel sleepy.
* Encourage athletes to eat at least 3 or 4 hours before athletic training or competition so that their food will be fully digested.

Sources:

Getlinger, M.J.; V. Laughlin; E. Bell. 1996. Food waste is reduced when elementary school children have recess before lunch. *Journal of the American Dietetic Association*. Sep; 96(9): 906-8.

Javierre, C.; J.L. Ventura; R. Segura. 1996. Is the post-lunch dip in sprinting performance associated with the timing of food ingestion? *Spanish Review of Physiology*. Dec; 52(4): 247-53.

Smith, A. and Ralph McNeill. 1991. Influences of meal size on post-lunch changes in performance efficiency, mood, and cardiovascular function. *Appetite*. Apr; 16(2): 85-91.

Smith, A.P. 1993. Meals, mood, and mental performance. *British Food Journal*. 95(9).

Team Versus Individual Sports: Which Creates More Anxiety in Athletes?

Sports psychologists say winning and losing in athletic competitions depends not only upon talent and ability, but on how athletes handle anxiety in competition. In essence, high anxiety can wreak havoc on self-confidence, concentration, and performance, report researchers Kirby and Liu (1999).

We know that uncontrolled anxiety is detrimental to cognition. It produces stress-related reactions in the brain and nervous system that stimulate the adrenal glands to release high amounts of the brain chemical cortisol. Scientists know that when cortisol levels are chronically high, learning processes in the brain's hippocampus region (important to memory formation) and other areas shut down.

Which types of sports tend to produce the most anxiety in athletes? Research suggests individual sports do. Kirby and Liu compared athletes competing in team sports (basketball) to athletes competing in individual sports (track and field) and found that subjects playing individual sports had significantly lower self-confidence and higher somatic anxiety than team sport athletes. These findings support earlier research conducted by Bejek and Hagtvet (1996), which demonstrated that figure skaters experienced greater cognitive and somatic anxiety prior to an individual competition than before team competition.

Thuot and colleagues (1998) suggest these results may be due to the fact that there is more diffusion or division of responsibilities in team sports than in individual competition—a factor that may reduce performance anxiety and enhance self-confidence. Similar suggestions have been made by Lloyd (1996) and others in research examining individual versus group study behavior.

Important gender differences have also been identified in levels of self-confidence and anxiety in sports participation. Females had lower self-confidence and higher somatic anxiety scores than males in a comprehensive study by Thuot and colleagues. This research also focused on the location of the athletic event, finding that away-games resulted in increased somatic anxiety and lower self-confidence for males and females both. The study also reported that adolescents, regardless of gender, experienced significantly higher anxiety and lower self-confidence as the ability of their opponents increased.

Action Steps

* Make sure that the individual athlete (or team) is both physically and psychologically prepared for what they will face in competition. Mental imagery and visualization exercises can be helpful in psychological preparation.
* Encourage relaxation methods, such as light running, brisk walking, meditation, and diaphragmatic breathing exercises before competition.
* Athletes should stay focused on the task at hand, a state that can be fostered through reassurance.
* Encourage athletes to give their best performance every time, regardless of how important or unimportant the competition might be.

Sources:

Bejek, K. and K. Hagtvet. 1996. The content of pre-competitive state anxiety in sports. *Anxiety, Stress and Coping: An International Journal*. 9: 19-31.

Kirby, J. and C. Liu. 1999. Anxiety-performance in team and individual sports. *Research Quarterly for Exercise and Sport*. 84: 93-103.

Lloyd, J.W. 1996. Group vs. individual reinforcement contingencies within the context of group study conditions. *Journal of Applied Behavior Analysis*. Summer; 29(2): 189-200.

Thuot, S.; S. Kavouras; R. Kenefick. 1998. Effect of perceived ability, game location, and state anxiety on basketball performance. *Journal of Sport Behavior*. Sept; 21(3): 311-21.

Chapter 7

Smart Nutrition

t's no secret that our brain requires good nutrition to function optimally, just as the rest of our body does. If we deprive this virtual 3-pound electrochemical factory of its essential nutrients, something must give, and it's usually our mental and physical energy. Malnourished students may show up to school, but sit slumped in their chairs, lethargic and inert. Learners with hyperglucose diets may show up to school, but not be able to settle down and focus.

Our brain "factory" does have its favorite foods: oxygen, water, and nutrients (glucose, trace elements, amino acids, and multi-mineral, multi-vitamins). These critical elements are sometimes in short supply not only among under-served or poor populations, but also across the socio-economic strata. Do federally-funded programs help? To a small degree, yes. But these programs tend to provide foods high in sugar and carbohydrates (cheaper to produce) and low in protein (more expensive). Although, there are numerous studies that support the value of multi-vitamin and multi-mineral supplements, about 25 percent of our nation's children are considered to be living at poverty level, so it is unlikely they can afford them. In addition to a high-protein, low-sugar meal at school, every schoolchild, regardless of income, ought to also have a daily multi-vitamin formula available to them on an optional basis.

Extending beyond the problem of adequate nutrition, neurophysiologist Carla Hannaford (1995) asserts that the average learner is often dehydrated—a condition that can also lead to poor learning performance. Hospitals have reported patient improvement when up to 20 glasses of water per day are consumed. Athletes know the importance of increasing water consumption for peak performance, as do actors and other professional presenters. Now, an increasing number of educators are also realizing the learning benefits of drinking plenty of pure water. Water is better for the body than coffee, tea, soft drinks, or fruit juices because it is free of diuretic agents and sugar, which can throw the body's natural rhythm off. Many teachers find that when they encourage their students to drink water as often as needed, behavior improves, as well as performance. Nutritionists recommend filtered water to ensure that it is free of contaminants.

In this chapter, we'll explore some recent studies that reveal just how much our brain depends on the vital elements of oxygen, water, and nutrients for optimal performance. So, jump right in and get started. Oh, by the way, did you remember your vitamins today?

Vitamins Pack a Cognitive Punch

Recent studies are revealing more about the importance of eating your spinach, oranges, bran cereal, seafood, chicken, and other vitamin-packed foods. Research also shows that individuals who follow a healthy diet benefit the most from vitamin supplements, and that vitamin deficiency among schoolchildren remains a serious concern.

Vitamins and other nutrients are essential to brain development, neural maintenance, and brain metabolism. Suffice it is to say that failure to consume a balanced diet will take its toll on brain function—from deficiency in memory and visuospatial ability to attention and planning problems (Ramakrishna 1999; LaRue, et al. 1997).

Minninger reported in 1984 that any diet under 2,100 calories per day is deficient in some vitamin, mineral, or trace element, unless tailored by a physician for a specific patient. After 3 months on a low-calorie diet, people exhibit faulty memory, increased error rates, clumsiness, panic, anxiety, and hostility, he found. In fact, even minor vitamin deficiencies can cause depression and mood disorders (ibid).

Especially essential to cognition are the brain-building vitamins: A, B, C, E, and folic acid. Minerals and trace metals such as zinc, iron, boron, and selenium are also crucial to alertness and memory.

In a study conducted by Riggs and colleagues (1996) on the cognitive effects of B-12, B-6, and folic acid, it was found that individuals with the highest levels of these vitamins in their blood performed significantly better on a battery of memory and spatial copying tests when compared to subjects with lower blood levels of these vitamins. Vitamin B-12 is found abundantly in shellfish; B-6 is found in chicken, fish, and whole-wheat products; and folic acid (or folate) is contained in fortified cereals and leafy green vegetables.

Brain-Friendly Supplements

Vitamins
Vitamin A
Vitamin B Complex
Vitamin C with Riboflavinoids
Vitamin E
Pyritynol (vitamin B-6)

Minerals
Magnesium
Zinc
Boron
Calcium
Selenium
Copper
Iron
Manganese

Drugs
Ampalex or CX-516 -
(ampakine)
Aricept™ - (donepezil)
Cognex™ - (tacrine)
Estrogen

Products
Phenylalanine
Glutamine
Tyrosine
RNA- (ribonucleic acid)
NADH - (nicotinamide adenine dinucleotide)
Acetyl-l-carnitine
DHEA - (dehydroepiandrosterone)
Ginkgo Biloba
Phosphatydyl Serine
Piracetam - (Nootropyl™ & Nootropil™)
Nimodipine - (Nimotop™ & Periplum™)
Pregnenolone
Phosphatidyl Choline
DMAE (dimethylaminoethanol) also
known as Deanol
Non-Steroidal Anti-Inflammatories
DHA (docosahexaenoic acid)
Hyperzine or Huperzine A (Hep A)

Beverages
Caffeine - (limit to moderation)
Cerebroplex - (mental-fitness capsules)
Smartz™ - (mental-fitness drink)

A research team led by LaRue (1997) concluded that vitamin supplements can yield cognitive benefits, but improvements are greatly enhanced if the person is already eating smart. The study followed 137 healthy seniors for 6 years and found that the vast majority of them improved their performance on memory and visuospatial and abstraction tests (initially given 6 years earlier) after taking supplements of vitamins C, E, A, B-6, B-12, and folate while routinely eating well-balanced meals.

With all that's been suggested about the importance of vitamins to cognition, vitamin deficiency among schoolchildren—especially students from low-income families—remains a serious concern. A 1995 study, published in *The Journal of the American Medical Association*, examined the breakfast-eating habits of 1,151 low-income second- and fifth-grade students in schools without federally-funded breakfast programs. The research team, led by Sampson, found that on any given day, 12 to 26 percent of the students attended school without having eaten anything. At least 36 percent of the students were obese, and a significantly greater portion of students consumed less than 50 percent of the required daily allowance for vitamins A, E, B-6, and folate. One quarter of the students were found deficient in vitamin C, calcium, and iron.

Action Steps

* Vitamin and mineral deficiencies result from either insufficient food intake, nutrient-poor food intake, or inadequate nutrient absorption by the body. Any of these conditions can cause fatigue, loss of appetite, poor concentration, failing memory, hostility, depression, and insomnia. If you suspect a problem among your learners, seek advice from a health/medical professional. Vitamin and mineral deficiencies can be determined by a simple blood test.

* If your school is located in a predominantly poor area, there is an increased chance that many students are not eating properly. Initiate steps to begin a federally-funded breakfast and lunch program at your school if one is not yet in place.

* Monitor the menu of your existing cafeteria lunch program and make suggestions for additional vitamin-nutritious meals.

* Provide instruction and handouts on the importance of vitamins and other nutrients to cognition and well-being.

* Megadoses of vitamins have no additional benefits and can be toxic. Stay within the required or suggested dosage range.

* Vitamin supplements are best absorbed when taken with other foods. Caffeinated beverages, alcohol, nicotine, aspirin, and other medications obstruct absorption. Since high levels of caffeine are known to block vitamin absorption, school district contracts that promote the increased presence of caffeinated beverage vending machines on campus may be adversely affecting nutrition and learning.

Sources:
Hannaford, Carla. 1995. *Smart Moves: Why Learning Is Not All in Your Head.* Arlington, Virginia: Great Ocean Publishers, Inc.

LaRue, A.; K.M. Koehler; S.J. Wayne; S.J. Chiulli. 1997. Nutritional status and cognitive functioning in a normally aging sample: A 6-year reassessment. *American Journal of Clinical Nutrition.* Jan; 65(1): 20-9.

Minninger, J. 1984. *Total Recall: How to Boost Your Memory Power.* Emmaus, PA: Rodale Press.

Ramakrishna, T. 1999. Vitamins and brain development. *Physiology Research.* 48(3): 175-87.

Riggs, Karen; A. Spiro; K. Tucker; D. Rush. 1996. Relations of vitamin B-12, vitamin B-6, folate, and homocysteine to cognitive performance in the normative age study. *American Journal of Clinical Nutrition.* Mar; 63(3): 306-14.

Sampson, Amy; S. Dixit; A. Meyers; R. Houser. 1995. The nutritional impact of breakfast consumption on the diets of inner-city African-American elementary school children. *Journal of the American Medical Association.* Mar; 87(3): 195-202.

Ginkgo: Forget Me Not

Its fan-shaped leaves come from one of the world's oldest trees, the ginkgo biloba, and its herbal potency has been respected for years in China. Today, research studies in the U.S. are concluding what Oriental medicine has long suspected: Ginkgo biloba is a brain booster.

Ever since Harvard scientists isolated one of ginkgo's most powerful compounds —Ginkgolide B—a decade ago, both animal and clinical research has noted the herb's powerful therapeutic effects (Gajewski & Hensch 1999; Oken 1999; Allain, et al. 1993). An important effect includes the expansion of blood vessels, which provides for increased blood flow to the brain. This, in turn, may help curtail or prevent the degeneration of memory in the hippocampus and other cognitive functions. In addition, Dr. Richard Firshein, founder of the Firshein Center for Comprehensive Medicine and a columnist for *Psychology Today*, says that studies suggest ginkgo, with its antioxidant properties, protects neurons from damage by free radicals.

But even before starting on a regimen of ginkgo, nutritionists strongly recommend that you already have a strong nutritional base on which to build memory improvement. This consists of eating substantial amounts of fruits, vegetables, fish, and other memory-enhancing foods.

Synaptic neural transmissions in the brain may begin to decline as early as age 30. As a result one's ability to recall names, dates, and other information may be negatively impacted.

In a quantitative analysis of published medical literature on the effects of ginkgo on Alzheimer's patients, Oken (1999) reported a small but significant effect on objective measures of cognitive function in Alzheimer's patients after 3 to 6 months of treatment with 120 to 240 milligrams of ginkgo extract.

And in 1997, Maurer and colleagues found that ginkgo biloba extract stabilized the condition of patients (ages 50-80 years) with mild to moderate dementia after 3 months of treatment. Doses of ginkgo extract also significantly improved the information-processing capabilities of elderly men and women during dual coding tests (Allain, et al. 1993).

Medical experts suggest taking ginkgo in a dose of 40 to 80 milligrams three times a day of an extract standardized to 24 percent flavenoid glycosides and 65 percent terpenoids—compounds known to play a role in fighting destructive free radicals. Persons following this regimen usually see an improvement in memory in about 8 weeks. Nutritionists also point out that similar memory enhancement can be derived by eating appropriate amounts of fruit, vegetables, and fish.

Ginkgo, however, should not be taken with anti-coagulants such as aspirin or warfarin, and should be avoided during pregnancy. Side-effects can include mild stomach or intestinal upset, an allergic skin reaction, and headaches.

Sources:

Allain, Herve; Pascale Raoul; Alain Lieury; Frank LeCoz; Jean-Marc Gandon; Pierre d'Arbigny. 1993. Effect of two doses of ginkgo biloba extract (Egb 761) on the dual coding tests in elderly subjects. *Clinical Therapeutics: The International Journal of Drug Therapy*. May-June; 15(3): 549-58.

Firshein, Richard. 1998. There's no forgetting ginkgo. *Psychology Today*. Sept/Oct; p. 26.

Gajewski, Ann and S.A. Hensch. 1999. Ginkgo biloba and memory for a maze. *Psychological Reports*. Apr; 84(2): 481-4.

Mauer, K; R. Ihl; T. Dierks; Lutz Froelich. 1997. Clinical efficacy of ginkgo biloba special extract (Egb 761) in dementia of the Alzheimer type. *Journal of Psychiatric Research*. Nov-Dec; 31(6): 645-55.

Oken, Barry S. 1999. The efficacy of ginkgo biloba on cognitive function in Alzheimer disease. *The Journal of the American Medical Association*. Feb 3; 281(5).

Vitamin A's Link to Learning and Memory

In a recent study conducted at the Salk Institute for Biological Studies, researchers reported that "Vitamin A is a type of molecular key that unlocks one of the most powerful functions of the human brain, namely learning" (Chiang, et al. 1998). The researchers found that the hippocampus (a brain area linked to learning and memory) has particular cell receptors (RARbeta and RXRgamma) for vitamin A, activating brain-cell activity. These receptors are also present in other tissues of the body where vitamin A is detected, and they help control complex genetic networks.

The scientists say it is too early to suggest whether or not vitamin A supplements will aid older patients suffering from memory problems associated with dementia, or that boosting amounts of the vitamin can improve an individual's memory or learning ability. However, what the researchers do conclude is that complete absence of vitamin A is detrimental to brain function.

The results underscore concerns about the consequences of vitamin A deficiency, estimated to affect 190 million children worldwide, including 32 percent of socio-economically disadvantaged preschool children in America (Spannaus-Martin, et al. 1997).

Until now, vitamin A was best known for its role in aiding night and color vision, its probable role as an antioxidant, and its role in the development of the nervous system in embryos. A diet deficient in vitamin A impairs immune function and makes a person more susceptible to infections and illness. A lack of this vitamin can also lead to night blindness and, in extreme cases, total blindness.

Vitamin A is a type of molecular key that unlocks one of the most powerful functions of the human brain, namely learning.

Action Steps

Dietary levels of vitamin A can be increased in the following ways:

* Cow liver is a direct source of vitamin A, and fatty foods such as egg yolks, milk, and cheese are also good sources.
* Vegetables such as carrots, kale, turnip greens, spinach, broccoli, red and green peppers, pumpkin, and sweet potatoes contain beta-carotene, the precursor of vitamin A.
* Fruits such as apricots, cantaloupes, peaches, and mangos are also good sources of vitamin A.

Sources:
Chiang, M.Y.; D. Misner; G. Kempermann; T. Schikorski. 1998. An essential role for retinoid receptors: RARbeta and RXRgamma in long-term potentiation and depression. *Neuron*. Dec; 21(6): 1353-61.
Spannaus-Martin, D.J.; L.R. Cook; S.A. Tanumihardjo. 1997. Vitamin A and vitamin E statuses of preschool children of socio-economically disadvantaged families living in the Midwestern United States. *European Journal of Clinical Nutrition*. Dec; 51(12): 864-9.

Is Chocolate Good for Learning?

The smooth, rich taste of chocolate has provided sensory pleasure to our palates for centuries, so much in fact that chocolate craving is considered the most common craving in North America (Michener, et al. 1994). This may not be all bad, however. According to recent research, chocolate, including chocolate candy bars (and sugar in general) when moderately consumed, can enhance our mood and receptiveness to learning (White 1998; Steelman 1996; Wurtman 1986).

Researchers are discovering that the roots of our attraction to chocolate may lie deep in our brain. Of particular interest is chocolate's dual capability of being both a mood relaxant and mood elevator—states good for cognition.

Sugar or carbohydrates found in chocolate release serotonin, formed from the amino acid tryptophan, which can result in a positive sense of well-being and calmness (Wurtman 1986). Impacting the brain's chemical balance, the stimulants trigger the brain's pleasure center, believed to be the median forebrain bundle, which runs parallel to our pain center.

Chocolate may also act as a mood elevator, says Wurtman. The sugar and fat in chocolate (the average candy bar is almost 10 percent protein and more than 30 percent fat) may trigger endorphins, or "feel good" brain chemicals, similar to those produced by aerobic exercise (Steelman 1996). In addition, chocolate contains three substances—caffeine, theobromine, and phenyethylamine—all considered to be mood elevators and anti-depressants (ibid).

Research by Di Tomaso and colleagues (1996), in fact, linked the pharmacological components of chocolate, namely caffeine and theobromine, to the stimulation of the brain's natural cannabinoid receptors, producing, in some individuals, feelings of euphoria similar to those produced by marijuana and other cannabinoid agents.

However, scientists are especially puzzled why depression, stress, eating disorders, pre-menstrual syndrome, and the onset of menstrual cycles are known to increase one's craving for chocolate and other sweets and carbohydrates (Willner, et al. 1998; Moller 1992). Consumption of chocolate temporarily relieves symptoms of these conditions, suggesting that a deficiency in serotonin and hormonal levels may be the culprit (Rozin, et al. 1991).

Chocolate, including chocolate candy bars (and sugar in general) when moderately consumed, can enhance our mood and receptiveness to learning.

Action Steps

* Before studying or taking a test, students may benefit from eating a pure chocolate candy bar.

* Chocolate candies, especially ones that also have peanuts or some other source of protein in them, can provide quick energy, alertness, and recall-enhancement after mental exercise.

* A child's psychological dependence on chocolate, or sweets in general, can be a sign of other underlying conditions. Consult the school nurse and/or notify the student's parents.

* Although chocolate's calming and mood-lifting properties can be beneficial in learning situations, remind students that the same effects can be had through more balanced foods, such as bran muffins, granola bars, and grain-based cereals (for mood-calming), and fruits and fruit juices (for energizing).

Sources:

Di Tomaso, E.; M. Beltramo; D. Piomelli. 1996. Brain cannabinoids in chocolate (letter). *Nature*. Aug. 22; 382(6593): 677-8.

Michener, W. and P. Rozin. 1994. Pharmacological versus sensory factors in the satiation of chocolate craving. *Physiol. Behavior*. Sept; 56(3): 419-22.

Moller, S.E. 1992. Serotonin, carbohydrates and atypical depression. *Pharmacol Toxicol*. 71 Suppl;. 1: 61-71.

Rozin, P.; E. Levine; C. Stoess. 1991. Chocolate craving and liking. *Appetite*. Dec; 17(13): 199-212.

Steelman, G.M. 1996. Can you change your mood with food? *One Source*. Winter; 16(2).

White, Norman M. 1998. Cognitive enhancement: An everyday event? *Journal of Psychology*. Apr; 33(2): 95-105.

Willner, P; D. Benton; E. Brown; S. Cheeta; G. Davies; J. Morgan; M. Morgan. 1998. Depression increases craving for sweet rewards in animals and human models of depression and craving. *Psychopharmacol*. (Berl) Apr; 135(3): 272-83.

Wurtman, Judith J. 1986. *Managing Your Mind and Mood through Food*. New York: Harper & Row Publishers.

Fish: A Potent Brain Food

There's good reason that fish is considered one of the most potent brain foods. Fish and shellfish represent an excellent source of protein, niacin, vitamin B12, iron, selenium, zinc, and other nutrients essential to optimal brain function and development.

In addition, fish, especially fatty fish (such as salmon, mackerel, herring, sardines, and trout), provides an important dietary source of omega-3 polyunsaturated fatty acids (PUFAs), and contains antioxidants such as selenium and vitamin E, report Innis (2000), Connor (2000), and others.

The Brain and Nutrition

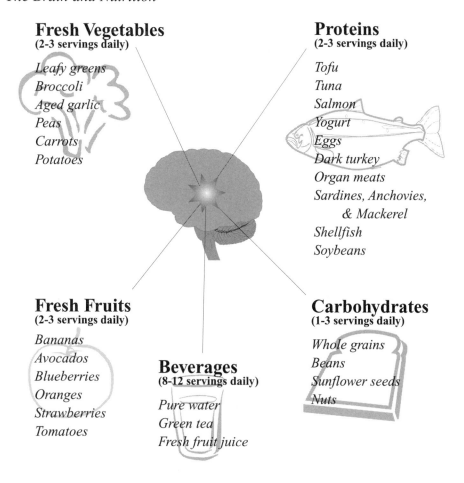

Fresh Vegetables
(2-3 servings daily)

Leafy greens
Broccoli
Aged garlic
Peas
Carrots
Potatoes

Proteins
(2-3 servings daily)

Tofu
Tuna
Salmon
Yogurt
Eggs
Dark turkey
Organ meats
Sardines, Anchovies,
* & Mackerel*
Shellfish
Soybeans

Fresh Fruits
(2-3 servings daily)

Bananas
Avocados
Blueberries
Oranges
Strawberries
Tomatoes

Beverages
(8-12 servings daily)

Pure water
Green tea
Fresh fruit juice

Carbohydrates
(1-3 servings daily)

Whole grains
Beans
Sunflower seeds
Nuts

Connor emphasizes that omega-3 PUFAs are important for brain and retinal development, maturation of the visual cortex, and motor development, and may also help regulate the duration of quiet sleep episodes in infants. Egeland and Middaugh (1997) report that during the third trimester of pregnancy, large amounts of omega-3 PUFAs and long-chain omega-6 acids are mobilized to meet the demands of increased neural and vascular growth. And during optimal infant development, 50 percent of the total fatty acids in areas of the cerebral cortex consist of cell membrane phospholipids (a component of omega-3 that is essential to cell membrane maintenance, memory, learning capacity, attention, and concentration). This finding suggests the need for omega-3 PUFA supplementation during pregnancy, Kidd (1996) reports.

In addition, fish consumption has also been closely linked to reduced risk of coronary artery disease, Connor and others have found, noting that fatty acids in fish help reduce the stickiness of the blood so the blood is less likely to clot. This is important in lowering cholesterol and triglyceride levels, which in turn play a role in lowering the risk of stroke and heart attack.

And, fatty acids found in fish can play an essential role in protecting the brain against age-related cognitive decline (Solfrizzi, et al. 1999), in reducing behavior and learning problems in children, and in treating depression and schizophrenia in adults (Stevens, et al. 1996; Maes, et al. 1999).

Fish and shellfish represent an excellent source of protein, niacin, vitamin B12, iron, selenium, zinc, and other nutrients essential to optimal brain function and development.

Action Steps

* Monitor your school cafeteria menu for adequate inclusion of fish and shellfish.
* Invite a dietician to speak to your students on the importance of fish and other "brain" foods in the diet. (Omega-3 fatty acids are also found in nuts, seeds, whole grains, and lean meats.)
* Encourage your learners to go easy on the fish sandwiches in fast-food outlets. The breading and frying make them higher in fat than a burger. Also, frozen fish that is breaded and/or battered is also generally high in fat.
* Canned salmon (with the bones mashed in) is an excellent source of bone-friendly calcium.
* Shellfish (such as lobster, crab, and scallops) provide a great source of protein as well as being rich in important vitamins and minerals. Shellfish is also low in fat and can be part of a low-fat diet (provided that it is not dipped in butter or rich, creamy sauce).
* If you buy canned tuna, reduce your intake of fat and calories by choosing the water-packed variety.
* Since the effects of fish oils are believed to be important to the development of a baby's brain and nervous system, pregnant and nursing moms should include fish in their diets.

Sources:

Connor, W.E. 2000. Importance of n-3 fatty acids in health and disease. *American Journal of Clinical Nutrition*. 71(1 supplement): 171S-5S.

Egeland, Grace and John Middaugh. 1997. Balancing fish consumption benefits with mercury exposure. *Science Magazine*. 278(5345): 1904-5.

Innis, S.M. 2000. Essential fatty acids in infant nutrition: Lessons and limitations from animal studies in relation to studies on infant fatty acid requirements. *American Journal of Clinical Nutrition*. 71(1 supplement): 238S-44S.

Kidd, Parris. 1996. Your aging brain: A program to rebuild declining function. *Total Health*. Aug; 18(4): 42-4.

Maes, M.; A Christophe; J. Delanghe; C. Altamura. 1999. Lowered omega-3 polyunsaturated fatty acids in serum phospholipids and choleteryl esters of depressed patients. *Psychiatry Research*. March 22; 85(3): 275-91.

Solfrizzi, V.; F. Panza; F. Torres; F. Mastroianni. 1999. High monounsaturated fatty acids intake protects against age-related cognitive decline. *Neurology*. May; 52(8): 1563-9.

Stevens, Laura; Sydney Zentall; Marcey Abate; Thomas Kuczek. 1996. Omega-3 fatty acids in boys with behavior, learning, and health problems. *Physiology & Behavior*. Apr-May; 59(4-5): 915-20.

Cafeteria Food and Cognition

Schools, teachers, and cafeteria staff are in a unique position to promote healthful eating habits, such as reinforcing nutrition education themes learned in class and providing opportunities for students to practice healthful food choices. In addition, researchers are learning that the quality of school meals can contribute significantly to the cognitive health of schoolchildren.

How are schools faring in the important role of feeding schoolchildren? Fair to midline with much room for improvement, according to a 1999 report by the American Dietetic Association and a comprehensive national study of 413 school districts and 607 individual schools at the K-12 level (Pateman, et al 1995). The researchers found that while many schools are taking measures to make more nutritious food choices available in cafeterias, as per U.S. Department of Agriculture guidelines, more effort is needed to reduce total calories from fat in school meals. In addition, the study recommends increased education and training standards for professional food preparation staff, and more attention to regulation of established contracts with fast food restaurants and vending machine companies.

We know that school meals are an important source of vitamins and minerals for many students, especially those from low socio-economic backgrounds. And we know that vitamins and other nutrients are essential to brain development, neural maintenance, and brain metabolism—all factors that influence attention, alertness, visuospatial ability, and planning. Especially important to cognition are the brain-building vitamins A, B, C, E, and folic acid. Minerals and trace metals such as zinc, iron, boron, and selenium are also crucial to alertness and memory. While vitamins and minerals enhance cognition, too much dietary fat, especially trans-fatty acids and saturated fat, is known to slow the thinking process, reduce alertness (Chamberlain 1996), and increase the risk of obesity and diabetes, certain cancers, and coronary artery disease.

The American Dietetic Association (ADA) notes that more than 26 million children, or 66 percent of children aged 6 through 12 years, participate in the National School Lunch Program daily. And for some 10-year-olds, approximately 50 to 60 percent of their total daily intake of energy, protein, cholesterol, carbohydrate, and sodium are obtained from these meals (ADA

1999). In addition, school meals account for 45 to 77 percent of daily intake for vitamins and minerals for participating students, the ADA reports.

With so many children depending upon the nutritional value of school meals, it is incumbent upon schools to increase their efforts to improve meal quality and management, Pateman and colleagues maintain.

Particularly disturbing, suggests the Pateman study, is that the majority of school districts and individual schools are not consistently practicing nutrition-enhancing techniques when preparing meals. For example, less than half reported using ground turkey or lean ground beef in place of regular ground meat on a fairly consistent basis; less than half reported regularly washing browned meat with water to remove grease before adding other ingredients; only 31 percent admitted to removing skin from poultry before or after cooking; and less than half trim the fat from beef or other meats before serving. In addition, only 7 percent reported making available low-fat salad dressing, and less than half reported reducing the amount of sugar in recipes.

The study also found that less than half of all middle/junior and senior high schools offer fresh (as opposed to canned or frozen) fruits and vegetables daily. These findings are important, the ADA study notes, when one considers that in the past 10 years, the number of children who are overweight has more than doubled, especially among low-income children. Currently, more than 11 percent of American children are overweight, and an additional 14 percent have a body mass index between the 85th and 95th percentiles, which puts them at increased risk of becoming overweight, the ADA reports.

The ADA also reported these findings:

* Ninety-one percent of children (especially African-Americans and Latinos) between the ages of 6 and 11 are not consuming the recommended minimum of five servings of fruits and vegetables per day.
* Approximately 80 percent of children consume snacks regularly, accounting for 20 percent of their daily energy intake and 19 percent of total fat and saturated fat intake. And 67 percent of children between ages 6 and 11 years old consume food away from home regularly.

*   Physical activity (known to enhance childhood cognition, reverse obesity, and prevent osteoporosis in later life) is on the decline among children. Forty-eight percent of girls and 26 percent of boys do not exercise vigorously on a regular basis. And, at the same time, participation in school-based physical education classes is declining. Daily enrollment in such classes dropped from 42 percent of students in 1991 to 25 percent in 1995.

Pateman reported that more than 77 percent of all middle/junior and senior high schools have vending machines on campus, which can dissuade students from choosing a more nutritious school meal. More than 37 percent of middle and high schools have been approached by fast food restaurants wanting to offer school meals, while 17 percent have established contracts with such restaurants.

Increased collaboration with school cafeteria staff and teachers on health and nutrition-related education is also needed, Pateman and colleagues claim. Only 19 percent of teachers reported having nutritionists, dieticians, or cooks from the food-service staff as guest speakers in classrooms, and only one-third of the teachers admitted involving food-service staff in health-related activities or projects (ibid).

The training and educational level of food service managers is another concern. Only 3 percent of all schools had a registered dietician in food management; 11 percent had a food service staff person with a four-year nutrition-related degree; 3 percent had a graduate-degreed staff member; and 8 percent had staff with an associate's degree (ibid).

Too much dietary fat, especially trans-fatty acids and saturated fat, is known to slow the thinking process, reduce alertness, and increase the risk of obesity, diabetes, and coronary artery disease.

Action Steps

* Encourage students to consider the school cafeteria an extension of classroom learning where they can put nutrition information into practice.
* Monitor the daily menu of your cafeteria for its nutritional value; meet with school meal planners to review and upgrade the menu.
* Encourage cafeteria management to solicit from students healthful additions to the menu.
* See to it that vending machines on campus offer healthful choices such as nuts, raisins, and fruit juices.

Sources:

(The) American Dietetic Association: 1999. Position of The American Dietetic Association: Dietary guidance for healthy children aged 2 to 11 years. *Journal of the American Dietetic Association.* Jan; 99(1): 93-8.

Chamberlain, J.G. 1996. Fatty acids in human brain phylogeny. *Perspectives in Biology and Medicine.* 39(3): 436-45.

Pateman, Beth Collins; Patricia McKinney; Laura Kann; Meg Leavy Small; Charles Warren; Janet Collins. 1995. School food service. *Journal of School Health.* Oct; 65(8): 327-32.

Chapter 8
Enrichment

nrichment can be viewed in two ways—from a scientific and an educational perspective. Educators have traditionally viewed enrichment as "more" or "harder," than a standard curriculum. Neuroscientists describe enrichment as the process by which favorable changes occur in the brain that would not otherwise be anticipated or predicted. Traditionally, these changes have included evidence of larger cell bodies, greater dendritic branching, enhanced glial cell production, increased synapses, and multiple synaptic contact sites. The discovery that humans can and do grow new brain cells—a process called neurogenesis—is another benefit elicited by enrichment. At first, it was thought that these cells only grew in the dentate gyrus of the hippocampus. Now we know that they grow in the frontal and parietal lobes, as well. Neuroscientists have identified more than seventeen factors that can impact neurogenesis, including genetic aberrations, serotonin, nerve growth factor, and exercise.

All of these factors are the subject of a tremendous amount of neuroscientific scrutiny, but the precise neural mechanisms are still not fully understood. Nonetheless, it is widely accepted that enrichment is good for learning. Some of these approaches include exposure to challenge, novelty, repetition, feedback, positive social bonding, and meaningful experiences. However, these approaches also stimulate the positive neural changes that scientists are studying. Either way you look at it, enrichment ultimately enhances cognition and improves learning. This chapter explores some of the research that supports this analysis and the resulting applications that enrich classroom environments, expand learners' minds, and help students succeed.

Neuroplasticity: How We Change Our Own Brain

Only a few short years ago, neuroscientists believed that the brain was fixed at birth, that humans could not grow new brain cells, and that the physical shape of the brain was predetermined. These beliefs have since been disproved. And what we've discovered in the process has staggering implications for learning.

Brain Connections

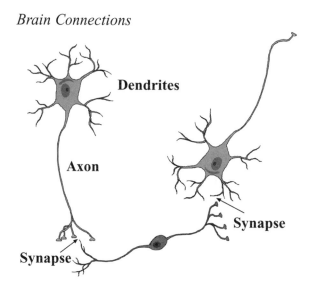

Studies demonstrate that the frontal, parietal, and temporal lobes are all receptive to neural changes (Brown & Chattarji 1995). The examples of neural rewiring are abundant. A team of researchers led by neuroscientist Michael Merzenich demonstrated that when monkeys repeatedly used a specific digit in experiments, they developed greater mass in the corresponding area of the brain that controlled the movement (Allard, et al. 1991). Studies examining cochlear hearing implants have shown that patients with certain kinds of hearing loss can rewire and gain mass in the auditory cortex enabling them to learn to hear again (Merzenich, et al. 1996). Musicians are known to have a larger cortical representation for sensory areas involved in making music than non-musicians (Elbert, et al. 1995). Salk Institute neuroscientist Fred Gage and colleagues discovered that rats who exercised, grew more brain cells in the hippocampus (van Praag, et al. 1999), and a Swedish team verified similar results in humans (Eriksson, et al. 1998).

The following predictions are just a few, among the many, implied by these discoveries: (1) We will discover how to grow new brain tissue to replace damaged parts; (2) We will learn how to help paraplegics walk again; and (3) We will use brain-based video games to customize skill and content learning.

But what specifically drives change in the brain? First, cortical changes are restricted to novel input. Doing something that you already know how to do will not add complexity or mass to the brain. This argues for the value of novelty. But a price is paid for excess novelty: more cortisol and noradrenaline. The brain's response to constant or incoherent novelty is distress. Thus, novelty must be balanced with predictability in the environment, as well. It is recommended, therefore, that teachers and managers maintain predictable rituals (morning announcements, reviews, relaxation exercises, team activities, songs, etc.) as part of every learning or work day.

Second, neural changes are restricted to activities that are meaningful to the organism. The organism has to pay attention, make choices, and be intentionally vested in a coherent activity. Animal studies have shown that processing novel, random input patterns alone will not produce cortical changes (Ahissar, et al. 1992). How the brain determines which input is meaningful is not fully understood at this time, but we believe emotions play an integral role. Assigning complex, challenging projects, therefore, with some learner choice in the process, is recommended.

Third, it's essential that learners receive feedback on their learning. The brain's neural network system is heavily weighted towards utilizing feedback. In fact, if a single neuron sends output to 10,000 neurons, which in turn connect with other neurons just twice more, a single signal will return to its starting point in just a few seconds. This feedback loop enables the brain to extract generalized patterns from many bits of information. The more specific, frequent, and accurate the feedback, the faster learning will occur. Yet most learners are starved for feedback. The best learning environments "build-in" dozens of non-directed, informal feedback devices. They may include discussions, peer editing, posted charts, checklists, completed models, videotaping, and graphing.

The final ingredient? Studies suggest that *time* is an important factor in learning (Wilson & McNaughton 1994). The hippocampus, a small C-shaped structure in the midbrain, processes single learning events and distributes them to the cortex. By design, the hippocampus is fast at learning but has a small capacity. The cortex is slow at learning with a larger capacity. This means the hippocampus must process information that it receives quickly, or it will decay and be lost (short-term memory). In this way the hippocampus serves as a "trainer" to the cortex, repeatedly packaging and sending it information.

This learning is represented in the cortex as alterations in the strength of synaptic connections. The long-term effect is adaptation and generalization in the brain's neural networks. This system argues for the value of short bursts (5 to 15 minutes) of new information, content, or skill-building activity. Learn it, process it, then take a break. In fact, many studies have shown this to be far more effective than 30 minutes or more of continuous content input (Spitzer 1999).

Action Steps

* Incorporate both novelty and predictability into your curriculum. Providing new and challenging topics in addition to familiar ones will stimulate interest and engage minds. But do not overuse novelty; ensure stability by maintaining a regular routine (i.e., morning announcements, reviews, relaxation exercises, team activities, and songs).

* Introduce new information that is meaningful to your learners. The brain generally has difficulty absorbing and assimilating random bits of data and isolated facts. Ensure relevance by associating new information with prior knowledge and providing context for new ideas and topics. Work with students to see how one piece of information fits into the larger whole, especially in its real-world context.

* Provide frequent and specific feedback via classroom discussions, computer instruction, peer editing, group work, checklists, posted charts, models, videotaping, graphing, and students' own self evaluations.

Sources:

Ahissar, E.; E. Vaadia; M. Ahissar; H. Bergman; A. Arieli; M. Abeles. 1992. Dependence of cortical plasticity on correlated activity of single neurons and on behavioral context. *Science.* 257: 1412-5.

Allard, T.; S.A. Clarc; W.M. Jenkins; M.M. Merzenich. 1991. Reorganization of somato-sensory area 3b representations in adult owl monkeys after digital syndactyly. *Journal of Neurophysiology.* 66: 1048-58.

Brown, T.H. and S. Chattarji. 1995. Hebbian synaptic plasticity, in *Handbook of Brain Theory and Neural Networks.* Arbib, M. (Ed). Cambridge, MA: MIT Press.

Elbert, T.; C. Pantev; C. Weinbruch; B. Rockstroh; E. Taub. 1995. Increased cortical representation of the left hand in string players. *Science.* 270: 305-7.

Eriksson, P.S.; E. Perfilieva; T. Bjork-Eriksson; A.M. Alborn; C. Nordborg; D.A. Peterson; F.H. Gage. 1998. Neurogenesis in the adult human hippocampus. *Nature Medicine*. Nov: 4(11): 1313-7.

Merzenich, M.M.; W.M. Jenkins; P. Johnston; C. Svhreiner; S.L. Miller; P. Tallal. 1996. Temporal processing deficits of language-learning impaired children ameliorated by training. *Science*. 271: 77-81.

Spitzer, Manfred. 1999. *The Mind Within the Net*. Cambridge, MA: MIT Press.

van Praag, H.; G. Kempermann; F.H. Gage. 1999. Running increases cell proliferation and neuro-genesis in the adult mouse dendate gyrus. *Nature Neuroscience*. March: 2(3): 266-70.

Wilson, M.A. and B.L. McNaughton. 1994. Reactivation of hippocampal ensemble memories during sleep. *Science*. 265: 676-9.

Growing New Brain Cells, Even As We Age

It was once widely accepted that neurons, the functional cells of the central nervous system, stop multiplying about the time children lose their baby teeth, and then begin to slowly die off into old age. But new evidence continues to demonstrate that this may not be true.

A landmark study by Ericksson and colleagues (1998) found that the human hippocampus, the area of the brain linked to learning and memory, retains its ability to generate neurons throughout life, even into old age. The study also demonstrated for the first time that new brain cells, including neurons in the adult human brain, originate in a brain area known as the dentate gyrus.

While Ericksson and his team say their findings may hold promise for future treatment of brain-damaged patients, they caution that it's still unknown whether newly grown brain cells in adults, especially the elderly, function normally. Moreover, the exact function of these new cells is still being investigated.

The study's conclusions do lend credence, however, to the power of mentally stimulating activities such as reading, puzzles, traveling or field trips, group activity, and physical exercise, not only during childhood, but as we mature. Previous research showed that mice reared in stimulating environments generated new brain cells faster and performed better on learning and memory tests than the control group.

The Ericksson study was conducted on terminal cancer patients (up to age 72) who underwent a diagnostic procedure that identified actively dividing cells. Following their death, the patients' brains were examined for the presence of new brain cells. The results suggest that all of the subjects had evidence of recent cell division in the hippocampus. The authors stated, "It is interesting to note that this was not a particularly young or healthy group of patients, so new cell growth may be even more prominent than we observed."

These findings are not only important to cognitive research, they also have significant clinical implications. If even a few cells with the power to regenerate can be harvested from victims of stroke and brain disorders, doctors may be able to induce new cells to grow in a laboratory dish and then graft them back into diseased areas.

Action Steps

✳ Expose your learners to enriched learning environments and experiences—field trips, reading, music, stimulating guest speakers, mentally challenging games, physical exercise, and constructive feedback.

✳ If you work with maturing adults and the elderly, the above suggestion is even more important.

Source:
Ericksson, Peter S.; E. Perfileva; T. Ejork-Ericksson; A.M. Alborn; C. Nordborg; D. Peterso; Fred Gage. 1998. Neurogenesis in the adult human hippocampus. *Nature Medicine*. Nov; 4(11): 1313-7.

Self-Reflection and Feedback: Keys to Learning from Our Mistakes

We know that a good deal of the learning process involves interacting with and learning from others, but it also includes self-reflection. It is, in fact, during this "incubation" period that we come face-to-face not only with our goals, dreams, and accomplishments, but also with our mistakes and short-comings. Recent studies suggest that learners mentally process and cope with their failures more successfully when a healthy dose of self-reflection and feedback is applied (Frydenberg & Lewis 1999; Shafrir & Eagle 1995).

While self-reflection may give our brain's frontal lobe region a chance to filter external stimuli, it also helps us face our problems and explore possible solutions. Without external feedback regarding our behavior or performance, however, the value of self-reflection is lessened. Turning our thoughts inward in self-reflection can undoubtedly be a source of relaxation and meaning, but it can also be a source of stress, especially if low self-esteem and negative or non-constructive feedback is involved. In the latter case, self-reflection can trigger the brain's amygdala, or emotional-memory center, to elicit harmful "fear and threat" responses that can shut down learning.

When constructive feedback is provided, however, feelings of threat and uncertainty are reduced, the pituitary-adrenal stress response remains even, thereby helping learners exhibit better coping skills. Constructive feedback makes us feel valued and cared for, triggering the release of such "feel good" neurotransmitters as endorphins and dopamine.

Shafrir's study (1995) found that even past mistakes can benefit learning in healthy elementary-school students when constructive self-reflection is involved. In his examination of 88 fifth- and sixth-graders, Shafrir concluded that students who spend long periods of time in reflection about their mistakes were not only better learners and problem-solvers, but developed better corrective strategies than subjects who did not spend a lot of time contemplating their errors. The former group was also found to make more use of constructive feedback in decision-making and to take a more serious view of failure, even when the source of the failure did not involve learning.

The role of feedback in self-evaluation is further illustrated in a 1995 study by Waung and colleagues. This study found that students who rated high in self-satisfaction and academic performance tended to raise their goals and expectations when receiving supportive feedback after committing errors. Conversely, students rated low in self-esteem were found to lower their goals after receiving negative feedback.

Reports suggest that when the feedback is also specific and consistent, it can especially help learning disabled students who are attempting to incorporate and apply new learning. Receiving specific information on how and why an error has occurred, coupled with instruction on how to correct the error, helps these students master skills more effectively. Kline and colleagues (1991) found that this form of instruction, called "elaborated feedback" can significantly reduce the instructional time required for learning disabled students to master certain educational goals. They assert that without such feedback, these learners often practice incorrect responses, thus delaying the mastery of targeted skills.

Action Steps

* Encourage learners to actively reflect on their errors and shortcomings by asking them, for example, how they might improve next time.
* Feedback is most effective when it is specific, stated affirmatively, multi-modal, timely, and learner-controlled.
* Praise students for learning from past mistakes, and for positive aspects before focusing on the places where there is room for improvement.
* When appropriate, allow students to re-take a quiz or exam after discussing errors and giving them time to reflect on their mistakes.
* Provide feedback as close to the time the error is made as possible.
* Provide positive feedback, as well.

Sources:

Frydenberg, Erica and Ramon Lewis. 1999. Things don't get better just because you're getting older: A case for facilitating reflection. *British Journal of Educational Psychology*. Mar; 69(1): 81-94.

Kline, F.; J. Schumaker; D. Deshler. 1991. Development and validation of feedback routines for instructing students with learning disabilities. *Learning Disability Forum*. 14: 191-207.

Shafrir, Uri and Morris Eagle. 1995. Response to failure, strategic flexibility, and learning. *International Journal of Behavioral Development*. Dec; 18(4): 677-700.

Waung, Marie; M. MacNeil; V. Maurya; R. Vance. 1995. Reactions to feedback in goal choice and goal change processes. *Journal of Applied Social Psychology*. Aug; 25(15): 1360-90.

Brain Teasers Enhance Creative and Analytical Thinking

You may not realize it, but while having fun with such brain teasers as the Rubik's Cube, the Tangram, the Tower of Hanoi, crossword puzzles, various word games, and mathematical puzzle books, you are actually enhancing your problem-solving ability, research shows.

Studies by Fan and Gruenfeld (1998), Subhi (1999), and others show that such activities not only result in higher scores on problem-solving tests, but also improve emotional and social skills (or emotional IQ) in children and adults. Findings reported by Malouff and Schutte (1998) suggest that brain-teasers stimulate activity in the brain's frontal lobe, impacting creative thinking, analytical skills, planning, decision making, and social conduct. This keeps the brain's neural connections flexible for future problem solving, the researchers suggest.

The Malouff and Schutte and Fan and Gruenfeld studies also report that puzzles and similar activities not only give the brain a break from more serious concerns, but may contribute as well to the development of thinking skills, creativity, and individual discovery. The benefits are compounded, Gebers (1985) found, when two or more learners work together on puzzles and brainteasers. Such use, she maintains, not only promotes cooperative social interaction but provides constructive classroom activity when the teacher is engaged in one-on-one activity with other students.

Beyond the school setting, Wenzler and Chartier (1999) noted that game-play, when conducted in a cooperative organizational setting (such as corporate training sessions and retreats), tends to enhance teamwork, motivation, and company pride.

Zaika and Lantusko (1997) found in a study of Russian school-age children that mentally challenging games and exercises especially benefited those children who are bright and active outside the classroom, but seem unable to pursue their full intellectual potential in formal learning situations.

Action Steps

* Make a habit of giving games and puzzles to children starting at an early age, gradually progressing to more sophisticated and challenging ones.
* Adults can also benefit from these activities by keeping brain neurons active.
* Leave games (various levels) and puzzles in break rooms and waiting areas.
* For added feedback and interaction, encourage teamwork during problem solving with games and puzzles.

Sources:

Fan, Elliot and D. Gruenfeld. 1998. When needs outweigh desires: The effects of resource interdependence and reward interdependence on group problem solving. *Basic & Applied Social Psychology*. Mar; 20(1): 45-56.

Gebers, Jane. 1985. Jigsaw puzzles: Rest for the left side of the brain. *Academic Therapy*. May; 20(5): 548-49.

Malouff, John and N. Schutte. 1998. *Games to Enhance Social and Emotional skills: Sixty-Six Games that Teach Children, Adolescents and Adults Skills Crucial to Success in Life*. Springfield, IL: Charles C. Thomas Publishing.

Subhi, T. 1999. The impact of LOGO on gifted children's achievement and creativity. *Journal of Computer Assisted Learning*. June; 15(2): 98-108.

Wenzler, Ivo; and Don Chartier. 1999. Why do we bother with games and simulations: An organizational learning perspective. *Simulation & Gaming*. Sept; 30(3):375-84.

Zaika, Evgeniy and G. Lantusko. 1997. Games for the formation of cognitive emancipation in schoolchildren. *Voprosy Psikhologii*. 58-62.

Field Trips Can Cement Classroom Learning

Going on thought-provoking, well-planned field trips, during which learners can apply theory and knowledge learned in the classroom to real life, does cognitive wonders for students, research suggests. A trip to the local historical museum, zoo, fire station, state capitol building, or the like helps promote important aspects of cognitive development.

Manner (1995) reported that such activities motivate students through increased interest and curiosity, which improves long-term retention of concepts. Powers (1999) and Orion (1993) found that field trips enhanced the learning of abstract concepts and helped students view learning as a practical component of life and not just a structured classroom activity. In addition, Smith (1995) noted that out-of-classroom activities increased student-to-student and student-to-teacher social interactions, enhanced communication, and furthered development of social skills.

Studies suggest that complex environments enhance rat brain growth (Black, et al. 1990), and we know that enrichment aids the human brain by bringing increased meaning and recall to learning. Getting students out of the classroom also gives them the opportunity to view what is learned in the classroom from a different perspective—by how it fits into the real world. This, in turn, enhances critical thinking and analytical skills.

Action Steps

* Make sure outings are well organized and that they complement classroom learning.
* Make students explicitly aware of the connections between the trip and classroom subject matter.
* Include as many hands-on experiences as possible for students during the outing.
* Upon your return to class, discuss the field trip; evaluate its effectiveness; encourage students to verbalize what they learned; and provide clarification and feedback where necessary.

Sources:

Black, J.E.; K.R. Issacs; B.J. Anderson; A.A. Alcantara; W.T. Greenough. 1990. Learning causes synaptogenesis while motor activity causes angiogenesis in cerebellar cortex of adult rats. *Proceedings of the National Academy of Sciences.* 87: 5568-72.

Manner, Barbara. 1995. Field studies benefit students and teachers. *Journal of Geological Education.* 43: 128-31.

Orion, N. 1993. A model for the development and implementation of field trips as an integral part of the science curriculum. *School Science and Mathematics.* 93(6): 325-31.

Powers, Kelli. 1999. The field trip as an active learning strategy: TAs in science and engineering. *Teaching Technologies.* 3(1).

Smith, George. 1995. Using field and laboratory exercises on local water bodies to teach fundamental concepts in an introductory oceanography course. *Journal of Geological Sciences.* 43: 480-4.

Guest Speakers Bring Real Life to the Classroom

Research examining the effectiveness of guest speakers (Mooney 1998) suggests that when learning is reinforced in a stimulating environment and from varied sources, students' interest in learning increases and the brain's transformation of learned material from short-term to long-term memory is facilitated. We know that shared experiences from the real world add legitimacy and cognitive substance to what students learn in class, and asking guest speakers to address your students is a stimulating way to accomplish this.

For example, having an historian from the local university or historical society come to speak about the most important battles of the Civil War and how such conflicts shaped the war's outcome, can do wonders for reinforcing what students have already learned in class. This approach also exposes students to different viewpoints.

Mooney reports that guest speakers also provide an effective means for bringing workplace learning into the classroom at all grade levels. Presentations by career professionals can aid students' understanding of the links between learning and career preparation, how learning relates to personal development, and how it applies to society as a whole.

Research conducted by Shipman-Campbell (1995) found that guest speakers can be effective in motivating students to higher standards of learning.

In a study of 63 Latino and African-American high-school students, Shipman-Campbell found that motivational guest speakers contributed to the increased number of students successfully completing English Advanced Placement Examinations.

And Boutwell and Sistrunk (1993) found in a study of 29 second graders and 29 fifth graders that having guests from the community (such as parents, former teachers, and local TV personalities) come to class and read stories improved students' reading scores and interest in reading.

Action Steps

* Add stimulation to learning by bringing interesting guest speakers into the classroom.
* Conduct your own research to find the most appropriate speaker for your class and topic. Speakers should not only be knowledgeable, but also experienced and adept at speaking to the age level of your students. The more "kid-friendly" visuals the speaker is able to bring, the better.
* Schedule speakers at least 3 weeks in advance to accommodate busy schedules. Give the speaker important information about the class (i.e., number of students, grade level, level of understanding about the topic, the objectives to be accomplished by the visit, and specific questions that students would like answered).
* Provide your students with background information about the speaker and enough time to prepare specific questions for the guest. Encourage students to write the guest a thank-you letter after the visit. This reinforces good social and communication skills.
* Don't forget to consider students' parents when looking for potential speakers.
* The local Chamber of Commerce or Business and Industry Councils are good resources for guest speakers from various fields in the community. And many local universities, large companies, and museums have existing speaker bureaus that you can call upon.

Sources:

Boutwell, Lydia and Kim Sistrunk. 1993. The effect of guest readers on reading attitudes of second- and fifth-grade children. Paper presented at the annual meeting of the Mid-South Educational Research Association. New Orleans, LA: Nov 10-12.

Mooney, Linda. 1998. Pitching the profession: Faculty guest speakers in the classroom. *Teaching Sociology*. July; 26(3).

Shipman-Campbell, Alice. 1995. Increasing the number and success rate of junior honors English students in taking English Advanced Placement Examinations. *Educational Psychology*. 36(4).

Positive Role Models Are Essential for At-Risk Students

Research conducted by Lockwood and Kunda (1999) indicates that the brain responds well to the influence of positive role models, especially if these relationships are interactive and include regular intervals of feedback. Such interaction lessens the brain's fear response to new and difficult experiences, enhancing a sense of safety, acceptance, and meaning. These conditions, in-turn, stimulate long-term memory and learning. However, while many children are fortunate enough to be surrounded by an ample array of positive role models (parents, family members, teachers, and clergy), economically- and educationally-disadvantaged youth are often not so fortunate.

Because disadvantaged youth run an increased risk of attending impoverished schools, having less access to professional help, and living in chaotic conditions, exposure to positive role models is often limited (Assibey-Mensah 1997). This lack of positive role modeling is especially prevalent among young African-American and Latino males, he found.

In a nationwide survey of 4,500 African-American youngsters between the ages of 10 and 18, Assibey-Mensah found that the subjects' overwhelming choice of role models was well-known athletes and sports figures. Parents were very seldom named, and none of the participants indicated an educator as a role model. What Assibey-Mensah also found disturbing is the lack of physical interaction that these youth have with a positive figure on a regular basis.

To solve this problem Assibey-Mensah and Drummond and colleagues (1999) call for the establishment of role model/mentorship programs in the inner city. Such programs would bring disadvantaged youth in direct contact with positive role models to emulate.

Research conducted by Yancey (1998) bears out the effectiveness of such an approach. In a study using role models interactively with adolescents in a group foster home, Yancey found self-image and receptiveness to learning were improved with exposure to positive role models, especially among African-American and Latino youth.

Lockwood and Kunda concluded that a relationship with a positive role model tends to inspire and motivate students to establish higher hopes and achieve greater goals than they would have on their own.

Action Steps

* Increase your students' exposure to and direct contact with positive role models—a step that can significantly enhance students' self-image and receptiveness to learning.
* Teachers are in the perfect position to be role models for students. Begin to think of yourself as one before starting a bona fide program.
* Contact universities, corporations, and/or community organizations in your area to establish a role model/mentorship program at your school. Look for role models and mentors who can deal effectively with the educational needs of your particular students, and who can enhance students' goals and aspirations.
* Establish a mechanism to recruit, train, and maintain role models and mentors.
* Study successful programs that have already been established by other schools.
* Periodically evaluate the program for improvement.

Sources:

Assibey-Mensah, George. 1997. Role models and youth development: Evidence and lessons from the perceptions of African-American male youth. *Western Journal of Black Studies.* Winter; 21(4): 242-52.

Drummond, Robert; Heather Senterfitt; Cheryl Fountain. 1999. Role models of urban minority students. *Psychological Reports.* 84(1): 181-2.

Lockwood, Penelope and Ziva Kunda. 1999. Increasing the salience of one's best selves can undermine inspiration by outstanding role models. *Journal of Personality & Social Psychology.* 76(2): 214-28.

Yancey, Antronette. 1998. Building positive self-image in adolescents in foster care: The use of role models in an interactive group approach. *Adolescence.* 33(130): 253-67.

Exposure to Informal Learning Settings Enhances Creativity

We all know the saying: "Learning is all around us." This is especially true for preschoolers and kindergartners and their developing brains. Research suggests that exposing children early to informal learning settings (i.e., museums, storytelling, story reading, and family learning situations) enhances creativity, reading skills, and problem-solving (Ashman 1997; Schauble & Beane 1996; McCaslin 1996).

We know that much of the basis for future learning actually occurs in informal settings away from the classroom, such as when interacting with friends, family, and hobbies. These are often environments where we feel safe, accepted, and fulfilled. In such settings, the brain is free to filter through the experience and to select and connect information for future learning association. In addition, a greater variety of input may activate many prior associations in the temporal lobes, while stimulating new connections in the frontal lobes.

Children who engaged in storytelling and story reading in class and at home scored higher on creativity, problem-solving, and literacy tests compared to children who did not, reported Peters (1993). And Ashman (1997) reported that when children were allowed and encouraged to apply classroom learning with problem-solving strategies away from the classroom, learning increased.

Action Steps

* Expose young children to as many informal learning sessions as possible (field trips, show-and-tell, music listening, storytelling, etc.)
* Parents, work with teachers to help children apply classroom learning to related learning situations at home, such as through reading, play activity, and TV viewing.
* Provide constructive and positive feedback to children during informal learning.
* Allow learning to be a fun and natural process.

Sources:

Ashman, Adrian. 1997. A learning experience. *Journal of Cognitive Education*. 6(2): 75-9.

McCaslin, Mary. 1996. The informal curriculum. In *Handbook of Educational Psychology*. Berliner, David (Ed). New York, NY: Prentice Hall International, pp. 662-70.

Peters, Sandra. 1993. Where have the children gone? Storyreading in kindergarten and pre-kindergarten classes. *Early Child Development & Care*. July; 1-15.

Schauble, Leona and DeAnna Beane. 1996. Outside the classroom walls: Learning in informal environments. In: *Innovations in Learning*. Schauble, Leona (Ed). Mahwah, NJ: Lawrence Erlbaum Associates, Inc., pp. 5-24.

Chapter 9
The Early Years

reparation for "school readiness" begins in the womb. The 9 months prior to birth represent an important opportunity for nurturing the embryo in a way that paves the road for later school (and life) success. We know that drug and alcohol consumption, smoking, distress, nutrition, and environment all impact the developing embryo. Studies have revealed, for example, that even a single alcoholic drink during a critical time in pregnancy can have a negative and lasting impact on the baby.

By month 5 the fetus is already well on its way to having the 50-100 billion brain cells that are normal at birth. These cells, called neurons, connect to other neurons to form a vast and complex network that represents cognition. To put the potential of the human brain into perspective, consider that a *newborn* enters the world with more than one thousand billion (or a trillion!) neuronal connections already established in their brain.

The developing brain grows so fast that at its peak it generates new cells at a rate of 250,000 per minute or 15 million per hour. Interestingly, studies indicate that "preemies" (born pre-term by 10 weeks or more) are at greater risk for having learning delays. While researchers have always known that the first years of life are crucial to the emotional, physical, and cognitive health of a child, we're just now learning *how* critical. Wayne State University neurobiologist Dr. Chugani, says "the experiences of the first year can completely change the way a person turns out. The infant's relationship with his/her primary caretaker," he adds, "strongly influences whether the child will have learning or emotional problems later."

Naturally, there are many factors that influence the health of the developing brain, such as family dynamics, parental care, stress, nutrition, violence, television, day care, school experiences, physical activity, environmental toxins, language, and culture. But even before a child is born, the road is paved or not for them.

This chapter presents some of the studies that are informing our understanding of the critical nature of "the early years." The "take-home" message here is that we really need to do a better job, both collectively and individually, at preparing our children for school, beginning at the time of conception.

Your Touch Can Work Cognitive Wonders

Research abounds on the crucial ways brain development is enhanced through touch. The cognitive benefits are especially essential in the formative years of infancy and early childhood when touching, holding, rocking, gentle stroking, and other positive physical contact from others provides the child with much needed reassurance, comfort, relaxation, and a sense of security. Such contact, scientists know, sends stimulating signals to the brain and helps the child connect with her/his surroundings in a meaningful way.

Studies suggest that behaviors such as rocking, cuddling, and holding an infant not only create a sense of safety and warmth similar to the womb experience, but they also send stimulating signals to the baby's brain (Gatts, et al. 1992). Conversely, the absence of touch produces stress and seems to slow the rate of biological processes (Fleming, et al. 1999).

Simply put, babies and children need touch to "grow the brain," says pediatrician Bruce Perry, Executive Director of the Child Trauma Program at The Baylor College of Medicine. "A child's interaction with caregivers such as parents and early childhood teachers plays a key role."

In a controlled, 16-week study of 90 healthy infants, Gatts and colleagues exposed 45 newborns to a specially designed cradle that closely simulated the motion, sound, weightlessness, containment, and reduced light found in the womb. Unlike infants in the control group, who were placed in an ordinary crib for certain periods throughout the day, newborns in the experimental group cried significantly less, slept for longer periods at night, slept throughout the night sooner, and scored significantly higher in mental orientation evaluations.

Newborns experience a rapid change in environment at birth—departure from their intrauterine world brings about the sudden and dramatic loss of warmth, quiet, darkness, soothing background noise, weightlessness, containment, and intermittent rhythmic motion. The new environment newborns enter is harsh by comparison. "These rapid changes are distressing to the neonate," Gatts reports, "as often evidenced by the infant's crying, disorganized motor responses, and physiologic stress responses."

Although it is still not fully understood, stimulating touch seems to promote growth and brain maturation, and may affect behavior by triggering certain hormones that control our responses to stress (Wheeden, et al. 1993). Absence of touch, on the other hand, produces stress and may trigger the slowing of metabolism (Fleming, et al. 1999).

In animal studies, Fleming and colleagues noted that the simple act of a mother licking her pups triggered a surprising subtle chain of biochemical events inside the baby's brain, ultimately inhibiting the production of a master stress hormone called CRH. High levels of stress in baby animals can impair growth and development of the brain and body.

To determine how these animal study insights might apply to human child rearing, researchers are now assessing the changing brain chemistry of children, and the attention they receive from their primary caregiver, be it mother, father, grandparent, nanny, or day-care provider. Scientists know that a child's brain is wired from birth to respond to a flood of sensory experiences, but when deprived of a stimulating environment either at home or in school (especially in an environment devoid of touch), cognition suffers.

At birth, our brain contains two hundred billion neurons, roughly as many nerve cells as there are stars in the Milky Way. During our first years of life, we form trillions of connections (or synapses) between neurons—more, in fact, than we can possibly use. Over the next 10 years of our life, however, the brain drastically "prunes" away excess neurons, thereby, shaping our "frame of mind" (for better or for worse) for life.

It is during the pre-pruning stage that touch plays such a critical role in forming and strengthening neural connections (Wheeden, et al. 1993; Field, et al. 1986). In a seminal study in 1986, Field found that infants who are rarely touched or have limited contact with others develop a 20 to 30 percent smaller brain than normal infants the same age. Conversely, she also found that newborns who were touched, stroked, and received limb movement for three 15-minute periods per day for 10 days averaged 47 percent greater weight gain per day, were more active and alert, and showed more mature orientation and motor behavior.

Scientists know that maternal or familial neglect can have lifelong cognitive consequences, including causing altered brain chemistry, which has long-term effects on learning and memory. However, touch can often offset the impact of neglect in infants and young children, researchers are learning. For instance, Wheeden reported in 1993 that 15 pre-term babies exposed to cocaine in utero improved dramatically after receiving 15-minute periods of massage for 3 consecutive hours over 10 days. The infant subjects averaged a 28 percent weight gain, showed significantly fewer post-natal complications, and demonstrated more mature motor behavior than a control group.

Even clinically depressed mothers (who often find it difficult to smile or speak words of affection while interacting with their babies) can have a positive impact by providing touch stimulation to their infants, concludes Palaez-Nogueras and colleagues (1996). This suggests that touch is often more important than facial or vocal expression in communicating with infants. Similar results were reported by Stack and Muir in 1992.

Unfortunately, we are fast becoming a society that is reluctant, and even afraid, to touch. For instance, in a 1999 national study of elementary- and high-school teachers by Anderson and Levine, it was found that 37 percent of survey respondents expressed concern about being falsely accused of child abuse; 70 percent advised against hugging or putting an arm around a student; and 42 percent advised a new teacher against being alone in a room with a student. With teens, as with all children, it is important to have sincere intentions and maintain clear boundaries, but keep in mind, we all benefit from periodic words of encouragement and a nurturing touch.

Action Steps

* Do not underestimate the soothing power of touch, including cuddling, rocking, stroking, and holding.
* Combine touch with such comforting actions as smiling, singing, humming, and affectionate words.
* Keep in mind that 60 percent of all learning in children takes place through tactile and visual experiences.
* Provide students with ample and appropriate levels of nurturing and physical contact (i.e. hugs, smiles, and affectionate words) during learning and recess periods. Be especially aware and sensitive to children who may not receive such loving attention at home.
* Bring in interesting objects for children to hold, touch, and share such as pets and artifacts.
* Student encouragement at the middle- or high-school level may best be expressed with a smile, high-five, positive verbal comments, or in writing.

Sources:

Anderson, Elizabeth and Murray Levine. 1999. Concerns about allegations of child sexual abuse against teachers and the teaching environment. *Child Abuse and Neglect*. Aug 23; (8): 833-43.

Field, Tiffany; S.M. Schanberg; F. Scafidi; C.R. Bauer; N. Vega-Lahr. 1986. Tactile/kinesthetic stimulation effects on pre-term neonates. *Pediatrics*. May; 77(5): 654-8.

Fleming, A.S.; D.H. O'Day; G.W. Kraemer. 1999. Neurobiology of mother-infant interactions: Experience and central nervous system plasticity across development and generations. *Neuroscience Biobehavioral Review*. May; 23(5)s: 673-85.

Gatts, James; S. Fernbach; Douglas Wallace; Turid Singra. 1992. Preliminary study data was presented at the annual meeting of the American Psychological Association, Washington, DC, August 14-17.

Palaez-Nogueras, M; T.M. Field; Z. Hossain; J. Pickens. 1996. Depressed mothers' touching increases infants' positive affect and attention in still-face interactions. *Child Development*. Aug; 67(4): 1780-92.

Perry, Bruce. 1999. 10 Things Every Child Needs (instructional video). KTXL Fox 40/Tribune Broadcasting.

Stack, D.M and D.W. Muir. 1992. Adult tactile stimulation during face-to-face interactions modulates five-month-olds' affect and attention. *Child Development*. Dec; 63(6): 1509-25.

Wheeden, A; F.A. Scafidi; T. Field; G. Ironson; C. Valdeon. 1993. Massage effects on cocaine-exposed pre-term neonates. *Journal of Developmental Behavioral Pediatrics*. Oct; 14(5): 318-22.

Children's Academic Success Is Shaped By the Words We Use

Recent studies suggest that the degree to which parents talk with their preschoolers is a strong determinant of children's subsequent academic success. In essence, infants and children whose parents talk to them more frequently and use bigger "adult" words often develop better language and other cognitive skills, concludes research by Evans and colleagues (1999) and Hart and Risley (1995).

Scientists know that babies become primed to receive and respond to speech in their first year when specialized neurons are formed in the auditory cortex of the brain. During this period, the left side of the brain, which plays a crucial role in language development, is also maturing to process rapid auditory information. The stage is therefore set for the child to hear language sounds and receive input from parents, siblings, and others in their environment.

Hart and Risley long suspected that quality family interaction was the reason why children from high income families often arrived at kindergarten and first grade with more developed language skills than their peers from poorer neighborhoods.

To test their theory, the researchers recruited 42 families with infants ages 7 to 12 months old. The parents were welfare recipients, blue-collar workers, or professionals. Once a month, an observer visited the families' homes and recorded the primary caretaker's verbal attention towards the child as they went about their normal routine. Observers also taped the families' conversations until the children reached age 3. The results revealed that the better-educated, professional families— regardless of their ethnic background—spoke to their children the most, while the poorer welfare families spoke to their children the least.

The study also revealed that, on average, the welfare child heard just 600 words per hour, while the working class child heard 1,200 words per hour, and the professional child heard 2,100 words per hour. To add further credence to the significance of early language skills, the study revealed that 3-year-olds from *talkative* professional families had higher IQ and vocabulary scores than the others. Not only did children from highly verbal families hear more words, but their parents asked them more questions and repeated or expanded upon comments the children made more often. This positive feedback, the report concludes, reinforces children's verbal expression while enhancing learning.

A longitudinal study by Gottfried and colleagues (1998) again illustrates the difference that parental involvement can make. Gottfried tracked the development of 130 children (from widely diverse racial and socio-economic backgrounds) beginning in 1979. He found that parents who placed more emphasis on reading to their children and exposed them more to learning opportunities and activities had children who were more academically motivated.

Action Steps

* Expose children, as early as their fist year (and as often as possible) to a variety of sounds, especially the sound of your voice talking and reading, and to songs and rhythms.
* When talking to your child or young learner, use "adult" words frequently. This will help them develop better early language skills.
* When your child or young student talks to you, provide constructive feedback, letting the child know you are listening.
* To help expand the child's sense of awareness and learning, provide age-appropriate reference books, computer aids, and other enrichment materials in the home and classroom.

Sources:

Evans, Gary; Lorraine Maxwell; Betty Hart. 1999. Parental language and verbal responsiveness to children in crowded homes. *Developmental Psychology*. July; 35(4): 1020-3.

Gottfried, Adele; J. Fleming; Allen Gottfried. 1998. Role of cognitively stimulating home environment in children's academic intrinsic motivation: A longitudinal study. *Child Development*. Oct; 69(5): 1448-60.

Hart, Betty and Todd Risley. 1995. *Meaningful Differences in the Everyday Experience of Young American Children*. Baltimore, MD: Paul H. Brookes Publishing Co.

Perception Is Reality: Disturbing TV News Affects Children's Cognition

While news gleaned from television can be a positive educational experience for children, problems can arise when the images presented are violent or when news stories touch on disturbing topics, psychologist Joanne Cantor reports (1998) in her book *Mommy, I'm Scared: How TV and Movies Frighten Children and What We Can Do to Protect Them*. News reports on such subjects as mass murders, child abduction, and school violence can teach kids to view the world as a threatening, confusing, and unfriendly place, she says.

We know that how we feel about a situation determines our response to it: Our feelings trigger certain biochemical reactions that affect our cognitive perception. For instance, if we perceive an event as an immediate threat, the neurotransmitter adrenaline is released igniting the "flight or fight" response. With increased adrenaline we also produce the neurotransmitter cortisol which decreases our ability to learn and remember. If instead we choose to perceive the event as a learning experience, other transmitters like acetylcholine, interferon, and interleukins are released. These increase our ability to establish or reorganize neural networks that precede thinking and remembering.

In a related study on how children perceive and internalize disturbing occurrences, Cantor and Omdahl (1991) found that kids exposed to fictional depictions of realistic life-threatening events (i.e., dramatic versions of a house fire and drowning) subsequently rated these events as more likely to occur soon in their own lives than children exposed to benign depictions.

And research by Hoffner (1997) reports that children given pertinent information about a frightening scene (including its outcome) before viewing it, exhibited less anxiety than children who did not receive such information.

In her book, Cantor reports that starting at preschool age, what a child watches on television can be personalized and perceived as reality. To calm children's fear about the news—even about events that can't be controlled, like natural disasters and senseless killings—teachers and parents, she says, should be prepared to deliver "calm, unequivocal, but limited information." In other words, deliver the truth, but only as much as the child needs to know. In the case of the Polly Klaas murder, for example, a teacher or parent might say that she was killed by a very sick man, but spare the child unnecessary details. If there are concrete things that children can do in certain cases to protect themselves from harm—such as ways to prevent fires, what to do in case of an earthquake, or how to be on guard against suspicious strangers—take the opportunity to provide this information.

Action Steps

* Discuss current events with children on a regular basis. Help them think through stories they see on television or read about in newspapers. Ask them questions: What do you think about these events? How do you think these things happen? Encourage them to express their views and opinions.
* Put disturbing news events in proper perspective for children. Explain that certain events are isolated or rare. Discuss how one event might relate to another to help a child better understand the big picture.
* Watch the news with your children to filter and explain stories as they watch them.

Sources:

Cantor, Joanne. 1998. *Mommy, I'm Scared—How TV and Movies Frighten Children and What We Can Do to Protect Them*. New York: Harcourt Brace & Company.

Cantor, Joanne and B. Omdahl. 1991. Effects of fictional media depictions of realistic threats on children's emotional responses, expectations, worries, and liking for related activities. *Communication Monographs*. Dec; 58(4): 384-401.

Hoffner, Cynthia. 1997. Children's emotional reactions to a scary film: The role of prior outcome information and coping style. *Human Communication Research*. Mar; 23(3): 323-41.

Cognitive Impact of Divorce on Children Is Significant, but Can be Minimized

Parental divorce or separation can undoubtedly have a significant emotional and cognitive impact on young schoolchildren, but research suggests that these effects can often be minimized if the child receives adequate emotional support from the custodial parent and is exposed to other resources designed to help cope with these events.

Children experiencing the divorce or separation of their parents can be left with a sense of abandonment, confusion, anxiety, self-blame, and other feelings that can impact the child's self-image and sense of security (Entwisle & Alexander 1996; Rubin 1988; Williams 1990). This, in turn, can adversely affect the child's academic adjustment, reducing their receptiveness and motivation to learn, report Smith (1995) and Call and colleagues (1994).

Further impacting the situation for the child is how the custodial parent adjusts to divorce or separation. Research indicates that recently divorced or separated mothers experiencing high degrees of emotional stress, depression, and insecurity were more likely to have schoolchildren with lower concentration, hyperactivity, and poorer academic performance (Entwisle & Alexander 1996; Rubin 1988). On the other hand, it was found that divorced mothers who expressed high expectations for their children while making adequate use of formal and informal social support networks, had children who were better adjusted at home and school.

Scientists know that even in less than desirable situations, the brain responds well to positive reinforcement—encouragement, stability, security, and a sense of order—reducing the fear response in our brain's amygdala and enhancing well-being and cognition.

But even for fairly well-adjusted children, parental divorce can be a critical event in their academic development. And adequate childhood adjustment takes time, reports Mulholland and colleagues (1991). In a study of sixty 10- to 15-year-olds with divorced parents, the Mulholland study found that such children showed significant deficits in grade point averages and scholastic motivation compared to a control group of children from intact families. The disparity in grades between the two groups remained for at least 2 years. Similar results were borne out in a study involving 116 fourth through sixth graders (Call, et al. 1994).

Research by Bisnaire and colleagues (1990), which included a 3-year follow up, demonstrates the advantage of *both* divorced parents being involved in the child's academic adjustment. While 30 percent of the subjects from divorced families still showed a decrease in academic performance during follow up, those who had access to both parents showed the least. In addition, the study revealed that mothers with more education tended not only to provide better psychosocial home environments, but also had children who spent more time with the noncustodial parent.

In one of the first studies examining parental divorce on the academic performance of college students, Jennifer and Jay Kuntz (1995) found in an investigation of 169 university undergraduates that students from divorced families had significantly lower grade-point averages than students from intact families.

Action Steps

* If a student's academic performance drops dramatically and/or consistently, speak privately with the student and with at least one of the student's parents.
* Recommend counseling for the student if his or her performance continues to decline.
* Nurture the student with additional support and provide a stable environment at school.
* Encourage a healthy social-support network with peer learning and cooperative group opportunities.
* Consider whether the student might benefit from a personal tutoring and mentoring situation.

Sources:

Bisnaire, Lise; P. Firestone; David Rynard. 1990. Factors associated with academic achievement in children following parental separation. *American Journal of Orthopsychiatry*. 60(1): 67-76.

Call, Garrett; Joe Beer; John Beer. 1994. General and test anxiety, shyness, and grade-point average of elementary school children of divorced and nondivorced parents. *Psychological Reports*. 74(2): 512-4.

Entwisle, Doris and Karl Alexander. 1996. Family type and children's growth in reading and math over the primary grades. *Journal of Marriage & the Family*. 58(2): 342-55.

Kuntz, Jennifer and Jay Kuntz. 1995. Parental divorce and academic achievement of college students. *Psychological Reports*. Jun; 76(3, Pt. 1): 1025-6.

Mulholland, Debra; Norman Watt; Anne Philpott; Neil Sarlin. 1991. Academic performance in children of divorce: Psychological resilience and vulnerability. *Psychiatry*. Aug; 54(3): 268-80.

Rubin, Julie. 1988. *The Effects of Parental Divorce on Infant Emotional and Cognitive Development*. Dissertation Abstracts International. Feb; 48(8-B): 2477.

Williams, Barbara. 1990. *A Learned Helplessness Explanation of Children's Post-Divorce Adjustment*. Dissertation Abstracts International. Feb; 50(8-A): 2439-40.

Smith, Thomas. 1995. What a difference a measure makes: Parental separation effect on school grades, not academic achievement. *Journal of Divorce & Remarriage*. 23(3-4): 151-64.

Learning a New Language in Early Childhood Requires Less Brain Effort

Have you ever wondered why children learn a second language more easily than adults? Recent research by Kim and colleagues (1997) suggests that children's more flexible neural connections may allow them to rely on just one critical patch of brain tissue when learning both the native and newly acquired tongue.

Adult language learners, in contrast, must recruit nearby groups of brain cells to accomplish the same tasks, the Kim study found. Related studies suggest that a second language is optimally learned between the ages of 2 and 6 (Genessee, et al. 1995; Mayo, et al. 1997).

According to the Kim study, bilingual individuals who acquired a second language during childhood displayed elevated activity in the same part of Broca's area (a frontal lobe area of the brain crucial to language expression) regardless of which language they used. In contrast, people who learned a second language later in life exhibited neural activity in spatially separated parts of Broca's area. The researchers used a non-invasive technique known as magnetic resonance imaging (MRI) to measure changes in blood flow in the brains of the 12 bilingual subjects. Researchers in the Kim study say the findings may reflect either Broca's area sensitivity to language exposure during childhood, or the existence of marked differences in the ways that children and adults learn languages.

Other studies have noted that children learning two languages simultaneously during infancy go through a stage in which they cannot differentiate their two languages (Genesee, et al. 1995; Genesee 1989). During this period they mix elements from both tongues. These results have been interpreted as evidence for a unitary, undifferentiated language system in the brains of bilingual children.

Action Steps

* Begin exposing children to age-appropriate foreign language learning aids such as sing-along tapes, talking books, and videos as early as one-and-a-half years old. Practice and review these exercises with the child regularly while maintaining a fun-filled atmosphere.
* When an individual first begins learning a new language, the brain's right hemisphere takes on most of the load. The left hemisphere takes on its share in the later stages. Thus, initially gear instruction toward the right (intuitive, creative) hemisphere, using such techniques as brainstorming, concrete visuals, and hands-on learning strategies.

Sources:
Genesee, F. 1989. Early bilingual development: One language or two? *Journal of Childhood Language*. Feb; 16(1): 161-79.
Genesee, F.; E. Nicoladis; J. Paradis. 1995. Language differentiation in early bilingual development. *Journal of Childhood Language*. Oct; 22(3): 611-31.
Kim, K.H.; N.R. Relkin; K.M. Lee; J. Hirsch. 1997. Distinct cortical areas associated with native and second languages. *Nature*. Jul 10; 388(6638): 171-4.
Mayo, L.H.; M. Florentine; M. Buus. 1997. Age of second-language acquisition and perception of speech in noise. *Journal of Speech, Language, and Hearing Research*. Jun; 40(3): 686-93.

Childcare Centers Can Have Cognitive Drawbacks for Preschoolers

While quality day-care centers have been shown to play a role in enhancing preschoolers' overall verbal and social skills, continual full-day exposure to day care, especially to poorly-run centers, can often be more stressful on children than home environments, according to studies by Dettling and colleagues (1999) and Tout and colleagues (1998).

The Dettling and Tout studies both measured levels of the stress-sensitive hormone cortisol in children attending full-day childcare centers and found that levels increased progressively from morning until afternoon. Conversely, cortisol levels in most of these same youngsters were found to decrease throughout the day (in accordance with the normal circadian rhythm of cortisol) when they stayed at home. Cortisol-level increases were especially prevalent among boys and among children attending low-quality childcare centers.

Cortisol is produced by the adrenal glands and is released in response to stress as a means for helping us withstand noxious or threatening events. Essential to our survival and to memory and learning, cortisol stimulates glucose production and moderates the activity of other stress-response systems, including the immune system.

In the United States, 4.74 million children under the age of 5 spend between 20 to 60 hours per week in organized childcare settings. Dettling and Tout both speculate that the day-care centers are often more stressful for children because they can involve continual separation from home and family; they are often poorly staffed; and the setting requires children to use underdeveloped social and coping skills to interact with multiple adults and peers.

The Tout study examined 75 preschoolers at two large urban childcare centers for a month and found that 81 percent of the participants had steady cortisol-level increases throughout the day while at the center. The Dettling study examined 36 preschoolers at five centers and noted that cortisol levels rise throughout the day in more than 70 percent of the subjects. Both researchers indicate that the stress in these situations often manifests as aggression, poor self-control, limited attention span, and introversion.

Action Steps

✳ Be sure that any childcare facility you're associated with is adequately staffed and equipped.

✳ In large day-care facilities, encourage children to develop a positive relationship with one or two day-care staffers at a time before exposing them to multiple adult workers.

✳ To help children develop familiar and positive interaction with peers, establish play groups, nap groups, and other pairing strategies.

✳ Encourage movement and exploration with periodic recesses, exercise, and physical play.

✳ Allow children to bring photos, toys, blankets, and other things that remind them of home and family. Create a "storytelling" session each day to allow kids to talk about what they brought.

Sources:

Dettling, Andrea; Meagan Gunnar; and Bonny Donzella. 1999. Cortisol levels of young children in full-day childcare centers: Relations with age and temperament. *Psychoneuroendocrinology*. 25(5); July; 519-536.

Tout, Kathryn; Michelle de Haan; E. Kipp-Cambell; Meagan Gunnar. 1998. Social behavior correlates of cortisol activity in child care: Gender differences and time-of-day effects. *Child Development*. Oct; 69(5): 1247-62.

Good Reading Skills Begin at Home, but Not in Front of the TV

Research suggests that excessive TV viewing among young children can deprive developing minds of the social interaction (particularly nurturing interaction with parents and other adults) necessary for developing life-long learning skills such as reading, creativity, and problem solving (Tonge 1990; Healey 1990; Hannaford 1995).

Recent studies by Huston and colleagues (1999) and Koolstra and colleagues (1997) indicate that children with high reading skills often watch fewer hours of television and come from home environments that foster and encourage good reading habits.

This is not to say that TV cannot contribute to childhood development, says Kotulak (1996) and others. When used appropriately and under the guidance and supervision of adults (especially later in childhood), TV can serve as a useful adjunct to learning. For example, TV and other visual mediums are known to enhance the long-term recall of reading material in older school children and adults. However, television should not serve as a "babysitter," or the primary source of the child's interaction with the world.

The seeds for reading skill development are planted in the early months of infancy. Vision development in the brain's occipital lobe, for example, occurs particularly in the first 4 to 6 months of life. And as early as 9 months, the cerebellum is ready for thinking via tactile learning. At this stage, the foundation for speech and comprehension of words, letters, and numbers is also being laid in the brain's left (or logical) hemisphere. Additionally, neural circuits in the infant's auditory cortex are formed in the first year and are enhanced by the sounds of the parents' voice, accent, and word pronunciation.

Reading skills are best developed in a supportive home environment where TV viewing is limited. Consider the following recent studies:

✱ Research by Huston and colleagues (1999) used time-use diaries to examine how groups of 2- and 4-year-olds spent their time over a 3-year period. Results indicated that as the children's time spent in educational and social activities increased, their time watching leisure TV decreased. And children with enriched home environments were more likely to view educational TV versus entertainment TV. In a similar study involving 2,200 third and fourth graders, Harrell and colleagues (1997) report that girls tend to watch entertainment TV slightly more than boys (30 percent versus 28 percent of boys), but girls also prefer to read more (23 percent versus 19 percent of boys).

✱ A study examining the reading and language scores of 295 children, first during kindergarten and later in second grade, found that children coming from home environments that encouraged library visits, limited TV viewing of 1 to 2 hours daily, adult-to-child reading, and the availability of ample reading material at home, scored dramatically higher on such tests (Griffin, et al. 1997).

Additional research indicates that some TV viewing by children can be helpful, such as the reading-oriented segments of programs like Sesame Street. Age-appropriate educational TV can create positive attitudes among youngsters for reading and motor-skill development, reports Blok (1995). Koolstra and colleagues (1997) report that watching subtitled foreign TV programs stimulates the development of reading decoding skills. And Beentjes and Van der Voort (1993) found that TV news stories result in more inferential learning than print stories and more long-term or delayed recall of news information.

Action Steps

* Understand the importance of reading to your children. Encourage reading in your family and monitor TV viewing. Unfortunately, studies show that fewer than 25 percent of American households follow these guidelines.
* Reading and comprehending what is read requires focus and concentration; therefore, when reading, avoid distractions such as TV and radio. The brain can only concentrate on one source of stimulation at a time.

Sources:

Beentjes, Johannes W. and Tom H. Van der Voort. 1993. Television viewing versus reading: Mental effort, retention, and inferential learning. *Communication Education*. Jul; 42(3): 191-205.

Blok, H. 1995. Children's reactions to Sesame Street in relation to their reading attitude. *Pedagogische Studieen*. 72(3): 221-34.

Hannaford, Carla. 1995. *Smart Moves*. Arlington, VA: Great Ocean Publishing Co.

Harrell, Joanne S.; Stuart A. Gansky; C.B. Bradley; Robert G. McMurray. 1997. Leisure-time activities of elementary school children. *Nursing Research*. Sept-Oct; 46(5): 246-53.

Healy, Jane. 1990. *Endangered Minds: Why Our Children Can't Think*. New York: Simon and Schuster.

Huston, Aletha; John Wright; Janet Marquis; Samuel Green. 1999. How young children spend their time: Television and other activities. *Developmental Psychology*. Jul; 35(4): 912-25.

Koolstra, Cees; Tom Van der Voort; Leo Van der Kamp. 1997. Television's impact on children's reading comprehension and decoding skills: A 3-year panel study. *Reading Research Quarterly*. Apr-Jun; 32(2): 128-52.

Kotulak, Ronald. 1996. *Inside the Brain*. Kansas City, MO: Andrews McMeel Publishing.

Tonge, B.J. 1990. The impact of television on children and clinical practice. *Australian and New Zealand Journal of Psychiatry*. 24(4): 552-60.

Chapter 10
The Fragile Brain

hat forces detract from the brain's ability to learn? Neglect, violence, trauma, illness, toxins, drugs and alcohol abuse, hormonal imbalances, neurological and genetic defects, malnourishment, stress, and injury are just some of the factors that play a role. With so many possibilities for obstruction, it's surprising that we learn at all. In fact, nearly 40 percent of students suffer from some form of cognitive impairment. But not all unhealthy brains under-perform. Many find ways to compensate. And research continues to provide us with greater understanding of the neurological mechanisms involved. Nonetheless, countless serious problems related to the brain continue to plague students, parents, teachers, and administrators, and more research remains to be done. Clearly, we face a difficult challenge.

Following are a few of the conditions that impact our fragile brain and the percentage of the population affected:

✳	Hyperactivity/hyperkinetic disorders	2-5 %
✳	Oppositional disorder	5-7 %
✳	Attention-deficit disorder	3-10 %
✳	Learning delays	5-8 %
✳	Abuse and attachment disorders	8-10 %
✳	Traumatic brain injury	3-8 %
✳	Depression	4-6 %
✳	Nutritional deficiencies	15 %
✳	Dyslexia	8-12 %
✳	Auditory processing deficits	10 %
✳	Delayed sleep disorder	75 %

* Toxic exposure or allergies   10-15 %
* Nutritional deficiencies   15 %
* Marijuana and alcohol abuse   25 %
* Learned helplessness   5 %

Although these disabilities are mostly treatable, they can involve lifestyle changes, extensive school resources, parental support, teacher training, medications, and therapy.

Perhaps the most important message gained from the research is that the brain is a fragile organ and more vulnerable to insult and debilitation than many realize. Schools, classrooms, and teachers create busy, complex environments that trigger complex responses, many of which are difficult to identify. Sometimes, symptoms of a learning impairment occur only under specific conditions. Other symptoms may be more generally apparent. Some cognitive disorders require immediate medical treatment, while others may simply be outgrown. Recognizing these differences is vital.

The studies presented in this chapter help piece together a complex picture of the reasons why learners of all ages may not learn. *The real message, however, is one of hope.* The more we understand the brain, the more students we'll eventually reach.

The Biology of Violence: Exploding the Myths

When students commit acts of violence or a worker goes berserk, what's really going on? The common answers like, "no one listened to his plea for help," or "he just lost control of his life, family, money, etc.," only serve to distract us from the real problem. To truly understand the phenomenon of violence, we must look inside the brain. If the cause of violence, however, is physiological, is there really anything we can do to reduce the chance of such an episode in our own school or workplace? The answer, fortunately, is yes. Let's begin by examining some of the myths.

The first myth is that some people are born with genes for violence. This is unfounded: Our genetic code does not cause us to pick up a gun and shoot another person. Human beings, in fact, represent the only species in the animal kingdom given the awesome responsibility, power, and capability for making conscious, rational decisions. This is our genetic heritage. But why then do some make bad decisions that have tragic consequences?

Factors that are often overlooked include (1) injury to the brain from an accident, fall, or illness; (2) injury to the brain from prolonged distress, threat, and trauma; and/or (3) injury to the brain from drug or alcohol abuse. The potential physiological results of these circumstances include insufficient prefrontal cortex activity, hypothalamic-pituitary-adrenal (HPA) dysfunction, attention-deficit hyperactivity disorder (ADHD), post-traumatic stress disorder (PTSD), and dopamine or serotonin dysfunction—the primary cause of depression and other mental disorders.

Another myth is that violence is caused by an environmental stimulus, like a rude co-worker or an insensitive teacher. The truth is that the seed for violence is planted long before any such environmental stressor(s) might trigger an attack. The HPA axis plays an important role here. The brain can actually reach a critical mass of distress, after which any emotional disturbance can prompt the hypothalamus and pituitary gland to release adrenocorticotropic hormone (ACTH). In healthy human beings, this physiological response stimulates the adrenal glands to secrete the stress hormone cortisol, which helps us escape danger and deal with stress. In the normal brain, a feedback system inhibits the release of excess cortisol, but in the overly stressed brain, excess ACTH perpetuates the distress cycle with no relief. As we've seen over and over again, the results can be disastrous.

Comb and colleagues (1987) demonstrated that cortisol can modulate genetic transcription factors. This means that cells may get encoded with the effects of cortisol; thus, impacting future cell responses. In this way, our genes are, indeed, inextricably connected to our environment. The violent outbursts we hear about in the news are not likely seeded the year (or even decade) before. Rather, the damage was probably sustained early in life.

In contrast, depressed levels of cortisol can create problems, as well. In studies involving repeat juvenile and adult offenders, significant reductions in cortisol have been found to be common (Virkkunen, et al. 1994). Children with oppositional disorder have also been shown to have lower cortisol values than their peers (Vanyokov, et al. 1993). Over and over we hear the same story: To function properly, the brain needs just the right balance of neurotransmitters (our chemical messengers) and hormones.

Another myth about violence is that it is simply an issue of character. It is true that humans have the power to make good choices, but fundamental to all understanding of human behaviors is that *only healthy brains can make healthy choices*. A student with ADHD can try as hard as he wants, but his attention span will be limited. In fact, the harder he tries, the worse his concentration becomes. And a depressed student simply doesn't *want* to make choices. But if she were healthy, the story would be different.

An area slightly below our forehead and behind our eyes, known for "executive function," inhibits irrational, aggressive tendencies. Vulnerable to dopamine irregularities and brain insults, this frontal lobe area when damaged, disrupts normal inhibition (or inner restraint). The frontal lobe also mediates our working memory, which is crucial to comprehension and decision-making. When this area is damaged, the combination of reduced inhibition and lack of self- control with short-term memory dysfunction can be a volatile mix.

The ability to represent and hold knowledge is what allows one to make good decisions—weighing risks against benefits, and thoughts against feelings in a microsecond. People with distress, disease, or damage to the frontal lobe area, however, may experience inaccurate, incomplete, and illogical thinking—the kind that can compel one to feel and say something like, "Everyone hates me anyway; I'll show them. I'm going to get a gun."

So how can we reduce the risk of violence if this is what is happening in the brains and minds of some in our community? "Contrary to popular belief, a neurobiological perspective emphasizes the possibility of change," says Deborah Niehoff, author of *The Biology of Violence*. What percentages can we impact? A definitive number is still unclear. "Some people will commit violent crimes no matter what; however, there is a large group for whom the correct environmental changes will make a *huge* difference," says Larry Siever, author of *The New View of Self*. Our schools and workplaces will become safer places when the fragile brain is not only better cared for by individuals, but by our society as a whole.

*To truly understand the phenomenon of violence,
we must look inside the brain.*

Action Steps

* Recognize the importance of the first 3 years of a child's life. Stability without threat, enriching environments, and frequent trusting interactions are crucial. Whatever can be done to support parents and primary caregivers in this process, *has* to be done.
* Provide these three important elements at your school or workplace: (1) safety; (2) structure; and (3) attachment. Include the use of teams, binding social rituals, trusting relationships, daily opportunities for personal expression, and skill building in emotional intelligence.
* Encourage cognitive behavioral therapy and pharmacological intervention for those who are likely to be or are current aggressive offenders.

Sources:

Comb, M.; S.E. Hyman; H.M. Goodman. 1987. Mechanisms of trans-synaptic regulation of gene expression. *Trends in Neuroscience*. 10: 473-8.

Niehoff, Deborah. 1999. *The Biology of Violence*. New York: The Free Press.

Siever, Larry. 1997. *The New View of Self*. New York: Macmillian Press.

Vanyokov, M.; H.B. Moss; J.A. Plail; et al. 1993. Antisocial symptoms in preadolescent boys and their parents: Associations with cortisol. *Psychiatric Research*. 46: 9-17.

Virkkunen, M.; R. Rawlings; R. Tokola; et al. 1994. CSF biochemistries, glucose metabolism, and diurnal activity rhythms in alcoholic, violent offenders, fire setters, and healthy volunteers. *Archives of General Psychiatry*. 51: 20-7.

Brain Injury: Do Children Recover Better than Adults?

Brain damage, especially that which results in concussion and coma, can have a significant impact on language and learning skills. Research suggests, however, that the prognosis for regaining moderate or full use of such skills following injury is increasingly good. This seems to be especially true for children, although researchers are not precisely sure why.

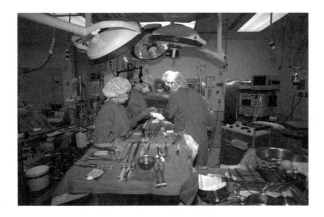

Aram (1999) and Stiles (1998) suggest that it may be due to the brain's plasticity— the brain's dramatic ability to grow and heal itself—a condition especially prevalent in the early stages of a child's developing brain. In addition, researchers have identified a neurotransmitter that plays a key role in brain recovery. Whishaw and colleagues (1996) found that sufficient levels of noradrenaline—a key neurotransmitter that regulates sympathetic arousal, metabolic rate, and emotions—may facilitate healing in the brain's frontal lobes.

In Aram's study of 40 children and young adults (ages 7 to 21) with left-hemisphere or right-hemisphere lesions, the young subjects experienced more marked recovery of language, spatial, and learning skills compared to the young adult subjects with similar brain lesions.

Kriel and colleagues (1995) reported similar results in a 1-year follow-up of 30 children and adults (ages 4 to 29) who had been unconscious for at least 90 days following traumatic and non-traumatic brain damage. And in a 10-year follow up of children who had suffered stroke either in utero or as infants, Stiles reported that such children are likely to develop into fully functioning adults.

Bagnato and Neisworth concluded in 1986 that brain-injured infants and preschoolers tend to have the most significant developmental recovery in the first 3.5 to 4 months post-injury, while significant recovery in adults often takes 6 months or longer.

Brain damage, such as closed head injury and infectious and metabolic brain injury, can alter mental function. Brain areas affected include the frontal lobe, which controls planning, concentration and decision making; the hippocampus, which is responsible for memory processing; the temporal lobes, which are involved in learning, balance, and memory storage; and the occipital lobes, responsible for vision and visual perception. Symptoms of such damage include headache, dizziness, lack of concentration (especially during complex tasks), confusion, personality change, and problems with sleep and balance.

Action Steps

* Be aware of the cognitive effects that brain injury (such as head trauma and concussion) can have on learning and employee performance, especially in terms of memory, concentration, attention span, and visual perception. Seek the counsel of Special Education Services or an Employee Assistance Program if necessary.

* Recognize that young children with head injuries have increased odds of recovering fully and more quickly than when damage occurs later in life.

* During recovery, consider placing the student or employee on a study/work regimen that does not demand high mental stress, immediate recall of facts, or performance of complex tasks.

* Place the student/employee in a supportive group study or work environment.

* Provide accommodation and understanding to the victims of traumatic head injury.

Sources:

Aram, Dorothy. 1999. Neuroplasticity: Evidence from unilateral brain lesions in children. In: *The Changing Nervous System: Neurobehavioral Consequences of Early Brain Disorders*. Sarah Broman (Ed). New York, NY: Oxford University Press, pp. 254-73.

Bagnato, Stephen; John Neisworth. 1986. Tracing developmental recovery from early brain injury. *Remedial & Special Education*. Sept-Oct; 7(5): 31-6.

Kriel, Robert; Linda Krach; Michael Luxenberg. 1995. Recovery of language skills in children after prolonged unconsciousness. *Journal of Neurologic Rehabilitation*. 9(3): 145-50.

Stiles, Joan. 1998. The effects of early focal brain injury on lateralization of cognitive function. *Current Directions in Psychological Science*. Feb; 7(1): 21-6.

Whishaw, Ian; Robert Sutherland; Bryan Kolb; Jill Becker. 1996. Effects of neonatal forebrain noradrenaline depletion in recovery from brain damage. *Behavior & Neural Biology*. Nov; 46(3): 285-307.

How Child Abuse Impacts Academic Performance

Child abuse can have both immediate and long-term psychological effects on its victims, but what has not been adequately studied is how these effects impact academic performance. However, a recent major study of 165 abused children sheds some light on the cognitive deficits that can result from such abuse, including significantly lower achievement test scores and higher rates of behavioral problems (Kinard 1999).

Kinard's study compared achievement test scores of abused children (mean age of 9) and other factors with that of 169 non-abused children. Abused students scored significantly lower on achievement tests, and they had lower grades in academic subjects overall. In addition, they were absent more days and were more often enrolled in special education classes.

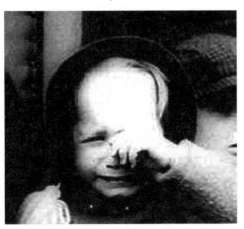

Ultimately, they tended to repeat grades more often and had more behavioral problems than did non-abused children. The study indicated that abused children also had less parental support.

What happens to the brain during emotional trauma, and how does it affect learning? Scientists know that child abuse, like other traumatic events, triggers anxiety and fear—two primary components of post-traumatic stress disorder (PTSD). Fear and anxiety, accompanying prolonged emotional trauma, often manifest as nightmares, frightening thoughts, emotional numbness, depression, incontinence, intense guilt, anger, and sleep disturbances.

Fear, the brain's automatic and unconscious response to danger, triggers the production of abnormal levels of the stress hormones cortisol and epinephrine. The hippocampus—a brain area involved in learning and memory—is highly susceptible to these hormones. When abnormal levels of these chemicals are produced during acute long-term stress, they can kill brain cells and severely inhibit cognition, including long-term memory.

In addition, victims of child abuse and other traumatic experiences are also known to produce high levels of natural opiates, which temporarily mask the pain associated with trauma (Daleiden 1998). Most victims continue to produce these high levels, even after the danger has passed, which may explain the blunted emotions often associated with post-traumatic stress disorder, according to the National Institute of Mental Health (1999).

Helping a student overcome the obstacles of child abuse or other emotional trauma can be one of the most challenging tasks faced by a teacher because a threatening or stressful situation always takes priority over cognitive functioning. Daleiden (1998) noted that memory in anxious children was especially hindered during conceptual tasks.

Action Steps

* Learn to recognize the subtle and not-so-subtle signs of child abuse. These include visible marks or injuries to the body, withdrawal from others, depression, emotional numbness, intense feelings of shame or guilt, substance abuse, behavioral problems, and sudden decline in academic performance.

* Consult school officials immediately if you suspect child abuse or have questions about dealing with its symptoms.

* Since students suffering from child abuse usually experience a "downshift" in cognitive function, teachers should take care to provide a supportive learning environment. This includes providing feedback that is prompt and specific, involving the student in appropriate group or team settings, and avoiding the assignment of duties which require conceptual thinking.

Sources:
Daleiden, E.L. 1998. Childhood anxiety and memory functioning: A comparison of systematic and processing accounts. *Journal of Experimental Child Psychology*. Mar; 68(3): 216-35.
Kinard, E. Milling. 1999. Psychosocial resources and academic performance in abused children. *Children & Youth Services Review*. May 21(5): 351-76.
National Institute of Mental Health. 1999. Reliving Trauma: Post Traumatic Stress Disorder (fact sheet). Bethesda, MD: The Anxiety Disorders Education Program.

Working With the Angry Learner

A climate that is tinged with anger or emotional distress is toxic to learning. These intense emotions, if not addressed, can seriously affect morale, concentration, and memory (Iezzi, et al. 1999; Jamison, et al. 1988; Dufton 1989). The impact is not only felt by the distressed person, but by those around him or her, as well. In a recent study of 73 patients with chronic pain, Iezzi and colleagues (1999) found that subjects with high emotional distress experienced more learning difficulties than those with low emotional distress.

Anger can take many forms, ranging from depression and pessimism to verbal and physical outbursts. Research indicates that healing can take place when a person expresses the anger without getting angry (Ironson, et al. 1992). In other words, verbalize it, deal with it, and leave it behind. But this is often easier said than done, especially if the emotional wound is long-held and severe.

While the almond-shaped region of the brain called the amygdala, located in the limbic system, has been strongly implicated as the "rage center," recent studies have identified other overlapping and distinct brain areas (associated with learning, language, and verbal expression) that are also stimulated by anger and anxiety. For example, Kimbrell and colleagues, in a 1999 study of self-induced anger and anxiety in 16 healthy adults, reported increased cerebral blood flow in both the left-inferior frontal lobe and the left-temporal pole after inducement. Anger itself was associated with the right-temporal pole and the thalamus (a key sensory relay station).

Anger, like other forms of stress, mobilizes the body for one of three responses: freeze, fight, or flight, and signals the hypothalamus—which coordinates basic metabolic and related functions—to initiate distinct physical changes such as the dilation of pupils, the constriction of arteries, the shut down of digestion, and the activation of the adrenal glands. The adrenal glands trigger increased levels of cortisol and other critical neurotransmitters like norepinephrine and epinephrine, which in turn feed aggression. All of these changes can seriously impede the cognitive process (Black 1991).

In addition, pent-up emotions trigger a complex series of physiological reactions that can drain the body's ability to fight off disease, according to Miller and colleagues (1999), Mills and colleagues (1996), and Baltrusch and colleagues (1991). Unexpressed anger is known to alter cell structure in the immune system, including natural killer cell activity and leukocyte and platelet volume (Baltrusch 1991; Mills, et al. 1996). Cynical hostility and other similar emotions have been linked to increased blood pressure and heart rate especially among men (Miller, et al. 1999). All in all, the physiological changes resulting from anger spells a heightened susceptibility to such conditions as infection, cancer, heart disease, rheumatoid arthritis, addictions, and mental illness, as well as a decrease in concentration and memory.

How do we prevent stressors like anger from getting a foothold in our life? Control may be the best solution (Ironson, et al. 1992). If we resign ourselves to the inevitability of long-term stress, it will continue to ravage our bodies. But if we decide that we have some degree of control over the situation, we can limit, prevent, and even reverse altogether the negative effects of stress.

Action Steps

* Learn to recognize the signs of an angry learner—open hostility, inability to concentrate, pessimism, physical aggression, alienation, bullying, depression, and problems with attendance and tardiness.
* Do not let anger control or disrupt the learning environment. If inappropriate behavior occurs, ask the individual to leave the room and cool off before discussing the situation with them. Document the incident, and discuss the situation immediately with parents.
* Encourage the learner to express what is bothering them—either to you or someone else they trust (therapist, physician, close friend, relative, or clergy member). Many times the problem has nothing to do with you or the immediate environment, but a past emotional wound.
* If appropriate, encourage the person to seek the help of a mental health professional or physician.
* Initiate support techniques in the classroom such as peer tutoring and cooperative learning groups.
* To help relieve the everyday stressors that can trigger anger and anxiety, do not underestimate the effectiveness of initiating stretch breaks, physical/aerobic exercise, relaxation techniques and humor.

Sources:

Baltrusch, H.J.; W. Stangel; I. Titze. 1991. Stress, cancer and immunity: New developments in biopsychosocial and psychoneuroimmunologic research. *Acta Neurol.* (Napoli). Aug; 13(4): 315-27.

Black, I.B. 1991. *Information in the Brain: A Molecular Perspective.* Cambridge, MA: MIT Press.

Dufton, B.D. 1989. Cognitive failure and chronic pain. *International Journal of Psychiatric Medicine.* 19(3): 291-7.

Iezzi, T.; Y. Archibald; P. Barnett; A. Klinck; M. Duckworth. 1999. Neurocognitive performance and emotional status in chronic pain patients. *Journal of Behavioral Medicine.* June; 22(3): 205-16.

Ironson, G., et al. 1992. Effects of anger on left ventricular ejection fraction in coronary artery disease. *American Journal of Cardiology.* Aug; 70: 281-5.

Jamison, R.N.; T. Sbrocco; W.C. Parris. 1988. The influence of problems with concentration and memory on emotional distress and daily activities in chronic pain patients. *The International Journal of Psychiatric Medicine.* 18(2): 183-91.

Kimbrell, T.A.; M.S. George; P.I. Parekh; T.A. Ketter; D.M. Podell; A.L. Danielson; J.D. Repella; B.E. Benson; M.W. Willis; P. Herscovitch; R.M. Post. 1999. Regional brain activity during transient self-induced anxiety and anger in healthy adults. *Biological Psychiatry.* Aug. 15; 46(4): 454-65.

Miller, G.E.; J.M. Dopp; H.F. Myers; S.Y. Stevens; J.L. Fahey. 1999. Psychosocial predictors of natural killer cell mobilization during marital conflict. *Health Psychology.* May; 18(3): 262-71.

Mills, P.J.; J.E. Dimsdale; R.A. Nelesen; E. Dillon. 1996. Psychological characteristics associated with acute stressor-induced leukocyte subset redistribution. *Journal of Psychosomatic Research.* April; 40(4): 417-23.

How Much Stress Is Too Much?

Research reveals that psychological stress is not inherently bad. In fact, moderate stress levels can have a motivating effect in the school environment (Kellogg, et al. 1999; Hardy & Parfitt 1991). moreover, when we are *under*-aroused we usually lack the stimulation to perform optimally and boredom sets in. Project deadlines, accountability pressures, and delays are

just some of the stressors that are part of our daily lives. These stressors, however, also help drive us to achieve our goals.

Scientists know that even moderate stress levels trigger the brain's hypothalamus to manufacture and release two primary stress hormones, cortisol and adrenaline, which put the body on alert for danger. When this occurs, our sensory perception sharpens, our physical strength and energy increase, and our senses and memory are enhanced. Unlike highly stressful or threatening situations, which cause cortisol to be released in high cognitive-impairing amounts, moderately stressful events trigger small amounts of the hormone, resulting in increased arousal, motivation, action, and long-term memory.

Kellogg found that moderate stress induced by a timed arithmetic performance test actually motivated both anxious and non-anxious students to more accurately apply previously learned principles. And in a study in which experienced collegiate basketball players were asked to shoot baskets under varying levels of cognitive stress, Hardy and Parfitt found that players operating under moderately high levels of stress significantly outperformed those under low cognitive pressure.

Action Steps

✻ Set deadlines by which assignments should be completed.
✻ Hold individuals accountable for their assigned tasks and learning goals. Accountability is a known motivating force.
✻ Set and maintain high, but reasonable, standards for learners.
✻ Introduce a healthy dose of peer competition, and appropriate use of cooperative teams for project accomplishment.

Sources:
Hardy, L. and G. Parfitt. 1991. A catastrophe model of anxiety and performance. *British Journal of Psychology*. May; 82(Pt. 2): 163-78.
Kellogg, J.S.; D.R. Hopko; M.H. Ashcraft. 1999. *Journal of Anxiety Disorders*. Nov-Dec; 13(6): 591-600.

Sports, Head Trauma, and Cognitive Damage

Recent findings on head trauma sustained by teenagers participating in popular contact sports reveal that these injuries may pose more serious cognitive threat than previously realized. In a comprehensive study of 393 college football players, Collins and colleagues (1999) found that two or more significant sports-related blows to the head, especially blows causing mild to severe concussion, can harm young athletes' thinking abilities for years to come.

Each year across the country, more than 62,800 high-school athletes competing in such sports as football, basketball, soccer, wrestling, and hockey suffer at least one concussion, according to a recent study (Powell, et al. 1999). The study noted that the sports which resulted in the highest incidence of concussion were football (63 percent, or 1 out of 3 players); wrestling (10.5 percent); girls' soccer (6.2 percent), and boys' soccer (5.7 percent). This finding reflects a serious public health issue.

To better understand the cognitive damage that can result, let's examine what a concussion really is. Contrary to popular belief, a concussion means more than just being knocked out or dazed. A traumatic blow to the head can alter mental function in the brain's frontal lobes (planning, concentration and decision making), the hippocampus (memory processing), the temporal lobes (learning, balance, and memory storage), and the occipital lobes (vision and visuoperception). Symptoms of head injury include headache, dizziness, lack of concentration (especially during complex tasks), confusion, personality change, and problems with sleep and balance.

The Collins study—the largest of its kind examining the prevalence of head trauma among young football players— found that subjects who had sustained two or more concussions had greater difficulty on tests measuring their ability to learn new words, think quickly, and perform reasoning tasks compared to uninjured athletes. Both the Collins and Powell studies confirm previous research that suggests multiple mild concussions are more likely result in long-term cognitive problems. However, these findings also shed light on the high incidence of head trauma among teenage athletes, the learning difficulties that can result, and the need to recognize the issue as a major public health concern.

In addition to football, researchers are also particularly concerned over the severity of head trauma suffered in other high-contact sports such as soccer. Master and colleagues (1998, 1999) found in a study of 53 professional Dutch soccer players that they exhibited significantly more impairment in memory, planning, and visuoprocessing than non-contact sport athletes in a control group.

The Master studies found similar results when examining soccer-related concussions among amateur players resulting from head impact with soccer balls, collisions with other players, and other serious incidents. Compared with of athletes non-impact sports in a matched control group, the amateur soccer players exhibited impaired performance on tests of planning (39% vs. 13%) and memory (27% vs. 7%). Twenty-seven percent of the soccer players had suffered at least one soccer-related concussion, and 23 percent had suffered two to five concussions during their career.

Recent research on how head injury affects specific brain areas in children may pave the way for improved treatment of sports-related head trauma in school athletics. For example, Vicari and colleagues (1998) and other researchers have found that children with injury to the left hemisphere (which controls logic, speech, analysis, and sequence cognition) perform better on spatial tests than children with injury to the right hemisphere (spatial perception, language and pattern interpretation, and creativity).

Shum and colleagues (1999) reported that children with severe traumatic brain injury had significantly less explicit memory (immediate recall of facts and information without coaching or priming) than other children. In addition, elementary- and high-school students with traumatic brain injuries are more than two times as likely to require special education services for learning and behavioral disorders after sustaining injury (Hux, et al. 1999).

However, encouraging news comes from Stiles (1998) whose findings suggest that the earlier in life a child suffers certain brain injuries, the better the chances of full recovery later. After a 10-year follow up study on the progress of children who had suffered stroke and other non-traumatic brain impairment, either in utero or as infants, the researcher found that such children are likely to develop into fully-functioning adults. This is due, she says, to the brain's powerful ability to heal itself, especially in the early development stages.

Action Steps

* Take inventory of the procedures and safety measures in place to prevent and deal with head injuries, including quality and condition of sports equipment, immediacy of access to medical consultation during and after athletic competition, and degree of sports-related injury awareness among athletes and educators. Instruct athletes on maneuvers and techniques to avoid blows in competition and practice.

* Be aware of the cognitive effects that head trauma and concussion can have on student performance, especially involving memory, concentration, attention span, and visuoperception. Increase learners' awareness of the risks. Seek the counsel of Special Education Services in your school district as necessary. In working with students who have suffered head injury, consider the available options, such as placing the student on a class/study regimen that does not demand immediate recall of facts, and/or performance of complex mental tasks. Having the student participate in a supportive group study environment may also help.

Sources:

Collins, M.W; S.H. Grindel; M.R. Lovell; M. Dede; B. Phalin; W. Nogle; D. Cordry; K. Daugherty; S. Sears; G. Nicolette; P. Indelicato; D. McKeag. 1999. Relationship between concussion and neuropsychological performance in college football players. *Journal of the American Medical Association*. Sep 8; 282(10): 964-70.

Hux, Karen; J. Marquardt; S. Skinner; V. Bond. 1999. Special education services provided to students with and without parental reports of traumatic brain injury. *Brain Injury*. June 13(6): 447-55.

Matser, Erik; A. Kessels; B. Jordan; M. Lezak; J. Troost. 1998. Chronic traumatic brain injury in professional soccer players. *Neurobiology*. Sep; 51(3): 791-6.

Matser, Erik; A. Kessels; M. Lezak; B. Jordan; J. Troost. 1999. Neuropsychologic impairment in amateur soccer players. *Journal of the American Medical Association*. Sept 8; 282(10): 971-3.

Powell, John W. and Kim D. Barber-Foss. 1999. Traumatic brain injury in high-school athletes. *Journal of the American Medical Association*. Sept 8; 282(10): 958.

Shum, David; E. Jamieson; M. Bahr; G. Wallace. 1999. Implicit and explicit memory in children with traumatic brain injury. *Journal of Clinical and Experimental Neuropsychology*. Apr; 21(2): 149-58.

Stiles, Joan. 1998. The effects of early focal brain injury on lateralization of cognitive function. *Current Directions in Psychological Science*. Feb; 7(1): 21-6.

Vicari, S.; J. Stiles; C. Stern; A. Resca. 1998. Spatial grouping activity in children with early cortical and subcortical lesions. *Developmental Medicine and Child Neurology*. Feb; 40(2): 90-4.

Chronic Bullying Takes Cognitive Toll On Victims and Perpetrators Alike

Not only does the prevalence of bullying tend to increase during middle school, it impairs the cognition of both victim and perpetrator alike, recent studies suggest. Bartini and Pellegrini (1999), in a landmark longitudinal study of bullying, victimization, and peer affiliation, found that 4-out-of-5 middle-school students admit to acting like bullies at least once a month. Moreover, such acts increased with the initial transition from fifth to sixth grade and then usually declined. In addition, studies by Kaltiala-Heino and colleagues (1999) and others suggest that depression, low self-esteem, guilt, anger, and even suicide ideation are equally likely to occur among those who are chronically bullied *and* those who are *doing* the bullying.

Why do children sometimes resort to bullying? To satisfy an insecurity, which can manifest as a psychological need to dominate, especially in a peer group setting, say Bartini and Pellegrini. For the victims, the result is usually fear and intimidation. Fear is known to cause the brain's amygdala region (which controls our sense of safety and security) to release such critical brain chemicals as vasopressin and adrenaline, which in abnormal amounts, can impede learning.

Chronic bullying also leads to shame and guilt—not only for the bullies themselves, but also for the victims (Slee & Rigby 1993; Kaltiala-Heino, et al. 1999). Shame and guilt are known to result in stress, depression, and other psychological problems that can negatively impact cognition.

The Bartini-Pellegrini study reported that bullying was used by teens primarily to establish dominance in new peer groups as they made the transition from elementary to middle school. Once the dominance is established and their place with their new friends is secure, the aggression usually subsides. But some students bully throughout their school years, the study found, never feeling secure in their peer alliances.

Bartini and Pellegrini also found that boys engage in and support bullying behavior more than girls. In addition, girls were more likely than boys to intervene on behalf of victims. And, it was found that fifth-grade bullies often continued their behavior into sixth grade.

Action Steps

* Teach conflict resolution skills, practice effective communication techniques, and encourage cooperative groupings.
* Remember that bullying is a common behavior among children, but take all incidences seriously, especially when threats or acts of physical violence are involved. Report these incidences immediately to the appropriate authorities and take necessary disciplinary action.
* Be aware that victims of bullies, and bullies themselves, can both suffer emotionally and cognitively from such behavior. Symptoms include depression, shame, guilt, low self-esteem, and even suicide ideation. In serious cases, recommended psychological counseling for both parties.
* Bullying is especially prevalent as students make the transition from elementary to middle school. Encourage healthy peer interaction during this time including reciprocal peer tutoring, and peer-assisted learning during classroom work and test preparation sessions.

Sources:

Bartini, Maria and Anthony Pellegrini. 1999. Bullying and victimization in early adolescence—description and prevention. *Child Abuse and Neglect*. Dec; 23(12): 1253-62.

Kaltiala-Heino, R.; M. Rimpela; M. Martunen; A. Rimpela; P. Rantanen. 1999. Bullying, depression, and suicidal ideation in Finnish adolescents: School survey. *British Medical Journal*. Aug 7; 319(7206): 348-51.

Slee, P.T. and K. Rigby. 1993. Australian school children's self appraisal of interpersonal relations: The bullying experience. *Child Psychiatry and Human Development*. Summer; 23(4): 273-82.

Job Burnout: The Stress Connection

Job dissatisfaction is a complex state of mind that involves numerous factors such as compensation, benefits, job security, and the nature of the work. However, recent research suggests that no other factor is more influential in the scenario than the impact of job stress. Studies involving municipal workers, hospital professionals, teachers, clerical workers, and others indicate job stress plays a significant role in not only work dissatisfaction, but also job burnout, employee turnover, and employee health problems (Carlson & Thompson 1995; Belicki & Woolcott 1996).

In a study of burnout and job dissatisfaction among chronic care hospital workers, Belicki and Woolcott found that increased stress led to increased feelings of job burnout. Similar results were reported by Carlson and Thompson in a comprehensive study of turnover among public school teachers. Carlson and Thompson also found that stress management intervention significantly reduced stress levels. The researchers report that stress management intervention (i.e., breathing, stretching, exercise, meditation, and time management training) has proven effective in reducing burnout and feelings of overwhelm, while also improving workers' overall ability to deal with stress.

McEwen (1999) and others have demonstrated that although moderate *short-term* stress can actually benefit the body by causing a surge in the stress hormones cortisol and adrenaline (which act to boost the immune system), the effects of *chronic* stress can wreak havoc on cognition and health. Excessive stress, scientists know, causes heightened levels of such hormones as cortisol and glucocorticoids, which in excess can damage neurons in the hippocampus—a part of the brain critical to memory and learning. Chronic stress also causes the shutdown of regular maintenance functions in the body, a problem that can result in weakened muscles, bone loss, insulin resistance (causing weight gain), and lowered libido. In addition, stress can impair the brain's frontal lobe region, causing distraction, disorganization, and sometimes impulsive or inappropriate behaviors, McEwen and others report.

Job dissatisfaction is a complex state of mind that involves numerous factors such as compensation, benefits, job security, and type of work.

Action Steps

* If you feel stressed, perform breathing and stretching exercises at least two to four times daily. This can be done at your desk, during meetings, or at a break time. Brisk walking, meditation, weight training and aerobics are also beneficial.

* Be aware of the signs of chronic job stress and burnout: increased impatience, frustration, and irritability; feeling stifled in your personal and professional life; feeling a lack of guidance or direction in your life; feelings of inferiority, exhaustion, or depression; a loss of interest in daily activities.

* If necessary, seek professional counseling, medical treatment, and/ or the advice of your Employee Assistance Program.

Sources:

Belicki, K. and R. Woolcott. 1996. Employee and patient designed study of burnout and job satisfaction in a chronic care hospital. *Employee Assistance Quarterly*. 12: 37-46.

Carlson, B.C. and J.A. Thompson. 1995. Job burnout and job leaving in public school teachers: Implications for stress management. *International Journal of Stress Management*. 2: 15-29.

McEwen, B.S. 1999. Protective and damaging effects of stress mediators. *The New England Journal of Medicine*. 338: 171-9.

Compulsive Behavior:
Important Link to the Brain

Why do some individuals have difficulty withholding aggressive impulses or seem helpless against controlling unwanted obsessive thoughts? Researchers are closing in on the cause of an array of behaviors known collectively as obsessive-compulsive disorder (OCD). Once thought to be a rare condition, we now know OCD affects 2 percent of the population and usually manifests in childhood or by early adolescence.

Brain scan studies conducted by Mendlewicz (1999), Baumgarten and Grozdanovic (1998), and Rosenberg and colleagues (1997) indicate patients with OCD receive too much or too little of an important impulse-controlling neurotransmitter called serotonin. When overproduced by the brain, serotonin can cause highly anxious behaviors, such as repeated hand washing or constant rechecking of locked doors. And when under-produced, serotonin can cause aggressive, anti-social behaviors, such as uncontrolled violent anger and disregard for others, the researchers found.

Brain scans also indicate that an area of the brain known as the caudate nucleus is overactive in these patients. The caudate nucleus acts as a gate-keeper that prevents unwanted thoughts from establishing self-reinforcing circuits in the brain. Like a record needle stuck in the same groove, unwanted thoughts in OCD patients keep repeating themselves, thereby driving compulsive behavior.

While high and low levels of serotonin can seriously affect behavior and memory, normal levels are associated with clear thinking and well-adjusted social interaction. When serotonin production is at a balanced level, the brain can muster all of its resources in the environment and balance risks against benefits for effective decision-making.

With the help of medication and behavior therapy, Baumgarten and Grozdanovic (1998) and Ko (1996) report that OCD patients are able to curb unwanted thoughts and impulses.

Action Steps

* Provide a supportive, structured learning environment with defined boundaries.
* Engage OCD students as much as possible in controlled group learning and encourage others to be patient, supportive, and understanding of them.
* Consult a psychiatrist or psychotherapist for more advice regarding medication and behavioral therapy.

Sources:

Baumgarten, H.G. and Z. Grozdanovic. 1998. Role of serotonin in obsessive-compulsive disorder. *British Journal of Psychiatry*. Supplement; 35: 13-20.

Ko, S.M. 1996. Obsessive-compulsive disorder—A neuropsychiatric illness. *Singapore Medical Journal*. Apr; 37(2): 186-8.

Mendlewicz, J. 1999. Predicting response: Serotonin reuptake inhibition. *International Clinical Psychopharmacology*. May 14; Supplement; 1: S17-20.

Rosenberg, D.R.; M.S. Keshaven; K.M. O'Hearn. 1997. Frontostriatal measurements in treatment-naive children with obsessive-compulsive disorder. *Archives of General Psychiatry*. Sept; 54(9): 824-30.

The Role of Neurotransmitters in Addiction

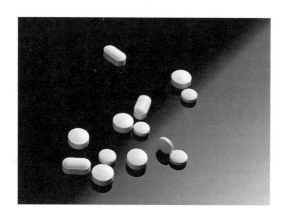

To investigate how substances like alcohol, tobacco, and drugs take their hold on the brain, scientists are increasingly turning to research on the interactions of drugs with neurotransmitters in the brain. In a study by Panikkar (1999) on the addictive effects of cocaine, it was found that the drug's pleasurable effects occur when a chemical messenger called dopamine—known to enhance relaxation, arousal, and mood—accumulates in the brain. The dopamine clusters around a group of circuits described as the brain's "reward pathway," located along the hypothalamic-pituitary-adrenal system.

Normally, the brain's cellular housekeeping mechanism removes excess dopamine, but cocaine is thought to obstruct this process by inhibiting a neurotransmitter called the dopamine transporter (Gardner 1999). Without this transporter, high levels of dopamine build up between brain cells, intensifying the feeling of reward and euphoria induced by the cocaine.

At the same time, however, brain cells are continually adjusting to the increased dopamine levels brought on by the cocaine, creating an ever-growing tolerance for the drug. It then becomes necessary to use greater amounts of it to create the same "high." This tolerance often leads to compulsive drug-seeking behavior (Panikkar 1999; Roberts & Koob 1997).

Gardner also reports on research using a strain of mice that were specifically bred without the dopamine transporter. To the surprise of scientists, these mice still self-administered cocaine by pressing a lever to receive the drug. When researchers studied the animals' brains, they found that cocaine was attaching to areas that were rich in receptors for another neurotransmitter, serotonin. Gardner suggests that, although the dopamine transporter is probably still a key factor in addiction, serotonin may also represent a new avenue of study in understanding addictive behavior.

Action Steps

* Have students research the personal and social health risks posed by drug and alcohol addiction. Have them present and discuss their findings in class.
* Invite guest speakers from the therapeutic community to your class to discuss the current research and medical implications of addiction.
* Coordinate a classroom debate or group discussion on innovative ways to reduce drug and alcohol addiction in your community.

Sources:

Gardner, Eliot. 1999. The neurobiology and genetics of addiction: Implications of the "reward deficiency syndrome" for therapeutic strategies in chemical dependency. In: *Addiction*. Elster, Jon (Ed). New York, NY: Russell Sage Foundation.

Panikkar, G. 1999. Cocaine addiction: Neurobiology and related current research in pharmacology. *Substance Abuse*. 20(3): 149-66.

Roberts, Amanda and George Koob. 1997. The neurobiology of addiction: An overview. *Alcohol Health & Research World*. 21(2): 101-6.

Appendix

Bibliography

Note:
Research citations are listed subsequent to each article throughout this book.

Reader Resources

Books on Learning, Teaching, and the Brain

The Brain Store features countless books, posters, CDs, and brain-related products. This innovative education resource company is all about the science of learning. You'll find resources for:

* **Teaching and Training**
* **Music and Dance**
* **Enrichment**
* **Organizational Change**
* **Staff Development**
* **Early Childhood**

To view all of our products, log on at: **www.thebrainstore.com**, or call (800) 325-4769 or (858) 546-7555 for a FREE color resource catalog.

Reader Resources Continued...

The LearningBrain Newsletter

If you enjoyed this book, get timely research-based articles, such as these, on a monthly basis. Log on to our online newsletter and stay abreast of the newest and most relevant information on topics like cognition, environment, nutrition, arts, memory, school policy, mind-body, and fragile brains. Save hundreds of hours in research time and expense. Gain twenty-first century teaching and training strategies. To get a free sample issue, log on at: **www.learningbrain.com** or call (800) 325-4769 or (858) 546-7555.

Conference: The Learning Brain Expo

A world-class gathering featuring more than fifty renowned speakers on the brain and learning. Session topics include music, movement, early childhood, emotions, memory, the fragile brain, and brain imaging. Get dozens of practical ideas and network with like-minded professionals. Held twice annually, you can attend this enriching event in either California or Texas. For more information, log on at: **www.brainexpo.com**, or call (800) 325-4769 or (858) 546-7555.

Free Samples

Go to **www.thebrainstore.com** to get free tips, tools, and strategies. You'll also find selected products at 40 percent savings. In addition, many books offer you a sneak online preview of the table of contents and sample pages, so you'll know before you order if it's for you. At The Brain Store, online shopping is safe, quick, and easy!

Trainings Facilitated by Eric Jensen

"How the Brain Learns" is a 6-day workshop for teachers, trainers, and other change agents with a focus on the brain, how we learn, and how to boost achievement.

"The Fragile Brain" is 3-day program for teachers, special educators, counselors, and other change agents with a focus on what can go wrong with the learner's brain and how to treat it.

For registration information, dates, and costs call (888) 638-7246 or fax (858) 642-0404.

About the Authors

Eric Jensen, M.A., is a visionary educator who is committed to making a positive, significant, and lasting difference in the way we learn. He's a member of the prestigious Society for Neuroscience and New York Academy of Sciences. A former middle-school teacher and college instructor, Jensen is the author of more than a dozen books on learning and teaching. He co-founded the world's first experimental brain-compatible academic enrichment program in 1982 that now has more than 30,000 graduates. Currently, he's a staff developer and consultant living in San Diego, California.

Other Books by Eric Jensen
Super Teaching, Student Success Secrets, The Learning Brain, Brain-Based Learning, Trainer's Bonanza, Teaching with the Brain in Mind, Joyful Fluency (with Lynn Dhority), *The Great Memory Book* (with Karen Markowitz), *Learning with the Body in Mind, Music with the Brain in Mind,* and *Different Brains, Different Learners.* Available through The Brain Store. Log on at: **www.thebrainstore.com**, or call (800) 325-4769 or (858) 546-7555.

Author Contact
Fax (858) 642-0404 or e-mail at eric@jlcbrain.com

Michael Dabney, M.Ed., is a medical and science writer specializing in media and public relations at the University of California, San Diego. He has written and edited numerous articles for the Mayo Clinic and *San Diego Review Magazine* and has worked as a freelance writer in Paris, France and Alaska. Mr. Dabney completed his graduate degree in Communication Arts at Xavier University in Cincinnati, Ohio, and has since spent two decades translating complex, technical subjects into lively, understandable science and news articles for both the media and general public.

Index